The Perfect
Afternoon Tea
Recipe Book

The Perfect Afternoon Tea Recipe Book

Over 200 classic recipes for every kind
of traditional teatime treat

ANTONY WILD AND CAROL PASTOR

LORENZ BOOKS

Contents

Introduction

In 1615 the first use of a word relating to tea is recorded in the English language, when an East India Company associate in Japan, Mr Wickham, writes to his friend Mr Eaton asking him to buy a 'pot of the best sort of chaw in Meaco', the place where the tea was grown for the Shogun, the chief military commander. It took a Portuguese princess, however, to introduce the British to the pleasures of drinking tea. In the summer of 1662 Catherine of Braganza arrived in England to become the bride of King Charles II. On landing at Portsmouth, the first thing she did was to ask for a cup of tea, taking the welcoming party completely by surprise (they had been preparing to serve her a glass of weak ale). Fortunately a potential diplomatic crisis was averted by a retainer in her entourage who was able to produce the tea, and so the English Court was introduced to an old custom of the Portuguese nobility. Portugal's long trading association with China and Japan had made the Portuguese accustomed to what was still, at the time, a novelty in England, and certainly one that the Court had previously looked upon with some suspicion.

Catherine's endorsement of tea meant that the unfamiliar beverage suddenly became all the rage in London society – music to the ears of the directors of the East India Company. Founded by Royal Charter in 1600, the company had been created to compete with the success of the Portuguese in capturing the hugely valuable spice trade from the East. However, the company had failed to dislodge its rivals, and its fortunes had fluctuated wildly. Its traders were aware of the existence of tea but at the time, the English were

reluctant to take up tea-drinking as a habit. Tea was to be found on sale at some of London's coffee houses, albeit in a medicinal role, but it was not until the arrival of Catherine in England that the habit of drinking tea became established.

Tea becomes the English drink of choice

As tea-drinking spread, the East India Company directors realized the popularity of the product. A Mrs Harris was hired to serve the drink at all the company meetings in the fine silver teapot presented to his fellow directors by Lord Berkeley in 1670. Two of the hallowed traditions of English business – the tea-lady and the tea-break – therefore owed their genesis, appropriately enough, to the company that first imported tea.

By the end of the 17th century, tea was in its ascendancy, with everyone from peasant farmer to the highest nobility in the land regularly drinking the beverage. Beer, the traditional drink of the working classes, was popular, and so was coffee in the coffee houses – but tea triumphed behind the drawing room doors of the middle classes, demanding to be served.

This Portuguese habit had taken the English by storm, although it was modified to reflect the unique character of the English. Fabulous outdoor tea gardens flourished at Vauxhall, Ranelagh Gardens and elsewhere in London. Here the fashionable set could see and be seen, and be entertained all the while as they took tea. Porcelain pots (their design adapted from Chinese wine jugs) were imported to brew the beverage in, and milk and sugar were added to the mix. The directors of the East India Company, which had the monopoly on the trade with China, rubbed their hands with glee: tea had become the single most valuable item of their trade.

The rise and fall of 'afternoon tea'

Tea was firmly established as the drink of choice, but the invention of the 'afternoon tea' meal, now seen as the quintessential English custom, did not occur until the 19th century. Although the innovation is usually attributed to the 7th Countess of Bedford, in

Left The famous tea clipper, the *Cutty Sark*, was designed to be the fastest of its kind in the world. Her maiden voyage was made to China in early 1870, and she returned later that year with the first of eight cargoes of almost 1,500 tonnes of tea. This method of transporting tea was later superseded by steamships, which were more suited to navigating the newly built Panama Canal.

Above Taking tea with friends in the afternoon was a social ritual valued by polite society.

fact the new habit was the result of the complex series of social and economic changes wrought over time by industrialization. Luncheon had been invented to fill the gap between breakfast and dinner, but this was a light meal. The evening meal of dinner was now served later than at any other time, and so a light snack in the afternoon became the way to stave off hunger. The custom of taking afternoon tea quickly became one of the defining rituals of English social life, giving rise to all manner of fashionable china and silver tea services as well as appetizing new snacks to accompany it. Many of the scenes in Oscar Wilde's most enduring play, *The Importance of Being Earnest* (1895), revolve around the afternoon tea table, its cakes and cucumber sandwiches, and when accused by a friend of eating too much, Algernon is able to respond with complete assurance, "I believe it is customary in good society to take some slight refreshment at five o'clock."

Initially a purely domestic phenomenon, by the end of the 19th century the serving of afternoon tea had been adopted by the large hotels which were springing up all over Britain – and in far-flung reaches of the British Empire. Elegant cafés followed suit, and even when silver cake stands and cucumber sandwiches were no longer to be found in homes, they could still be

found in cafés. The tradition continued widely but after the 1970s the cafés increasingly became self-service. Working practices changed for many people and with them came new social habits. Only a few bastions of the old tradition remained – mainly the grand hotels and the occasional little teashop in a quaint rural town, with gingham tablecloths and homemade cakes.

Teatime is now enjoyed by everyone
In the 1990s an increasing interest in quality teas came to the fore, against the all-pervasive coffee bar boom, to remind people that there was a way of eating and drinking socially in an unhurried, elegant manner, in a way that appealed to people's sense of nostalgia. Afternoon tea has returned to the national consciousness. While tea leaves remain an imported commodity, the tradition of teatime lends itself perfectly to the trend for creating delicious homemade delicacies. In hotels, department stores and cafés, and of course at home, the ritual of afternoon tea is enjoyed by many.

Although the fashionable private salons for taking afternoon tea in the style of the Countess of Bedford may no longer be found, the tradition of afternoon tea is still maintained, albeit as a treat rather than on a daily basis. Alongside the great variety of teas now available, hosts and hostesses like to delight their guests with a range of delicious traditional and original baked confections, all beautifully presented.

The afternoon tea table

The new 19th-century phenomenon of afternoon tea was not only good for tea importers, it heralded a growth in several attendant industries, such as the production of fine china and porcelain tea services and the manufacture of silverware.

The East India Company made huge profits out of the tea that they brought from China, and so did the government, who applied hefty taxes to the product. To increase sales, the importers quickly realized that their new customers needed something in which to brew the tea. The Chinese were used to brewing tea in powdered form in a teacup, but towards the end of the 14th century larger-leaved teas had become popular, requiring a brewing vessel, and the Chinese, who had made growing and brewing tea a skill akin to that of wine production, had adapted their traditional wine pots to this purpose, adding a handle and a spout.

The first appearance of the teapot

This appealing Chinese design found favour with the English when they became interested in drinking tea, and many stoneware pots of this kind were exported back to England. These in turn spawned imitators, principally in Staffordshire, and the familiar 'Brown

Betty' teapot evolved, a utilitarian vessel, with a high sheen glaze, reputed to make the best pot of tea. While not the most elegant of teapots, it had the virtue of durability – and given the sheer quantity of tea being brewed in Britain at the time, that was not to be underestimated. The design of the Brown Betty has stood the test of time and can still be seen in many households to this day, although nowadays every colour imaginable is available to co-ordinate with kitchen decor and home furnishings.

Fine china

Such workaday items as the Brown Betty teapot, however, were not suited to the elegant style of service that tea drinking demanded among the fashionable, well-heeled set. Consequently, it was Chinese porcelain which lent the most lustre to the new custom in Britain. This was the era of the craze for 'Chinoiserie', when Chinese silks, wallpapers, screens and porcelain were

Below In the grandest circles, the elegant tradition of taking afternoon tea necessitated an equally fine tea service to present it.

Below Industrialization also meant that pottery was widely available for everyone to purchase a tea set at reasonable cost.

Above Every fashionable house, teashop or hotel tearoom possessed an attractive fine china tea service, as porcelain became the refined material of choice for making and serving tea.

the must-have items for any distinguished household. The East India Company's merchants started to exploit these markets, eventually involving themselves in the design and production process in China. Many a noble house in the 18th century would display dinner services of fine porcelain emblazoned with their coats of arms, hand-painted on the other side of the world. Teapots, teacups and saucers were now added to the shopping list among a growing range of other tea-serving items.

The Chinese dominance of the porcelain industry, could not last, however. German alchemists discovered the formula for making porcelain, and later Josiah Wedgwood of England was credited with industrializing the production of pottery on a scale never seen before. Other manufacturers followed suit, and the distinctive elements of Chinese designs such as the ubiquitous 'Willow Pattern' and 'Blanc de Chine' were shamelessly plundered, remaining popular even now.

It was not just the demand for teapots that fuelled the porcelain boom. During the 18th century British tea drinkers discovered a taste for black teas (as opposed to the green teas they had drunk initially) and found that these bitter teas worked particularly well with the addition of milk and sugar. This was good news for

dairy farmers, West Indian sugar planters and porcelain manufacturers, who produced suitable vessels for the new additions. Then, in the last century, along came the idea of afternoon tea with its cakes and sandwiches, and yet more items were required to make up a tea service.

Silverware and linen
Alongside the East India Company – who retained their monopoly on the tea trade with China until 1834 – and porcelain manufacturers, others benefited commercially from the fashion for tea. Silver manufacturers were required to create sugar tongs, strainers, teaspoons, cake stands and small cutlery to enhance the daintiness of the offering, as well as teapots, milk jugs and sugar bowls for the top-notch tearooms. Linen mills, embroiderers and lacemakers did well likewise in producing tablecloths and napkins – even the innovation of the humble doily was a spin-off from the unstoppable growth in demand for tea.

But, the teapot always was and remains the undisputed star of the proceedings. Over the years endless sleek styling and technical innovations in design have been dedicated to the teapot during its illustrious career. Nonetheless, in Britain at least, the conservative, ever-reliable earthenware teapot remains the default pot style of choice in many households – and for that we have to thank an anonymous 14th-century Chinese craftsman.

The etiquette of afternoon tea

Over two centuries of tradition have led to a wealth of customs and codes of behaviour that must be followed if you wish to display proper teatime manners in genteel society. Smart clothes and good manners are always welcomed at the tea table.

When serving afternoon tea the host or hostess should bring all the essential items to the tea table on a large tray. The tray should be set down on the table and the individual items arranged appropriately. Platters of sandwiches and cake stands should be placed in the middle of the table and the teapot should be positioned with the spout facing the pourer. In front of each guest a teacup should be placed on a saucer with a teaspoon resting on the right side, a small plate with a fork for eating cake (or knife if you are serving anything that requires spreading) and a napkin. The milk jug and sugar bowl should be arranged near the centre.

Pouring the tea perfectly

A warm teapot should be filled immediately when the water boils, and be brought to the table on a tray where it can stand while the tea brews. When the tea is ready to pour, the pourer should take the teapot to each guest and pour carefully into each cup. Tea is traditionally served in a cup holding 120ml/4fl oz of liquid and should be three-quarters filled with tea. The size is not imperative, but a teacup should be shallower and wider than a coffee cup to allow the tea to cool slightly before drinking.

Demure tea drinking

Once the tea has been poured, guests may add milk or lemon (offered in delicate slices) and sugar. It is preferable to use gentle to-and-fro movements with the spoon rather than wide, noisy circular motions. The teaspoon should be placed on the saucer to rest.

If seated at the table, the correct etiquette is to lift the teacup only to drink the tea and replace it on the saucer between sips. If there is no table, the saucer should be held in the left hand on your lap and the teacup in your right hand. It should be returned to the saucer when not in use. The cup should be held daintily by the handle between the thumb and fingers, with the little finger extended for balance. Never hold the teacup in the palm of your hand or loop your fingers through the handle, and by no means should you wave the cup around. Tea should be drunk in small, silent sips from the cup with as much grace and elegance, and as little slurping, as possible.

Elegant eating

The correct size of plate to use for serving sandwiches, cakes, pastries and other delicacies at afternoon tea is between 15 and 20cm (6 and 8in). The hostess must ensure that guests are provided with the necessary cutlery

for the food that is served. It is customary to serve wafer-thin sandwiches cut into triangles and with crusts removed from purposely designed bread and butter plates. Finger food can also be served. A slice of cake, scones with jam and cream, or a selection of biscuits, are appropriate, in dainty sizes.

When enjoying afternoon tea at a table, place the napkin on your lap and, if you leave the table temporarily for any reason, set the napkin on the seat.

All food should be eaten in delicate bites, with the utmost attention to detail. Think about how you will appear to your fellow guests at the tea table. When not in use forks should be rested on the side of the plate with the tines down. Never place them back on the table once they have been used. Similarly, place used knives on the side of the plate.

A social event
Above all, afternoon tea is a sociable occasion to be enjoyed with friends and family. So smile and make polite conversation (between mouthfuls, of course) and savour this most quintessential of English traditions.

Below Even for a more informal afternoon tea at home, it is worth making the effort to use a clean tablecloth, pretty crockery, an elegant stand for the food and, if you have one, a teapot warmer.

A perfect pot of tea

Whether your preference is for green, black, herbal or flavoured, there is nothing more refreshing in the afternoon than a pot of freshly brewed tea. Aficionados have maxims of their own on what constitutes the perfect cup of tea, and many blends are mentioned here, but they all agree that utmost care should be taken in making it. Step-by-step instructions for brewing are given in this chapter. If you prefer a cool drink on a hot day, or you wish to offer a choice, there are also some suggestions for suitable alternative beverages to serve at the tea table.

Left Perfectly brewed tea, served in china cups and accompanied by delicious food, is one of life's great pleasures.

Teas of the world

There is a wonderful variety of teas, ranging from the fabled imperial 'monkey-picked' tea of China, so-called because it was collected from inaccessible locations, or the rare Ceylon 'Silver Tips', to special blends like Earl Grey and machine-harvested black brews.

India, China and Sri Lanka dominate the tea-producing world. Together India and China produce more than half of all tea consumed. India produces enormous amounts of tea – its 14,000 plantations employ one million people. Kenya, Turkey, Indonesia and Malawi are also tea producers. Teas of a particular country or region of origin, high-quality single-estate loose-leaf teas, are known as speciality teas.

Picking tea
Tea is picked from the plant *Camellia sinensis*, which is a hardy bush, not unlike the common privet hedge, and is kept to a height of about 1.2m (4ft) on tea plantations. The quality and taste of tea are affected by many factors including the time of year that the tea is picked, the way it is picked, the climate of the region where the plantation is situated, the altitude and direction that the plantation faces, as well as the quality of the soil. Consecutive years may produce completely different qualities of crop from the same plantation.

The tea plants are dormant through the winter, turning green in spring. The youngest 'two leaves and a bud' are handpicked from the bush in early spring,

and then sometimes up to two or three times a week at peak harvest times. The first tips picked in spring have collected the most essential oil and are known as golden (or silver) tips – the most expensive picking.

Tea manufacturing
Broadly speaking, there are three principal methods of treating tea leaves and all are carried out on or near the tea plantation.

Leaves can be immediately 'fired', that is quickly heated in a metal pan to dry them out, the leaves being gently rolled at the same time. This method produces green tea, the backbone of the China tea industry.

The second method involves 'withering' (a gentle initial drying), and then the leaves are cut and torn by machines opening their cell structure up to oxidation, or 'fermentation' as the industry calls it. The blackened fragments of the tea leaves are then dried further in their final stage of production, and finally graded by size. 'Orange Pekoe' and 'Broken Orange Pekoe' are the two largest sizes remaining, the smallest being 'Fannings' and 'Dust'. These sizes of leaf are black teas, which form about 90 per cent of the world's production today.

Below Oolong tea is halfway between green and black tea in appearance and flavour. The best have a hint of peach in taste.

Below Lapsang Souchong, a Chinese tea, has a smoky flavour derived from drying the tea leaves over spruce fires.

Above White tea, with its delicate, sweet flavour, is made from very young, tender leaves that are quickly dried.

Above Green tea is becoming the drink of choice for those concerned with improving their health.

Halfway between green and black teas is 'Oolong', a semi-fermented tea mainly produced in China and Taiwan, and much prized by connoisseurs for its peachy flavour. Oolong is often referred to as a blue-green tea because of the colour of the leaves of the plant.

To the varieties of green, black and Oolong must be added other variations. The most well- known are Lapsang Souchong, a Chinese black tea which has been smoked over a fire of spruce, and Jasmine tea, a green or black China tea blended with jasmine petals.

Black teas

The black teas that dominate today were initially developed by the British on new plantations in Sri Lanka and India. Not wishing to emulate the extremely labour-intensive production methods of China, the British pioneered the idea of using machinery to speed the process up and bring the price down. Black teas were effectively the first industrialized teas, and enjoyed great worldwide commercial success. As a result the tea-producing colonies that made up the British Empire started consuming teas in vast quantities too. Today India, the world's largest producer, has to import tea in order to feed the habit they acquired from the British. The British tea 'estate' system was successfully exported to Britain's East African colonies, with the result that some of the finest blending teas in the world now come from Malawi and Kenya. Their bright orangey flavour makes these teas a brisk, refreshing brew.

Green teas

Almost all green teas originate in China – where tea has been produced for more than 2,000 years – and Japan, where a Buddhist monk introduced it in the 9th century and where it became central to Japan's famous tea ceremonies. In fact, 80 per cent of the tea that China produces is green tea, the daily drink of the Chinese people. Green tea was widely drunk in Europe before black tea became more popular. The health benefits of green tea in protecting against heart disease and certain types of cancer have been recognized of late, and it is now better known in the West than it used to be. Specialists can now be found dealing only in green tea. The most common of the Chinese ones is 'Gunpowder'. In this variety the leaves are tightly rolled into pellets. The astringent 'Sencha' is the best-known Japanese tea variety.

White teas

This little-known tea variety comes from the same plant as green, black and Oolong tea, but it is uncured and unoxidized. The fresh leaves have a white downy coat. Once picked, they are fast-dried rather than roasted. White tea comprises buds (or tips) and young leaves, which have been found to contain less caffeine than older leaves. White teas are thought to be the most beneficial to health, since they contain greater numbers of antioxidants, which are thought to help fight cancers. However, this tea needs brewing for a long time in order for the flavour to be released.

Tea blends

A blend is a mixture of leaves from different plantations. Blends are made in India as well as other countries, though, like olive oil and wine, blended tea is not perhaps for the purist. Some blends are machine-harvested teas and can play an undistinguished role in the proprietary mixtures of tea that are widely sold.

A few superior teas exist however, which are defined as speciality tea but which are created from a blend, for instance the blend known as Earl Grey, the bestselling and highly regarded tea. This blend of black teas is flavoured with essence of bergamot, and tea companies frequently claim to have some unique access to the original recipe. However, Earl Grey, the popular British prime minister who saw the Reform Act through Parliament in the 1830s, almost certainly had nothing to do with its formulation. Although the blend is supposedly of Chinese origin, in fact the bergamot fruit is a spontaneous mutation of the bitter orange, and has never been grown in China. Earl Grey tea is best enjoyed black, or with a splash of milk, or a thin slice of lemon.

Another blend that has speciality tea status is 'English Breakfast' (also known as 'Irish' and 'Royal Breakfast'), which could consist of teas from anywhere, the only consensus being that they should be of a reasonably high quality and have a strong flavour.

Speciality teas

These are the aristocrats of the tea world and are considered sufficiently refined and distinctive to be drunk unblended. India and Sri Lanka produce speciality teas from their distinct regions and plantations as well as blended teas. India is best known for its delicate Darjeelings and robust Assams. Assam is also known as British tea, because of the British preference to take this strong-flavoured tea with milk and sugar.

Clockwise, from top left

Ceylon tea is a black tea, with citrus notes to the flavour, grown on the island of Sri Lanka (formerly Ceylon).

India has three tea-producing regions – Darjeeling, Assam and Nilgiri – and a blend from these produces Indian tea.

Darjeeling tea, named after the Darjeeling region of West Bengal in India, has a unique, much sought-after muscatel flavour.

English Breakfast tea is a blended tea with a strong flavour intended to be offset by the addition of milk and sugar.

Earl Grey tea is infused with bergamot, the pungent oil of a citrus fruit. It is a popular tea in Britain and North America.

Assam tea, manufactured from leaves picked in the Assam region of India, has a full-bodied flavour.

The region of Darjeeling produces the 'champagne of teas', prized for its light colour and fine flavour. The first crop of the year is known as the 'first flush' and has a fanatical following in northern Germany. Darjeelings are all grown for export.

Assam, the other leading Indian tea, comes from the valley of the lower Brahmaputra River where indigenous tea plants were discovered in the 1840s. The Assam Company, which still exists today, pioneered the estate system there. The best Assams have a rich, almost tarry flavour. Lesser ones are often used to give strength to blends such as English Breakfast.

In Sri Lanka too, teas are often packaged according to the plantation or tea garden from which they are hand-picked. The government of that country still permits the use of the old colonial name of Ceylon in connection with its fine, golden teas. The two best-known are the pungent Uvas of the east and softer Dimbulas of the west. China, like India and Sri Lanka, produces many speciality teas.

Below It is worth taking the time to consider the flavour of the tea and choosing one that will complement the food on offer.

Herbal & flavoured teas

The average cup of tea contains about half the amount of caffeine as an equivalent cup of coffee. Many people, however, are concerned about consuming excessive quantities of caffeine. For them, herb and fruit teas, or tisanes, are the ideal substitute.

Herbal and fruit teas frequently, but not always, contain no 'real' tea (derived from the bush *Camellia sinensis*). The case against caffeine has led to an enormous surge in demand for herbal and fruit teas. Many of these tisanes offer a range of delights for the palate, and some herb teas may have genuine medicinal properties. The key issue in this respect is the level of essential oils left in the plant material used in the blends.

An anomaly exists here too: 'Moroccan mint' sounds as if it should be pure mint, but in fact is mint blended with black tea. The result of this proliferation is that the grocer's shelf is a minefield for those wanting to drink 'healthy', caffeinate-free tea. Reading the packet carefully is the only solution.

Herbal teas
The essential oils in all herb teas decay with oxidation and time, so the best way to reap the benefits is to buy them fresh, or preserved in sachets. Depending on where you live, some herb teas can be grown in your garden or window box, and there is something particularly pleasing about drinking a preparation of the leaves of a plant that you have grown yourself.

Below Fruit teas are infusions of dehydrated fruits and flowers.

Chamomile tea is associated with inducing sleep and a calmed state – making a fresh brew with leaves just picked ensures the essential oils go into the brew.

Other popular herb teas include peppermint and fennel, which act as aids to digestion, lime flower, nettle and verbena. Tea manufacturers have made considerable efforts over the last few years to create blends claiming specific effects. Teas with names like 'Tranquillity', 'Yogi' and 'Detox' are available, but check the essential oil content before you buy.

Fruit teas
The packets of fruit blends claim no such medicinal effects, and are drunk purely for their flavour, which like any new tea, is an acquired taste. However, it is possible to buy fruit teas that use purely natural ingredients, as opposed to artificial or 'nature identical', meaning created in a laboratory to replicate the flavour it purports to be. Such fruit flavours may well be tasty, but they have never had the benefit of sunshine or a warm breeze.

Beware though, many fruit teas have black tea as a base and are flavoured with the fruit rind or dried fruit as part of the manufacturing process. Lemon tea, made by adding lemon slices to black tea, may well be the precursor of fruit teas. Always read the label carefully.

A healthy balance
Many tea drinkers regard herb and fruit teas with suspicion, but these infusions are becoming increasingly popular as the health issues surrounding caffeine consumption become more widely recognized.

Clockwise, from top left
Chamomile tea is made using fresh or dried flowers.
Mint tea is easy to make, using the fresh herb peppermint. Pick a sprig and infuse in boiling water.
Ginger tea is made using slices of the fresh ginger root.
Naturally caffeine-free, Rooibos or red bush tea is derived from the plant of that name.
Ginseng tea is said to have many health benefits. The tea is made from the fleshy root.
Nettle tea is made from the young leaves of stinging nettles. Its flavour is unlike any other.

The art of brewing tea

The key ingredient of a perfect cup of tea is easily taken for granted – it is none other than water. This should be freshly drawn, which means that the cold tap should be allowed to run for half a minute, at the very least, before the kettle is filled.

Water that has been sitting in the pipes overnight is stale and flat. Likewise twice-boiled water is dull and lifeless, so empty the kettle before filling it with fresh. The hardness of your water supply has a great influence on the quality of your tea. Some manufacturers even go to the lengths of making specific blends for specific areas. Very soft water mutes the nuances of flavour in a tea, and very hard water tends to dull the appearance of the brew and can create an unpleasant scum. Filtering the water before boiling always improves its performance.

1 Always warm the pot before measuring in the tea. Either hold the inverted pot over the spout of the kettle as it boils, or swill the teapot with boiling water before adding the tea leaves.

2 There is no fixed amount of tea that should be used. Large leaf teas occupy more volume than small leaf ones, so adjust the measure accordingly.

3 Tea brews best at boiling point, so pour the water on to the tea leaves as soon as the water boils. Stir briskly. Allow to stand for at least 3 minutes.

4 Pour the tea through a strainer once it has brewed to your preferred strength, then add lemon, milk or sugar as desired.

Adding lemon Many people drink black tea with a slice of lemon for added zest – though some tea purists feel you shouldn't add anything. Never add milk to tea that is already flavoured with lemon.

Adding milk To temper the bitterness of black tea, milk can be added. It doesn't matter whether you add the milk before or after the tea – adding it first helps it to mix but adding it after gives more control of the colour.

Adding sugar As with the addition of lemon, sweetness is all a matter of individual preference. White sugar (loose or in lumps) can be added to black tea, to tea with milk, and to lemon tea.

Making tea with fresh herbs

The same general rules apply for brewing herbal infusions from fresh leaves as they do for brewing tea from dried leaves. The exception is fresh ginger tea made using thin slices of peeled root ginger: this should be allowed to steep for at least 5 minutes.

The difference between this technique and making tea is that you pick your own leaves, so correct plant identification is crucial. Fresh mint, in a variety of types (spearmint, chocolate mint) is one of the most popular. Use one sprig of your chosen herb per person.

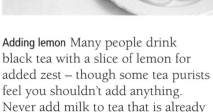

1 Either add the chosen herb leaves to the warmed teapot, as for tea, or, if you are making an individual cup, you could put the sprig straight into the cup,

2 Pour on freshly boiled water and allow the herb to steep until the infusion has reached the desired strength. Remove the herb using a spoon or just leave it in the cup, or strain it from a teapot as you serve. Add a little sugar, if you like.

Other drinks

In addition to tea and herbal infusions, you can of course enjoy many other drinks at teatime. Coffee is the obvious choice, whether hot or cold, along with hot chocolate, and a wide selection of elegant thirst-quenchers for warm days or for those who avoid caffeine.

Fresh coffee

Simple filter coffee made in a cafetière is often best for afternoon tea, complementing rather than competing with the food.

SERVES 4

freshly boiled water (see page 20)
60ml/4 tbsp freshly ground coffee of your choice

milk, to serve (optional)
sugar, preferably raw sugar, in lumps, to serve (optional)

1 Prewarm the cafetière by half filling it with some of the boiling water or inverting it over the spout of the kettle as it boils. Pour away this water.

2 Put the coffee in the bottom of the cafetière and pour over the water, which should be just off the boil. Leave to stand for 3–4 minutes.

3 Stir with a spoon, then slowly push down the plunger. For an elegant touch, transfer the coffee into a warmed china coffee pot. Serve with milk and sugar.

Hot chocolate

Proper hot chocolate, made with good-quality chocolate, full-fat milk and, if you like, a hint of cardamom, is a sophisticated treat.

SERVES 4

900ml/1½ pints/3½ cups milk
2 cardamom pods, bruised (optional)

200g/7oz plain (semisweet) chocolate, broken into pieces
whipped cream, to serve (optional)

1 Put the milk in a pan with the cardamom pods, if using, and bring to the boil.

2 Add the chocolate and whisk until melted.

3 Using a slotted spoon, remove the cardamom pods and discard, if necessary.

4 Pour the hot chocolate into heatproof glasses, mugs or cups and serve with whipped cream, if you like, though this may be a bit much for afternoon tea.

Coffee: The nutritional information will vary according to the type of coffee you use, and how much milk and sugar, if any is added.
Chocolate: Energy 220kcal/924kJ; Protein 8.1g; Carbohydrate 25.3g, of which sugars 25.1g; Fat 10.4g, of which saturates 6.4g; Cholesterol 13mg; Calcium 248mg; Fibre 0.6g; Sodium 88mg.

Cinnamon iced coffee

For those who prefer coffee to the traditional afternoon drink, this beverage is perfect for hot summer days.

SERVES 2

5ml/1 tsp ground cinnamon
400ml/14fl oz/1⅔ cups milk
40g/1½oz/3 tbsp caster
(superfine) sugar

300ml/½ pint/1¼ cups strong cold espresso coffee
ice cubes, to serve
cinnamon sticks, to serve

1 Put the cinnamon and a quarter of the milk in a small pan with the sugar. Bring the milk slowly to the boil, then remove from the heat and leave to cool.

2 Turn the cinnamon milk into a large jug. Add the remaining milk and the coffee and whisk well, using a hand-held electric wand, until frothy.

3 Pour into glasses with ice. Serve with cinnamon stick stirrers.

Green tea latte

This Asian twist on an Italian classic is a delightful, sweet beverage. The green tea has a refreshing quality and distinctive flavour.

SERVES 4

1 litre/1¾ pints/4 cups milk,
preferably full-fat
60ml/4 tbsp green tea powder
or matcha, plus extra for dusting

30ml/2 tbsp sugar
120ml/4fl oz/½ cup whipping
cream

1 Heat the milk in a pan over a low heat until simmering. Add the green tea powder and half the sugar and stir well. Remove from the heat and pour the tea into a bowl or jug. Leave to cool before chilling.

2 When ready to serve the tea, whisk the cream until it begins to thicken. Then add the remaining caster sugar and continue to whisk until the cream is light and fluffy.

3 Pour the tea into glasses and top with whipped cream. Dust each glass with a little green tea powder and serve.

Iced Coffee: Energy 218kcal/915kJ; Protein 7.1g; Carbohydrate 30.8g, of which sugars 29.9g; Fat 8.2g, of which saturates 5.1g; Cholesterol 28mg; Calcium 251mg; Fibre 0g; Sodium 88mg.
Latte: Energy 269kcal/1126kJ; Protein 9.2g; Carbohydrate 23g, of which sugars 23g; Fat 16.4g, of which saturates 10.3g; Cholesterol 46mg; Calcium 323mg; Fibre 0g; Sodium 116mg.

Fresh orange squash

A league above store-bought cordial, this bright and zesty squash is packed with flavour, and makes a lovely alternative to tea.

**MAKES 600ML/
1 PINT, TO DILUTE**

90g/3oz/½ cup caster (superfine) sugar
100ml/3½fl oz/scant ½ cup water

6 large oranges
still or sparkling mineral water, to serve

1 Put the sugar in a pan with the water. Heat gently, stirring until the sugar has dissolved. Bring to the boil and boil rapidly for 3 minutes until syrupy. Remove from the heat and leave to cool.

2 Cut away the skins from three of the six oranges. Chop the flesh into small pieces. Chop the remaining oranges, with skins on, into similar-size pieces.

3 Push all the orange pieces through a juicer, then mix with the syrup. To serve, dilute to taste.

Barley water

Barley water is an old-fashioned but refreshing drink. It is usually served cold, but is equally delicious as a hot drink.

MAKES 10 GLASSES

50g/2oz/⅓ cup pearl barley, washed
rind and juice of 1 lemon
600ml/1 pint/2½ cups water

caster (superfine) sugar, to taste
still or sparkling mineral water, to serve

1 In a large pan cover the pearl barley with cold water. Bring to the boil and simmer for 2 minutes. Strain.

2 Return the barley to the rinsed pan. Add the lemon rind and the measured 600ml/1 pint/2½ cups water.

3 Bring to the boil over medium heat and simmer for 1½–2 hours, stirring occasionally.

4 Strain the liquid into a jug or pitcher, add the lemon juice, and sweeten to taste. Dilute with water to serve.

Orange: Energy 484kcal/2064kJ; Protein 2.2g; Carbohydrate 125.7g, of which sugars 125.7g; Fat 0.4g, of which saturates 0g; Cholesterol 0mg; Calcium 62mg; Fibre 0.5g; Sodium 40mg.
Barley: Energy 38kcal/161kJ; Protein 0.4g; Carbohydrate 9.4g, of which sugars 5.3g; Fat 0g, of which saturates 0g; Cholesterol 3.8mg; Calcium 21mg; Fibre 0g; Sodium 0.5mg.

Sparkling elderflower

This fermented drink made from fragrant elderflowers is sophisticated and refreshing – perfect for afternoon tea.

**MAKES 9 LITRES/
2 GALLONS**
24 elderflower heads
2 lemons
1.3kg/3lb/scant 7 cups granulated white sugar

30ml/2 tbsp white wine vinegar
9 litres/2 gallons/2.4 US gallons water

1 Find a clean bucket that you can cover with a clean cloth. Put all the ingredients into it.

2 Cover the bucket with a plastic sheet and leave overnight.

3 Strain the elderflower drink then pour into bottles, leaving a space of about 2.5cm/1in at the top.

4 Leave sealed for about 2 weeks in a cool place. A fermentation takes place and the result is a delightful, sparkling, refreshing, non-alcoholic drink.

Still lemonade

Fresh lemonade is often seen on the menu in smart contemporary cafés and tea shops. It is easy to make yourself, and tastes wonderful.

MAKES 4–6 GLASSES
3 unwaxed lemons
115g/4oz/generous ½ cup caster (superfine) sugar
900ml/1½ pints/3½ cups boiling water

Variation
You could make this drink with limes, oranges or grapefruit, if you like.

1 Pare the skin from the lemons with a vegetable peeler. Put the lemon rind and sugar into a bowl, add the boiling water and stir well until the sugar dissolves.

2 Cover and leave to cool.

3 Squeeze the juice from the lemons. Add it to the flavoured water, and mix well.

4 Strain into a jug or pitcher, and serve, garnished with mint leaves if you like.

Elderflower: Energy 1282kcal/5467kJ; Protein 1.7g; Carbohydrate 339.8g, of which sugars 339.8g; Fat 0g, of which saturates 0g; Cholesterol 0mg; Calcium 173mg; Fibre 0g; Sodium 20mg.
Lemonade: Energy 115kcal/489kJ; Protein 0.2g; Carbohydrate 30.4g, of which sugars 30.4g; Fat 0g, of which saturates 0g; Cholesterol 0mg; Calcium 17mg; Fibre 0g; Sodium 2mg.

Baking techniques

Good-quality ingredients are the foundation of deliciously successful cakes and bakes, so information is provided in this chapter on the characteristics of basic ingredients such as sugar, eggs, flour, fats and spices, as well as describing how and why certain pieces of equipment are used. The many methods of making cakes, such as creaming, all-in-one, rubbing-in, melting and whisking, are also described step by step to help you achieve perfect results, and there's a handy guide to what can go wrong and how to rectify the problem in the future. To finish a beautiful cake you may like to add some fabulous decorations in the form of buttercream or cream cheese frosting, colourful glacé icing, a sugarpaste covering, or moulded fondant embellishments.

Left Eggs, sugar, butter and flour are the basic ingredients for making tempting cakes for afternoon tea. Chocolate adds richness.

Essential ingredients

Basic ingredients have different properties, and these, combined with the particular cake method, are what makes such a wide variety of bakes possible. Most cakes are made by mixing sugar with fats, flour and eggs and then adding a variety of flavourings.

Sugars

Not only added for sweetness, sugars produce the structure and texture that make a cake tender, so it's important to use the correct type:

Caster (superfine) sugar is available in white and golden unrefined varieties. It blends easily with fats when beaten or 'creamed' into light sponge mixtures.

Granulated sugar may be coarse white or golden and unrefined and is used for toppings.

Demerara (raw) sugar is golden in colour and has a grainy texture. It is often used for recipes where sugar is melted over heat, or as a decorative topping.

Soft light and dark brown sugars cream well and usually form the base of a fruit cake or are used in recipes where a rich flavour is required. To prevent them from drying out store them in an airtight container.

Muscovado (molasses) sugar is natural and unrefined with an excellent dark colour and richer flavour. It makes fruit cakes and gingerbreads extra special.

Icing (confectioners') sugar is sold as a fine white powder or as an unrefined golden variety. It is used for icings, frostings and decorations. Store the sugar in a dry place, as it tends to absorb moisture. Sift the sugar at least once, or preferably twice before you use it, as it may form hard lumps during storage.

Golden (light corn) syrup, honey, treacle and molasses are thick liquid sugars. They can be used in cakes made by the melting method.

Eggs

Although eggs are often stored in the refrigerator, better baked results will be achieved if they are at room temperature when they are used. The eggs will whisk better than those kept refrigerated and achieve more aeration. Aeration gives more volume but also allows the eggs to blend into mixtures more easily. Cold eggs will tend to curdle a mixture more quickly.

Medium size (US large) eggs are used in this book, unless otherwise stated in the recipe.

Dried egg-white powder gives excellent results and can be substituted in royal icing recipes, or in recipes where you are unsure about the suitability of using raw egg whites. Raw eggs are unsuitable for the elderly, pregnant women, babies and young children.

Flours

Plain (all-purpose) flour provides the structure of a cake but contains nothing to make it rise. Richer cakes that do not need raising agents are made with plain flour.

Self-raising (self-rising) flour has raising agents mixed into it. These create air in the batter to make a cake rise, so self-raising flour is used for sponges and light mixtures that contain little or no fruit. If you have only plain flour, add 12.5ml/2½ tsp baking powder to every 225g/8oz plain flour to make it into a self-raising flour.

Wholemeal (whole-wheat) and brown flours contain bran from the wheat, which provides a good texture with extra fibre. This keeps bakes moist and gives a mellow flavour. If you are substituting brown flour for white, add extra liquid, as the bran will absorb more fluid.

Gram flour is made from ground chickpeas and retains moisture, giving a heavy, moist crumb.

SEPARATING YOLKS AND WHITES

When separating egg whites from their yolks, tip the whites into a cup one at a time so that if there are any specks of yolk or pieces of shell in the cup, you can remove these easily. If yolk is present in a bowl of whites it will prevent whisking and aeration. Even a tiny speck of yolk will stop the whites from whisking up to a foam and you will have wasted the whole mixture.

White flours can be kept in a cool dry place for up to 6 months, but wholemeal flours will not keep for as long because they have a higher fat content. Check the use-by date on packs of all types of flour. Don't add new flour to old, as eventually small micro-organisms that look like tiny black specks may form, and will spread into new flour. Keep all flour dry in a clean airtight container, as damp flour weighs more and therefore alters the measurements in a recipe, which could lead to failure. For a note on gluten-free flours, see page 47.

Raising agents

There are a number of raising agents that, when added to flour, make cakes rise. They produce an airy and light texture. As they are added in small quantities, it is important to be accurate when measuring them out.
Baking powder is a mixture of bicarbonate of soda (baking soda) and cream of tartar. When liquid is added, the powder bubbles and produces carbon dioxide, which expands during baking and creates an airy texture.

Above Flour, sugar, butter and eggs are the starting point for many cakes and bakes, along with raising agents, milk and other dairy products, and all manner of flavourings.

Bicarbonate of soda (baking soda) is a gentler raising agent than baking powder and is often used to give melted or spicy mixtures a lift. It can create a bitter flavour if too much is added.
Cream of tartar is a fast-acting raising agent that works immediately once it touches liquid, so bake the mixture as soon as possible after adding it.

Fats and dairy products

As well as giving flavour and texture to cakes, fats improve their keeping qualities. For cake-making (apart from mixtures that use the rubbed-in method), always use fats at room temperature. Fat and sugar should be beaten to a smooth, rather than grainy, batter.
Butter and hard block margarine can be interchanged in a recipe, but butter will always give the best flavour.

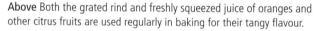

Above Both the grated rind and freshly squeezed juice of oranges and other citrus fruits are used regularly in baking for their tangy flavour.

Above All manner of dairy products are used in baking for structure, moisture, texture and flavour, and served as an accompaniment.

Soft tub margarine is suitable only for all-in-one sponge recipes where all the ingredients are quickly mixed together in one bowl. These cakes usually require an extra raising agent. Don't overbeat, as the mixture will become wet and the cake will sink. Do not substitute for butter or block margarine as it is a different kind of fat, and will not produce the same results.

Vegetable shortenings are flavourless but can be used to produce very pale, light cakes.

Cooking oils can be used in moist cakes such as carrot cake. As they do not hold air, the mixture cannot be creamed and these cakes have a dense texture.

Milk and buttermilk are both used widely in baking, to slacken and moisten mixtures. Buttermilk will also act as a raising agent in recipes that use bicarbonate of soda. The acidity in the buttermilk combines with the bicarbonate of soda to produce carbon dioxide, which raises the mixture as it cooks. If buttermilk is not available, you can make your own souring agent by mixing 300ml/10fl oz low-fat yogurt or milk with 15ml/1 tbsp lemon juice.

Cream adds richness to many recipes and is of course a luxurious finishing touch to numerous classic teatime treats, whether served clotted on scones or whipped for

a filling and topping for indulgent cakes and pastries.

Yogurt can be used to create a moist, tangy cake, usually in combination with oil. Use full-fat for preference.

Cheese French Brie and soft herb and garlic cheese add a light tart flavour to savoury recipes. Cheddar, Parmesan and Stilton each add robust flavour. Ricotta is used in cheesecakes, as is cream cheese, which together with mascarpone can appear in brownies and other bakes.

Fruits

Sultanas (golden raisins), raisins and currants are usually sold pre-washed and cleaned, but it is worth picking them over. Dried fruit benefits from soaking in alcohol or fruit juice, which will make it succulent.

Glacé (candied) and crystallized fruits, such as cherries, ginger or angelica, need to be rinsed and dried to wash away their sugary coating. If you do not do this, the coating may cause the fruits to sink during baking.

Fresh fruit such as berries may be partly cooked with sugar and butter before they are added to the batter. Mandarins or clementines can be boiled and puréed to make zesty cakes. Freshly squeezed juice and grated rind from lemons, limes and oranges are widely used in all manner of cakes, tarts and cookies.

Above Spices such as star anise, cinnamon, nutmeg and cloves bring warmth and their distinct flavours to many cakes, breads and cookies.

Herbs and spices

Frequently used spices for baking include nutmeg, ground ginger, cinnamon, cloves and mixed (apple pie) spice. Dried spices have a long shelf-life but will not keep indefinitely. Buy them in small quantities and keep them in a dark, cool and dry space. If you add spices to hot mixtures, don't measure them into the mixture from the jar, as steam may cause the spice to become damp.

Nuts

Because nuts are expensive and will deteriorate quickly, buy them in small quantities. If you buy a large pack of nuts that you are not going to use immediately, you can freeze them for up to 6 months.

Almonds are bought blanched, slivered, flaked, sliced, ground or whole. To remove the skins from shelled almonds, place the nuts in boiling water for 2–3 minutes. Drain and rub off the skins. Ground nuts have a fine, powdery texture.

Hazelnuts come whole, skinned, unskinned or ground.

Walnuts contain more oil than most other nuts and will quickly become rancid, so don't buy them in bulk. Walnut halves are more expensive, so if you need chopped walnuts, buy walnut pieces.

Chocolate

For a professional finish and fine flavour, buy the best-quality chocolate. Good chocolate is sleek and shiny and will snap easily. It also contains a higher percentage of real cocoa fat, which gives a superior flavour and texture. The amount of cocoa fat or solids will be noted on the wrapper of any chocolate. Those marked as 70 per cent or more cocoa solids will give the best results.

Cocoa powder needs to be cooked so that its flavour will be released. Blend it with boiling water to make it into a paste, then cool it before adding to a recipe.

Drinking chocolate contains milk powder and sugar. Don't substitute it for cocoa powder.

White chocolate may be difficult to work with. Grate it finely, or, if melting it, keep the temperature low.

Alcohol

The alcohol content of any drink you add will evaporate during baking, leaving a luxurious flavour. Calvados (apple brandy) enhances cakes made with pears, apples, or quince. Amaretto (almond-flavoured liqueur) adds to the flavour of peach, almond and apricot bakes. Marsala has a special affinity with pears, chocolate and coffee.

Vegetables

Versatile ingredients in bakes, vegetables should be finely grated before they are added to the batter. Use courgettes (zucchini), marrow, pumpkin, squash, onions, carrots, beetroot and sweet potato for sweet and savoury flavours.

MELTING CHOCOLATE

Melting chocolate needs care and attention. To melt chocolate, break the bar into small pieces and put it in a large heatproof bowl standing over a pan of warm water. Make sure the bowl containing the chocolate is dry and that steam cannot get into the bowl. Heat the water to a gentle simmer, and avoid over-stirring the chocolate as it melts.

Basic equipment

For successful cake-making you need an oven that will retain an accurate and even temperature and some basic equipment. If you're new to baking, start off with some mixing equipment and a few pans. A 900g/2lb loaf tin, a muffin tin and a 20cm/8in cake pan are useful sizes to have.

Baking papers, paper cases and foil
For lining tins and baking sheets use baking parchment, which is non-stick, or greaseproof (waxed) paper. Paper cases can be purchased in many different and convenient sizes to fit round or square cake tins (pans) or cupcake and muffin tins. Waxed paper is a useful surface to pipe royal iced decorations on to, as they will peel away easily once dry. Kitchen foil is handy for wrapping rich fruit cakes or for protecting wrapped cakes in the freezer.

Baking sheets
Choose large, heavy-duty baking sheets that will not buckle at high temperatures. Non-stick sheets are useful, but avoid thin, cheaper bakeware, which may bend during baking and cause sloping cakes or burnt edges.

Bowls
You'll need a set of different sizes of bowls for mixing and beating small and large amounts of cake batters, eggs, cream and other liquids.

Electric whisk
A hand-held electric whisk makes quick work of whisking cake batters and egg whites, and is an invaluable aid for cake-making.

Flexible scraper
A flexible scraper is perfect for getting the maximum amount of cake batter out of a bowl. They become softer with use.

Grater
A grater with a fine and a coarse side is useful for grating citrus rinds, chocolate and marzipan. You can also use a zester for citrus rinds.

Measuring spoons and cups
Use a set of standard measuring spoons for accurate measuring of small quantities of ingredients. Sets of plastic or metal measures are sold specifically for this purpose. Remember that all spoon measures should be level. Standard kitchen tablespoons or teaspoons may be inaccurate measures.

Metric and imperial measures are given in the recipes. Follow one set of measurements only, as they are not exact equivalents.

Graded measuring cups are used in many countries in place of kitchen scales and are handy for quick measuring. A measuring jug or cup is vital for liquids and it needs to be graduated in small measures.

Oven
Each recipe usually begins with the oven setting (unless some form of preparation needs to be done in advance). It is important to preheat the oven to the correct temperature before putting a cake in to bake. Before you switch on the oven, it is also important to arrange the shelves to the correct position.

Fan-assisted ovens circulate hot air around the oven and will heat up very quickly. If you are using a fan oven, you will need to reduce the temperature stated in the recipe by 10 per cent; for example, if the

Left Having the correct equipment makes producing perfect cakes and bakes much easier, and is well worth the investment.

baking temperature is 180°C/350°F/Gas 4, reduce it to 160°C/325°F/Gas 3. If the oven is too hot, the outside of a cake will burn before the inside has had time to cook. If it is too cool, cakes may sink or not rise evenly. Try not to open the oven door until at least halfway through the baking time when the cake has had time to rise and set, as a sudden drop in temperature will stop the cake rising and it will therefore sink.

Palette knives or spatulas
These are ideal for many jobs including loosening cakes from their tins, lifting cakes and smoothing on icing and frostings.

Pastry brush
This is necessary to brush glazes over cakes and to brush melted butter into tins. Brushes wear out and start to shed bristles if used regularly, so keep a spare one handy.

Scales
Weighing scales are important for accurate measuring of ingredients, a digital or electric scale is particularly good for tiny amounts. Also have a set of measuring cups.

Scissors
These are essential for cutting lining papers to size and snipping dried fruits or nuts into chunks.

Sieves
A large wire sieve or strainer is useful for sifting flour and dry ingredients. A smaller nylon sieve can be kept just for icing (confectioners') sugar.

Skewer or cake tester
A thin metal skewer is used to test if the inside of a cake is cooked.

Spoons
Keep a large wooden spoon aside just for baking, for beating mixtures, butters and creaming. Don't use one that has been used for frying savoury things such as onions, as the flavours may taint the cake batter. Use a metal spoon for folding flour into cake batter.

Tins and pans
Always use the size of baking tin (pan) in the recipe. If you use too large a tin, your cake may be too shallow when it is baked. Too small a tin may cause a peak in the mixture to form, which will crack or sink in the middle.

Choose good-quality rigid bakeware. When buying new tins, remember that top-quality tins will last longer and give better results. Non-stick coatings on some of

Above An electric whisk is one of the most useful pieces of equipment in the kitchen. Use a large mixing bowl so the content doesn't spray out.

the new ranges of bakeware need almost no greasing and cakes turn out beautifully, as do cakes cooked in the new heatproof flexible-type muffin and loaf moulds.

Sandwich tins and shallow round tins are designed to bake light sponges quickly.

Loaf tins in small and large sizes are ideal for teabreads and loaf cakes.

Deep round and square heavy-duty cake tins are ideal for baking rich fruit cakes.

Springform tins are round baking tins that have a clipped side that can be loosened and removed easily from delicate bakes such as light sponges or cheesecakes. A loose-based tin makes a good substitute.

Muffin tins are available in sets of six or twelve indentations and have deep-set muffin holes for larger individual cakes.

Fairy cake, bun or patty tins are similar to muffin tins but have shallower indentations in the individual tins for making smaller cakes. Line each indentation with a paper case.

Ring, bundt and Kugelhopf tins are round metal moulds with a hole or funnel in the centre and are specially designed for baking angel cakes and ring-shaped cakes. Grease these moulds well with melted butter and put small strips of baking parchment in the base of plain ring moulds to aid the release of the cake.

Wire racks
These cooling racks allow air to circulate around the hot baked cakes so that they will cool without becoming moist underneath.

Successful cake-making

Paying attention to the detail of a recipe will help to ensure a perfect cake. So, get all your equipment ready and prepare your cake tin. Take care with accurate measuring of ingredients, and know how to test that the cake is cooked.

Accurate weighing and measuring

Ensure that you have all the necessary ingredients before baking. Recipes usually specify imperial, metric or cup weights and you must stick to one set only and never combine these weights, as they are not exact equivalents. If the measurements are muddled, it will affect the quality of the baked goods. Use good kitchen scales for weighing or graded measuring cups and scoops. These cups should be levelled for accurate measuring unless the recipe calls for a 'generous' cup.

All spoon measurements must be level using a recognized set of metric or imperial spoon measures. Never estimate weights, as you will rarely achieve an accurate result. Do not measure ingredients over the mixing bowl in case you spill too much.

TINS AND COMPARABLE SIZING

If you use a tin (pan) that is a different size from the one stated in the recipe, the baking time, height, texture and appearance of the cake may be affected. Although you can use a square tin instead of a round tin, the equivalent sizes are not exactly equal, as they involve a 2.5cm/1in size difference. A square tin will have a larger area than its round equivalent; for example, a 20cm/8in round cake tin will take the same quantity of mixture as an 18cm/7in square tin.

Preparing tins

When recipes give instructions on how to prepare and line tins (pans), don't be tempted to skimp on them, or you may ruin the baked cake. If using tins without a non-stick coating, give them a light greasing before use. Line the base of a tin to help the cake turn out easily.

1 If lining a round tin: apply a thin film of melted butter with a pastry brush, or rub around the tin with kitchen paper and a little softened margarine.

2 Place the tin on a sheet of baking parchment and draw around it with a pencil. Cut out.

3 Cut a piece of baking parchment 2.5cm/1in wider than the depth of the tin and long enough to fit around the circumference. Make a fold along one long edge, about 2.5cm/1in deep. Snip this folded edge at regular intervals.

4 Line the sides of the tin using the strip, with the snipped edge at the base, lying flat. Smooth the baking parchment flat against the sides. Lightly grease any overlap of the edges so that it doesn't protrude into the cake batter. Lightly grease the snipped edges. If your tin has a loose base this will stop the baking batter from escaping and burning on the oven base.

5 Fit the rounds of paper in the base of the tin to cover the snipped edge of the side lining.

6 Tins for rich fruit cake batters are double-lined on the inside and lined on the outside. Cut a piece of baking parchment large enough to fold double and to stand 5cm/2in higher than the tin sides before continuing as for step 4. A layer of brown paper wrapped around the outside protects the cake from forming a dark crust.

7 If lining a square or rectangular tin: grease it well.

8 Cut a sheet of parchment larger than the tin, then cut into each corner on the diagonal.

9 Press the paper into place, smoothing it and folding in the snipped corners so they lie flat.

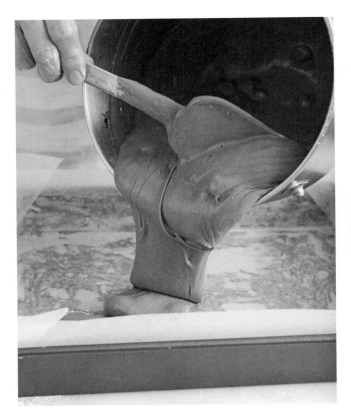

Above Be gentle when you pour cake batter into a prepared tin and spread it out – you want to retain as much air as possible.

Above Cake should be completely cold before you fill, ice, slice and store it, otherwise fillings and icing will melt and the cake won't slice neatly.

Filling a cake tin with batter

Pour batter into the centre of the tin and spread it out to the edges evenly. Do this lightly without removing too much air from the batter. Rub off any drips.

Checking to see if a cake is cooked

There are several clues to help determine whether a cake is ready. Has it baked for the suggested time? The baking times may need reviewing if you know that your oven temperature is inaccurate, if other items are being cooked at the same time, or if the oven door is opened in the baking process.

1 Cakes should be golden, risen and firm to the touch when pressed lightly in the centre. Lighter sponges and cakes should be a pale golden colour and the sides should shrink away slightly from the sides of the tin.

2 To test to see if a cake is baked through, insert a thin warmed skewer into the deepest part of the centre, which should take longest to bake. If the cake is cooked, the skewer should come out perfectly cleanly with no mixture sticking to it. If there is mixture on the skewer, bake the cake for a little longer and test again.

Releasing from the tin and cooling cakes

As freshly baked cakes are very fragile, they need time to stand in the tin to cool for a short time to firm them. Sponges and delicate cakes need 3–4 minutes standing time, but rich fruit cakes are very soft when freshly baked, so leave these in the tin for longer. To give a good shape to the edges, very rich fruit cakes such as wedding cakes should be left in the tins to go cold.

1 Loosen the cake sides by running a small metal spatula around the inside of the tin between the lining paper and the tin.

2 Turn the cake out to go cold on a wire rack. Put a wire rack on top of the cake tin, then turn the whole thing over so that the cake is upside down. Use oven gloves to protect your hands.

3 Peel away the lining papers from the base of the cake while it is warm. Turn the cake back the right way up. Leave to go completely cold before icing and storing.

Right To prolong their keeping qualities, cakes and bakes should be stored in an airtight container, in a cool dark place or a refrigerator.

Storing cakes

Make sure cakes are completely cold before storing, or condensation will form and cause the cakes to go mouldy. Plastic food containers will encourage cakes to keep moist, so are ideal for storing richer sponges, but an airtight cake tin is necessary to keep fatless sponge-type cakes dry. If you don't have a large cake container, invert a large mixing bowl over the cake on a flat surface.

Cakes with fresh cream fillings and decorations need to be kept in the refrigerator and ideally eaten on the day of filling with cream. Fatless sponges such as Swiss rolls (jelly rolls), will keep for only 1–2 days. Sponges with added fat will store for 3–5 days and richer cakes, such as creamed sponges, will keep for up to 1 week. Light fruit cakes will store for 2 weeks in a tin but rich fruit cakes will keep for up to 3 months after cutting.

Storing a rich fruit cake

Rich fruit cakes, such as wedding cakes, will mature in flavour and improve in texture if kept for 3 months before being eaten, especially if you feed them with alcohol two or three times during that 3 months' storage time. Store undecorated fruit cakes in their baking papers, encasing the original wrappings of the cake with clean baking parchment and sealing with tape. Wrap in a double layer of foil and seal well, then store in a cool dry place.

Feeding a fruit cake

Fruit cakes fed with alcohol have a mellow flavour. Prick the surface of the baked cake with a cocktail stick (toothpick) and brush with a little alcohol such as rum, brandy or sweet sherry. The alcohol should infuse the cake and help preserve it.

Freezing cakes

Most cakes will freeze well, undecorated. Cool each cake completely, then wrap in strong clear film (plastic wrap) or kitchen foil to exclude as much air as possible. Label and freeze away from strong-smelling foodstuffs such as fish. To use, unwrap and thaw it at room temperature on racks, allowing plenty of time for larger cakes.

Different methods of making cakes

There are just a few basic ways to make cakes. Each method gives the cake a different texture and consistency. To get perfect results, it's important to know how the different types of mixtures should be prepared and what to look out for.

Classic creaming method

Light cakes are made by the creaming method, which means that the butter and sugar are first beaten or 'creamed' together. A little care is needed to achieve the perfectly creamed mixture.

1 Use a large bowl, and either an electric whisk or a wooden spoon to beat the fat and sugar together until pale and fluffy. This should take about 5 minutes. You can also use a stand mixer, if you prefer, which leaves you free to weigh out the flour while the fat and sugar blend. As the sugar dissolves it blends with the fat, lightening it and making it very soft. Have the fat at room temperature to make beating it easier.

2 Now add the eggs one by one, beating after each addition, to form a slackened batter. Eggs for baking are always best used at room temperature to prevent the mixture from 'splitting' or curdling, which will happen with cold eggs. Adding a teaspoon of flour with each beaten egg will help to keep the mixture light and smooth and prevent the mixture from separating. A badly mixed and curdled batter will hold less air and be heavy, or it can cause a sunken cake.

3 Sift in the flour, holding the sieve high above the bowl so it aerates. Fold it in very gently, but thoroughly, using a figure-of-eight motion and a large metal spoon, which will cut through the mixture without removing air more effectively than a wooden spoon.

All-in-one method

This one-stage method is quick and easy, and it's perfect for those new to baking, as it does not involve any complicated techniques. It's an ideal method for making light sponges, but softened butter or tub margarine at room temperature must be used.

1 Place all the ingredients in a large bowl and quickly beat together using a wooden spoon or an electric mixer for just a few minutes until smooth. Do not over-beat, as this will make the mixture too wet.

Rubbing-in method

This method is used for easy fruit cakes and small buns such as rock buns. The fat should ideally be cold.

1 Rub the fat into the flour with your fingertips until the mixture resembles fine crumbs. Shake the bowl to allow larger lumps of fat to rise to the surface, then rub them in. Repeat until an even crumb is achieved.

2 Stir in the dry ingredients, then add enough liquid to give a soft mixture that will drop easily from a spoon.

MAKING FRUIT CAKES

Rich fruit cakes are usually made by the creaming method, then soaked dried fruits and nuts are folded in with the flour.

1 Cream the butter and sugar in a large bowl, add the eggs, a few spoonfuls of flour and treacle (molasses).

2 Add the flour and any spices, then add the dried fruits, stirring to incorporate all the ingredients. The batter for a rich fruit cake is usually quite stiff.

Melting method

Cakes with a moist and sticky texture, such as gingerbread, are made by the melting method. These cakes use a high proportion of sugar and syrup and may contain heavier grains such as ground nuts or oats, which means that although they rise, the texture is heavier than that of other cakes. They benefit from storing for at least a day before cutting, to improve their moisture and stickiness.

1 Over gentle heat and using a large pan, warm together the fat, sugar and syrup, until the sugar granules have dissolved and the mixture is liquid. If the heat is set too high, the sugar will burn before the fat has melted. Stir occasionally, but keep watching so that the sugar does not burn on the base of the pan.

2 Allow the mixture to cool a little before beating in the flour, eggs, spices and remaining ingredients to make a batter. Bicarbonate of soda (baking soda) is often used as a raising agent in this method, to help raise a heavy batter.

Whisking method

Light and feathery sponges are made by the whisking method. These are not easy cakes for beginners, and require a little skill and care or else they fall flat while baking. The only raising agent for this method is the air that has been trapped into the mixture during mixing. As the air expands in the heat of the oven, the cake rises. Fatless sponges such as a Swiss roll (jelly roll) are made by whisking.

1 A classic sponge is made by whisking eggs and caster (superfine) sugar together over a pan of hot water until the batter is thick enough to leave a trail when the whisk is lifted away from the bowl. When the mixture is pale, thick and airy, remove from the heat and continue to whisk until the batter is cool and doubled in volume.

2 Add the flour by sifting some over the surface and gently folding it in, using a large metal spoon, until all the flour is evenly blended. A metal spoon will cut through the batter retaining as much air as possible.

3 Be gentle with the mixture; it is essential not to knock out the air bubbles when folding in the flour.

Problem solving

If you accurately measure ingredients and follow the recipe steps carefully, your cakes should work out well each time, but if your cake does not turn out as expected, look at the following problems and solutions to find out what might have happened.

1 Why do cakes stick to the tin?
- You will not be able to turn a cake out of a tin if it was not greased sufficiently into all the corners or properly lined with paper.
- Poor-quality tins tend to produce bad results and can buckle in the heat, causing a misshapen cake.
- If the cake has been left in the tin for too long it may have dried to it.

2 Why does a cake sink?
- Too much raising agent used in proportion to the amount of flour and other ingredients.
- If the oven is too cool, the cake will be under-baked and sink.
- Mixture that is too wet, caused by over-beating when using soft tub margarine or adding too much liquid.
- If the mixture was cooked in a tin that is too small, it will not cook through properly.
- Opening or slamming the oven door during cooking.
- If the cake is under-baked, particularly in the middle, and the batter is damp and heavy, the cake will sink.

3 What causes a close and heavy texture?
- Too little raising agent, or adding too much fat, egg or flour.
- A mixture that is too dry or too wet.
- If the cake is not whisked or beaten sufficiently to incorporate air, the texture will be coarse.
- Too much sugar in the batter.
- Baking in an oven that is too cool.
- Fat and sugar not beaten enough before the other ingredients added.

4 Why do small fairy cakes spread?
- Small cakes spread out if the mixture is too wet or if there is too much mixture in each paper case; for best results half-fill the cases.
- Adding too much or too little raising agent.

5 What causes a cake with a dry texture?
- The cake is baked too slowly or contains too much raising agent.
- The mixture was not rubbed in or beaten sufficiently.
- The cake was over-baked, making it dry.

6 What causes a dark, hard outer crust?
- Too hot an oven or over-baking in a fan-assisted oven at a high temperature. If you are using a fan-assisted oven you will need to turn the temperature down by 10 degrees, or follow your instruction booklet.
- Rich fruit cakes taking several hours to bake should be protected by a double lining inside the tin and by brown paper and newspaper around the outside.

7 Why do cakes fail to rise?
- Insufficient raising agent or over-beating a mixture, which knocks out the air.
- If a mixture is too stiff and does not contain enough liquid or is baked in too cool an oven.
- If too large a cake tin was used.
- If the batter was left for a while before baking it will not rise.

8 What causes a crack or peak to appear in the top of the cake?
- If the tin is too small and contains too much mixture, the batter will rise up and the top will form a peak.
- Baking in an oven that is too hot, or baking the cake too near the heat at the top of the oven.
- The mixture is too wet or too dry.
- Too little liquid in the batter.

9 Why does the fruit sink in a sponge cake?
- All vine fruits must be dry when added to the mixture. Glacé (candied) cherries must be rinsed, dried and tossed in flour to prevent them sinking.
- If the mixture is too wet or if it contains too much raising agent.
- Using too cool an oven or opening the oven door too soon before the end of the baking time.

10 Why do large air bubbles and tunnels form in the centre of the cake?
- An uneven texture is caused by under-mixing when adding the flour or liquid.
- If the mixture is too dry it will tend to contain pockets of air instead of the air being evenly distributed.
- If the flour and raising agent are not sifted in or properly mixed together.

Successful icing

Having made the perfect cake, it's now time to decorate it. There are various different types of icing, from simple glacé icing and rich buttercream or cream cheese frosting to mouldable sugarpaste icing, used for covering the outside of cakes and for making decorations.

Buttercream or cream cheese frosting

Rich, sweet and spreadable, these types of icing are used both to sandwich cakes together and to decorate them.

It is important to make sure that your butter or cream cheese are at room temperature and easily spreadable.

1 Sift the icing/confectioners' sugar into a bowl.

2 Add the butter or cream cheese to the bowl. Using an electric mixer, whisk or beater, start to whisk very slowly at first (take care that the icing sugar does not explode in a dust cloud).

3 If called for in the recipe, add the milk gradually until the icing is thick and stiff and holds a peak when you lift up the beater.

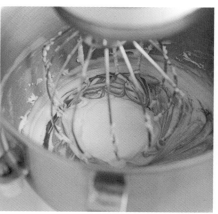

4 Whisk for a few minutes until it becomes light and airy. If it is too stiff, whisk in a little more milk. If you add too much milk and it does not hold a peak, whisk in more icing sugar.

5 Add any colouring you intend to use, and mix briefly until well blended and you have achieved an even colour.

6 Instead of or in addition to colouring your buttercream, you can add flavourings – for instance vanilla, cocoa powder, peppermint extract or citrus juice.

Glacé icing

Also known as water icing, glacé icing is made with finely sifted icing (confectioners') sugar and hot water, and makes a basic topping that is suitable for many cakes. The icing can be flavoured with vanilla, fruit juice and rind, chocolate, coffee or alcohol, and looks wonderful in delicate, pastel colours. It is important to get the consistency exactly right: too thick and it will not form a super-smooth glossy coating; too thin and it will run over the top and down the sides of the cake. Glacé icing sets to form a crisp surface, but never becomes rock-hard. The consistency determines how many cakes the icing covers.

MAKES ENOUGH FOR 16 CUPCAKES
225g/8oz/2 cups icing (confectioners') sugar
15–30ml/1–2 tbsp hot water
few drops of food colouring

1 Sift the icing sugar into a bowl, then gradually mix in the water, a few drops at a time, beating until the mixture is the consistency of cream.

2 Add one or two drops of food colouring (with caution). For a more vibrant colour use paste food colouring, available from specialist suppliers. Stir until evenly coloured.

3 Use the icing immediately, while it is smooth and fluid. Add any further decoration before the icing dries.

GLACÉ ICING VARIATIONS

Fresh fruit flavouring The strained juice from fresh berries such as raspberries, redcurrants or citrus fruits can be used to scent and softly colour plain icing and glazes. A more concentrated citrus hit can be achieved by adding finely grated rind or replacing some of the water used to make up the glacé icing with fruit juice.

Melting liqueur fondant Lift the flavour of icing with 15–30ml/1–2 tbsp crème de framboise (raspberry liqueur), limoncello (lemon liqueur), or another fruit-based liqueur, which add fruity tones.

Iced fruit Small bunches of redcurrants or cherries (with their stalks left on) dipped in melting liqueur fondant and left to set on baking parchment make a very appealing topping for summer cakes. You could also add small bunches of fruit to cake tops for pretty natural decorations.

Decorations Glacé icing is a great base upon which to stick other decorations, such as sweets, sprinkles, sugarpaste flowers, or even plastic toys for a children's birthday party. Work quickly though while the icing is wet. Once it starts to dry adding any decoration will cause the icing to crack and the smooth, glossy surface will spoil.

Sugarpaste

A versatile medium, sugarpaste – also known as fondant – can be rolled out like pastry and used to cover cakes with a perfectly smooth sweet coating. It can also be stamped, embossed and moulded to make decorations. It consists of a combination of liquid glucose, gelatine, glycerine and icing (confectioners') sugar, and can be bought ready-made. You can make it at home, but it is more convenient to buy it, though it is wise to check the brand is suitable if you have a food allergy. When you use it make sure that during and after use you keep it well wrapped with clear film (plastic wrap), or it will become dry and chalky in texture and unusable. If the paste is too sticky, mix in a little finely sifted icing sugar.

To tint sugarpaste

Subtle tones of sugarpaste often look much more appealing than bright ones. If you require a vibrant shade it is better to buy it ready-coloured because the quantities of colouring needed make the paste too wet.

1 To colour sugarpaste add a few drops of food colour or a few specks of paste to a ball of sugarpaste. (A)

2 Knead until the colour is evenly distributed. (B)

ROYAL ICING

Use royal icing to cover Christmas or wedding cakes to form a snowy-white surface, or as edible glue.

MAKES 500G/1LB2OZ
2 egg whites
500g/1lb2oz/5 cups icing (confectioners') sugar, sifted
5ml/1 tsp glycerine
10ml/2 tsp lemon juice

1 Put the egg whites into a grease-free bowl and whisk with a fork to break up the whites until foamy.

2 Sift in half the sugar with the juice and glycerine, and beat for 10 minutes, or until smooth.

3 Gradually sift in the remaining sugar and beat again until thick and smooth. Alternatively, use a hand-held electric mixer set on a slow speed.

4 Keep covered with a damp cloth until you are ready to use or refrigerate in a tightly lidded plastic container. Beat it again before use.

To mould sugarpaste shapes

Plastic chocolate moulds are a good investment for this skill. The fine texture of sugarpaste makes it ideal.

1 Place the paste on a working surface lightly dusted with sifted icing sugar, and knead until it is smooth and free from cracks. Colour it as required.

2 Divide the paste into portions and press each into a decorative mould. Press repeatedly to ensure the paste adheres. Trim the top so that it is smooth and level. (C)

3 Chill for several hours. Press the tip of a knife between the paste and the mould to create an air pocket. Prise out the shape and leave to soften. Smooth out any knife marks once the sugarpaste has softened sufficiently. (D)

To emboss sugarpaste

Imprint patterns in soft sugarpaste with decorative tools.

1 Use a decorative rolling pin or craft stamp, available from sugarcraft stores, and press on to thinly rolled-out paste to leave an imprint. Remove with care. (E)

2 Use a cookie cutter to cut a scalloped circle. Stick to the top of a cupcake with a little royal icing. (F)

To make sugarpaste plunger-cut flowers

The plunge mechanism in each cutter pushes the flower out of the cutter and makes the cupped shape. You just need to add a contrasting centre to finish off.

1 Lightly dust the work surface with sifted icing sugar. Roll out a small ball of coloured sugarpaste to 3mm/⅛in thick using a small rolling pin.

2 Use a plunger cutter to cut out flowers, then lift them using a palette knife or metal spatula to avoid squashing the edges of the petals with your fingers. (G)

3 Using a fine plain nozzle and a little royal icing in a piping bag, pipe a blob at the centre of each flower.

To make stamped sugarpaste flowers

Shaped cutters are available to suit every theme.

1 Roll out a small ball of sugarpaste on a light dusting of icing sugar to 3mm/⅛in thick and cut out each shape (H).

2 Use a ball modelling tool to manipulate the sugarpaste flowers into a cup shape, bending the petals up a little. Pipe the centre and add false stamens if you like. (I)

A

B

C

D

E

F

G

H

I

Successful pastry

Making your own pastry may seem daunting at first, but if you follow a few basic rules and stick to the right quantities, you will soon find it easy. The key is not to hurry and to keep your hands cool when handling the dough. The crisp, light results are always worth the effort.

Shortcrust pastry

This crumbly pastry is the best known and most frequently used type. The following makes enough for a 25cm/10in flan tin (pan) or ten 7.5cm/3in tartlet tins or mini quiche pans. Add the optional sugar if you are making a sweet tart or pie pastry.

MAKES 375G/13OZ

225g/8oz/2 cups plain (all-purpose) flour
pinch of salt
30ml/2 tbsp sugar (optional)

115g/4oz/½ cup chilled butter, diced, or half butter and half lard or white vegetable fat
45–60ml/3–4 tbsp chilled water

1 Sift the flour and salt together into a bowl. Add sugar, if using. Cut the fat into the flour using a pastry blender or use your fingertips to rub it in. Shake the bowl occasionally to bring any large pieces of fat to the top. Blend until the mixture resembles fine breadcrumbs.

2 Sprinkle 45ml/3 tbsp of the water over the mixture and mix with a round-bladed knife until the dough comes together. Add a little more water if the mixture is still too dry; it should just begin to hold together.

3 Gather together to form a ball. Incorporate any loose pieces of the rubbed-in mixture. Knead on a lightly floured surface for just a few seconds until smooth. Wrap in clear film (plastic wrap). Chill for 30 minutes.

Rich shortcrust pastry

Also known as pâte brisée, this is a richer version of shortcrust pastry. This quantity is enough for a 25cm/10in flan tin (pan) or ten 7.5cm/3in tartlet tins or mini quiche pans. Add the optional sugar if you are making a sweet tart or pie pastry.

MAKES 400G/14OZ

225g/8oz/2 cups plain (all-purpose) flour
pinch of salt
30ml/2 tbsp sugar (optional)

150g/5oz/⅔ cup chilled butter, cubed
1 egg yolk
30ml/2 tbsp chilled water

1 Sift the flour and salt into a large mixing bowl. Add sugar, if using. Rub with your fingertips or cut in the butter until the mixture resembles fine breadcrumbs. Cut the fat into the flour using a pastry blender or use your fingertips to rub it in. Shake the bowl occasionally to bring any large pieces of fat to the top. Blend until the mixture resembles fine breadcrumbs.

2 Mix the egg yolk and water together. Sprinkle over the dry ingredients and mix in lightly to form a soft dough.

3 Gather the dough together into a ball. Knead on a floured surface until smooth. Wrap in clear film (plastic wrap) and chill in the refrigerator for 30 minutes before using, or until required.

MAKING SHORTCRUST PASTRY IN A FOOD PROCESSOR

This method of making pastry is good for rich shortcrust, especially where the higher proportion of fat and sugar may make it harder to handle. It also helps to keep the dough cool in hot weather.

1 Put the flour, salt and sugar, if using, into the food processor. Process for 4–5 seconds. Sprinkle the cubes of chilled fat over the dry ingredients and process for 10–12 seconds only, or until the mixture resembles fine breadcrumbs.

2 Sprinkle over the water or other liquid and, using the pulse button, process until it starts to hold together. Pinch a little of the mixture between your finger and thumb; if the dough is too dry, add more water and process for 1–2 seconds more. Do not allow the pastry to form a ball in the food processor.

3 Remove the mixture and form into a ball. Knead on a floured surface for a few seconds until smooth. Wrap in clear film (plastic wrap). Chill for 30 minutes.

GLUTEN-FREE PASTRY

The recipes in this book can be made with gluten-free pastry by replacing the wheat flour with a gluten-free substitute. You may also be able to find quinoa flour or chestnut flour, which are also gluten-free and are suitable for making pastry. Other flours, such as oat flour or rice flour, may not be suitable, so check the information on the packet before using. Pastry that is made with gluten-free flour often needs a little more water than wheat flour, when mixing to a dough.

Baking blind

This process is used: to partly cook an empty pastry case so that it does not become soggy when the filling is added; to completely bake a pastry case when the filling cooks in a relatively short time and you need to ensure that the pastry is cooked through; when the pastry case is to contain a precooked mixture or an uncooked filling. Lining the case with baking parchment or foil and filling it with baking beans stops it from rising up.

1 Cut out a round of baking parchment or foil 7.5cm/3in larger than the flan tin (pan). Prick the base all over with a fork. Lay the parchment or foil in the pastry case or pie shell and press it over the base and up the side.

2 Put ceramic baking beans, or dried beans or peas, in the case, spreading them out evenly.

3 Bake in an oven preheated to 200°C/400°F/Gas 6 for 15 minutes, or until set and the rim is dry and golden. Remove the paper and beans. Return to the oven for a further 5 minutes until the base is completely dry.

Flaky pastry

It is convenient to buy ready-made puff pastry, but if you want to make it yourself, flaky is an easier method than puff pastry.

MAKES 450G/1LB

225g/8oz/2 cups strong white bread flour

pinch of salt

175g/6oz/¾ cup chilled butter, cubed

150ml/5fl oz/⅔ cup chilled water

1 Sift the flour and salt into a mixing bowl. Rub in 40g/1½oz/3 tbsp of the butter until the mixture resembles fine breadcrumbs.

2 Pour over 120ml/4fl oz/½ cup of the water and, using a round-bladed knife, mix to a soft dough, adding a little more water if needed.

3 Put on a floured surface and knead until smooth. Wrap in clear film (plastic wrap). Chill for 15 minutes.

4 Roll the dough out to a 30 x 10cm/12 x 4in rectangle. Cut another 40g/1½oz/3 tbsp of the remaining butter into small pieces and dot evenly all over the top two-thirds of the pastry, leaving a 1cm/½in margin. Fold the lower third of the pastry over the centre third, then fold the top third over that. Press the edges firmly with the rolling pin to seal.

5 Wrap in clear film and chill for 10 minutes. Repeat the rolling and folding process once more.

6 Roll out two more times, with the folded edges at the sides, using 40g/1½oz/3 tbsp of the butter each time. Roll out and fold once again (without fat). Chill for at least 1 hour before using.

Savoury treats

A traditional high tea includes little savouries, and here is a delectable selection of dainty treats to tempt the tastebuds. Serve exquisite cucumber or egg and cress sandwiches, thinly sliced with crusts removed, or choose from angels (and devils) on horseback, homemade fish mousse and potted cheese, sausage rolls, succulent little pastry tarts and quiches, and crisp crackers to go with flavourful spreads and pâtés.

Left Finger sandwiches are the ideal accompaniment to a pot of aromatic tea, whetting the appetite for the sweet treats to follow.

Classic cucumber sandwiches

Delicate cucumber sandwiches are synonymous with traditional afternoon tea.

SERVES 6

1 cucumber
12 slices white bread, crusts removed
butter, at room temperature, for spreading
ground black pepper, to taste

Cook's tip
It is best to use soft bread for these rather than types that are more robust, in order not to overwhelm the cucumber.

1 Peel the cucumber and slice thinly. Sprinkle with salt, drain in a colander for 20 minutes, then pat dry.

2 Spread each slice of bread with butter. Arrange the cucumber over six slices and sprinkle with pepper. Top with the remaining bread. Press down lightly.

3 Cut the sandwiches into fingers, squares or triangles. Arrange on a serving plate.

Cheese & pickle sandwiches

Sharp, mature cheese is complemented with tangy pickle in these dainty sandwiches.

SERVES 6

12 slices white bread, crusts removed
butter, at room temperature, for spreading
300g/10oz hard cheese, such as mature (sharp) Cheddar

90ml/6 tbsp pickle
watercress or rocket (arugula), to garnish
salt and ground black pepper, to taste

1 Spread each slice of bread with butter. Thinly slice the cheese and arrange on half of the bread, up to the edges.

2 Spoon 15ml/1 tbsp of pickle on to the cheese and season. Spread the pickle to the edges of the remaining bread, then use to close the sandwiches. Press down gently.

3 Cut each sandwich into three equal portions. Arrange on a plate and garnish with watercress or rocket.

Cucumber: Energy 174kcal/735kJ; Protein 6.8g; Carbohydrate 29.2g, of which sugars 3.3g; Fat 4.2g, of which saturates 1.1g; Cholesterol 5mg; Calcium 92mg; Fibre 1g; Sodium 307mg.
Cheese: Energy 429kcal/1793kJ; Protein 17.4g; Carbohydrate 31.8g, of which sugars 6.4g; Fat 25.6g, of which saturates 16.5g; Cholesterol 72mg; Calcium 433mg; Fibre 1g; Sodium 972mg.

Egg & cress sandwiches

A well-made egg and mayonnaise sandwich is a satisfying teatime snack.

SERVES 6

12 thin slices white or brown bread, crusts removed

butter, at room temperature, for spreading

4 small hard-boiled eggs, peeled and finely chopped

60ml/4 tbsp mayonnaise (see page 266)

1 carton of cress

salt and ground black pepper

slices of lemon, to garnish

1 Spread each slice of bread with butter.

2 To make the filling, gently mix together in a bowl the chopped hard-boiled eggs, mayonnaise, cress, and seasoning.

3 Spoon on to six slices of bread and spread out to the edges. Top each with another slice of bread and press down gently. Cut into triangles. Garnish with lemon.

Egg & tuna sandwiches

A tasty combination, these sustaining tuna fish sandwiches are enlivened with a squeeze of lemon juice and a dash of paprika.

SERVES 6

12 thin slices white or brown bread, crusts removed

butter, at room temperature, for spreading

4 small hard-boiled eggs, peeled and finely chopped

50g/2oz canned tuna fish in oil, drained and mashed

10ml/2 tsp paprika

squeeze of lemon juice

50g/2oz piece of cucumber, peeled and thinly sliced

salt and ground black pepper, to taste

1 Spread each slice of bread with butter.

2 To make the filling, gently mix together the hard-boiled eggs with the tuna, paprika, lemon juice and seasoning in a bowl.

3 Cover six slices of buttered bread with the cucumber, top with the tuna and egg mixture and finish with another slice of bread.

4 Cut each sandwich into three even fingers.

Cook's tip

All of these sandwiches will keep well for 2–3 hours. Cover with damp kitchen paper, then cover tightly in clear film (plastic wrap). Chill in the refrigerator and uncover at the last minute.

Egg & cress: Energy 320kcal/1337kJ; Protein 9g; Carbohydrate 26.8g, of which sugars 1.6g; Fat 20.5g, of which saturates 7.8g; Cholesterol 157mg; Calcium 89mg; Fibre 0.9g; Sodium 450mg.
Egg & tuna: Energy 273kcal/1145kJ; Protein 12.3g; Carbohydrate 25.7g, of which sugars 1.2g; Fat 14.6g, of which saturates 6.9g; Cholesterol 154mg; Calcium 58mg; Fibre 3.5g; Sodium 477mg.

Crab sandwiches

Bread and butter served with crab is a classic teatime treat. Slices of lemon and some cracked black pepper bring out the flavour.

SERVES 6

3 cooked crabs, about 900g/
2lb each
12 slices crusty wholegrain bread
butter, at room temperature,
for spreading

2 lemons, cut into quarters
rocket (arugula)
salt and ground black pepper,
to taste

1 Break off the crab claws and legs, then use your thumbs to ease the body out of the shell. Remove and discard the grey gills from the body and put the white meat in a bowl. Scrape the brown meat from the shell and add to the white meat. Season with salt and pepper, to taste.

2 Butter the bread and spread the crab meat on half of the slices. Add a squeeze of lemon juice and a little rocket. Top with the remaining bread slices and cut into triangles.

Turkey & cranberry sandwiches

Perfect for the festive tea table, turkey and cranberry sandwiches taste delicious and are a great use of leftovers.

SERVES 6

12 slices wholemeal
or wholewheat bread (or soft
white bread, if preferred)
butter, at room temperature,
for spreading

300g/10oz roast turkey, sliced
90ml/6 tbsp cranberry sauce

1 Spread each slice of bread with butter. Cover half of the slices of bread with roast turkey.

2 Spoon 15ml/1 tbsp of cranberry sauce on to the turkey and spread out to the edges. Season with salt and pepper, then top with another slice of bread.

3 Cut each sandwich into quarters diagonally to make small triangles. If preferred you could also trim off the crusts and slice them into quartered rectangles for daintier finger sandwiches.

Crab: Energy 526kcal/2209kJ; Protein 30.1g; Carbohydrate 56g, of which sugars 2.6g; Fat 21.7g, of which saturates 9.1g; Cholesterol 85mg; Calcium 117mg; Fibre 7.7g; Sodium 1150mg.
Turkey: Energy 312kcal/1314kJ; Protein 20g; Carbohydrate 35.4g, of which sugars 11.5g; Fat 11.3g, of which saturates 6.2g; Cholesterol 63mg; Calcium 40mg; Fibre 3.5g; Sodium 435mg.

Roast beef & horseradish sandwiches

Piquant horseradish sauce is a perfect accompaniment for roast beef.

SERVES 6

12 slices crusty white bread
butter, at room temperature,
for spreading
300g/10oz roast beef, thinly sliced
30–60ml/2–4 tbsp horseradish
sauce, to taste (see page 266)

rocket (arugula)
salt and ground black pepper,
to taste

1 Spread each slice of bread with butter.

2 Allowing about 50g/2oz of beef per sandwich, top half of the slices with meat and a little horseradish sauce.

3 Add some rocket to each sandwich. Sprinkle with salt and black pepper, to taste. Top each one with another slice of bread, and cut each sandwich into quarters.

Ham & mustard sandwiches

Cold ham sandwiches with hot mustard are an old-fashioned favourite.

SERVES 6

12 slices seeded bread
butter, at room temperature,
for spreading
300g/10oz roast ham, thinly sliced
15–30ml/1–2 tbsp English (hot)
mustard, to taste

salt and ground black pepper,
to taste
4 tomatoes and ½ carton of cress,
to garnish

1 Trim the crusts from each slice of bread, then spread with butter. Top half with slices of roast ham, then add English mustard to taste, spreading to the edges. Season.

2 Top each one with a slice of bread and press down gently, then cut each sandwich into three equal portions.

3 Garnish with tomato wedges and chopped cress.

Beef: Energy 505kcal/2125kJ; Protein 27.3g; Carbohydrate 58.5g, of which sugars 3g; Fat 19.6g, of which saturates 11g; Cholesterol 79mg; Calcium 148mg; Fibre 1.6g; Sodium 838mg.
Ham: Energy 275kcal/1157kJ; Protein 15.2g; Carbohydrate 28.8g, of which sugars 2.2g; Fat 11.9g, of which saturates 6.3g; Cholesterol 52mg; Calcium 55mg; Fibre 2.6g; Sodium 1171mg.

Anchovy toast soldiers

This classic old English favourite is redolent of Victorian high tea and gentlemen's clubs, but is equally welcome at a modern tea table.

SERVES 4

50g/2oz can of anchovy fillets in olive oil, drained
75g/2½oz/6 tbsp unsalted butter, softened
15ml/1 tbsp finely chopped fresh parsley

generous squeeze of lemon juice
ground white pepper
4–6 slices white bread

1 Using a mortar and pestle, crush the anchovies to make a thick paste. Add the butter, parsley and lemon juice and mix well, seasoning to taste with pepper. Cover and chill until required

2 To serve, toast the bread. Spread the anchovy paste on the hot toast, cut into fingers and serve immediately.

Cook's tip
If you have any anchovy paste left over, it makes a great brunch spread on toast and topped with a poached egg. Alternatively, stir it through some cooked spaghetti.

Potted shrimps

Potting brown shrimps in spiced butter is a time-honoured way to both preserve and serve them, and makes for a luxurious teatime treat.

SERVES 4

225g/8oz cooked, shelled shrimps
225g/8oz/1 cup butter
pinch of ground mace
pinch of salt
pinch of cayenne pepper
dill sprigs, to garnish

lemon wedges and thin slices of brown bread and butter, to serve

1 Chop a quarter of the shrimps. Melt half the butter slowly in a small pan. Skim off any foam, then stir in all the shrimps, the mace, salt and cayenne pepper and heat gently without boiling. Pour into four individual dishes and leave to cool.

2 Melt the remaining butter in a clean pan, then spoon the clear butter over the shrimps. When almost set, place a dill sprig in the centre of each. Cover and chill.

3 Remove from the refrigerator 30 minutes before serving with lemon wedges and brown bread and butter.

Anchovy: Energy 159Kcal/661kJ; Protein 4g; Carbohydrate 10.4g, of which sugars 0.7g; Fat 11.5g, of which saturates 6.7g; Cholesterol 32mg; Calcium 55mg; Fibre 0.4g; Sodium 512mg.
Shrimps: Energy 460kcal/1895kJ; Protein 9.6g; Carbohydrate 0.4g, of which sugars 0.4g; Fat 46.7g, of which saturates 29.4g; Cholesterol 193mg; Calcium 83mg; Fibre 0g; Sodium 555mg.

Potted cheese

Potting cheese is a good way to use up odd pieces left on the cheeseboard. Simply blend them with your chosen seasonings, adjusting the flavour before adding the alcohol, then serve with plain crackers, oatcakes or crisp toast for a satisfyingly savoury start to afternoon tea.

SERVES 4–6

250g/9oz hard cheese, such as mature (sharp) Cheddar
75g/2½oz/6 tbsp soft unsalted butter, plus about 30ml/2 tbsp for melting
1.5ml/¼ tsp ready-made English (hot) mustard
1.5ml/¼ tsp ground mace
30ml/2 tbsp sherry
ground black pepper, to taste
fresh parsley, to garnish
thin slices of toast or crispbreads, to serve

1 Cut the cheese into rough pieces and put them into the bowl of a food processor. Use the pulse button to chop the cheese into small crumbs.

2 Add the butter, mustard, mace and pepper and blend until smooth. Adjust the seasoning. Blend in the sherry.

3 Spoon the mixture into a dish, leaving about 1cm/½in to spare on top. Level the surface.

4 Melt some butter in a small pan, skimming off any foam that rises to the surface. Leaving the sediment in the pan, pour a layer of clear butter on top of the cheese mixture to cover the surface. Chill until required.

5 When you are ready to serve, garnish with parsley and serve spread on thin slices of toast or crispbread.

Variations
• Use some crumbled Stilton in place of the Cheddar and the same quantity of port in place of sherry.
• Chopped chives could be added instead of the hot mustard.

Energy 262kcal/1082kJ; Protein 10.7g; Carbohydrate 0.2g, of which sugars 0.2g; Fat 23.6g, of which saturates 15.2g; Cholesterol 70mg; Calcium 290mg; Fibre 0g; Sodium 363mg.

Salmon mousse

This light and delicate mousse is ideal for tea on the lawn on a balmy summer's afternoon. Garnish it with sliced cucumber and lemon wedges. Serve with thin plain crackers or Melba toast for a satisfying crunch.

SERVES 6–8

300ml/½ pint/1¼ cups milk
1 small onion, thinly sliced
1 small carrot, thinly sliced
2 bay leaves
2 sprigs of parsley or dill
6 whole peppercorns
15ml/1 tbsp powdered gelatine
350g/12oz salmon fillet

75ml/5 tbsp dry white vermouth
25g/1oz/2 tbsp butter
30ml/2 tbsp plain (all-purpose) flour
75ml/5 tbsp mayonnaise (see page 266)
150ml/5fl oz/⅔ cup whipping cream
salt and ground black pepper

1 Put the milk in a pan with half of each of the onion, the carrot, herbs and peppercorns. Bring slowly to the boil, remove from the heat, cover and leave to infuse for 30 minutes.

2 Meanwhile, sprinkle the gelatine over 45ml/3 tbsp cold water and leave to soak.

3 Put the salmon in another pan with the remaining onion, carrot, herbs and peppercorns. Add the vermouth and 60ml/4 tbsp water. Simmer, covered, for 10 minutes.

4 Flake the fish into a bowl, discarding the skin and bones. Boil the juices in the pan to reduce by half, then strain.

5 Strain the infused milk into a clean pan and add the butter and flour. Whisking continuously, cook until thickened, then simmer for 1 minute. Pour into a food processor, add the soaked gelatine and blend. Add the salmon and the cooking juices and pulse briefly.

6 Transfer to a bowl and stir in the mayonnaise and seasonings. Whip the cream and fold in. Pour into an oiled mould, cover and refrigerate before serving.

Energy 285kcal/1183kJ; Protein 12.6g; Carbohydrate 5.8g, of which sugars 3.2g; Fat 22.7g, of which saturates 8.7g; Cholesterol 57mg; Calcium 73mg; Fibre 0.2g; Sodium 103mg.

Smoked mackerel pâté

This recipe is an ideal way to use smoked mackerel – it's quick and easy, involves no cooking and is extremely versatile. It tastes wonderful spread on crisp toast or crackers, or can be used as a filling for dainty teatime sandwiches.

SERVES 4–6

225ml/8fl oz/generous 1 cup crème fraîche or plain Greek (strained) yogurt
finely grated rind of ½ lemon
few sprigs of parsley
225g/8oz smoked mackerel fillets
10ml/2 tsp horseradish sauce

15ml/1 tbsp lemon juice, or to taste
ground black pepper, to taste
crusty bread, hot toast or crisp plain crackers and lemon wedges, to serve

1 Put the crème fraîche and lemon rind into a blender or food processor. Add a few sprigs of parsley, keeping a few back for garnishing.

2 Flake the mackerel, discarding the skin and any bones. Add the flaked fish to the blender. Blend in pulses on a medium speed until the mixture is almost smooth – take care not to over-process it.

3 Add the horseradish sauce and lemon juice and blend briefly. Season to taste with pepper.

4 Spoon the mixture into individual dishes. Cover and chill until required.

5 When ready to serve, garnish with parsley and serve with crusty bread, hot toast or crackers and lemon wedges for squeezing over.

Variations
• You could use other types of smoked fish in this dish, such as trout or salmon, or try drained canned sardines.
• For a richer pâté, substitute some of the crème fraîche with some mascarpone or extra-thick cream.

Energy 344kcal/1421kJ; Protein 10.7g; Carbohydrate 0.5g, of which sugars 0.4g; Fat 33.3g, of which saturates 14.3g; Cholesterol 88mg; Calcium 57mg; Fibre 0.1g; Sodium 518mg.

Smoked salmon with warm potato cakes

A classic combination of ingredients, this a comforting high tea variation on blinis, with lovely little warm little potato cakes used as the base for smoked salmon.

SERVES 6

450g/1lb potatoes, cooked and mashed

75g/2½oz/⅔ cup plain (all-purpose) flour

2 eggs, beaten

2 spring onions (scallions)

a little freshly grated nutmeg

50g/2oz/4 tbsp butter, melted

150ml/5fl oz/⅔ cup sour cream

12 slices of smoked salmon

salt and ground black pepper

chopped fresh chives, to garnish

1 Put the potatoes, flour and eggs into a large bowl. Chop and add the spring onions. Season with salt, pepper and a little nutmeg, and add half the butter. Mix thoroughly and shape into 12 small potato cakes.

2 Heat the remaining butter in a non-stick frying pan and cook the potato cakes until browned on both sides.

3 To serve, mix the sour cream with some salt and pepper. Fold a piece of smoked salmon and place on top of each potato cake. Top with the cream and chives and serve immediately.

Cook's tip
If it is more convenient, you can make the potato cakes in advance and keep them overnight in the refrigerator. When they are required, warm them through in a hot oven for about 15 minutes before topping with the salmon and cream cheese, and serving.

Variation
You could also top the potato cakes with smoked mackerel and a squeeze of lemon juice, or even slices of thinly cut smoked ham, if you like.

Energy 326Kcal/1365kJ; Protein 21.9g; Carbohydrate 22.9g, of which sugars 2.3g; Fat 17g, of which saturates 8.6g; Cholesterol 119mg; Calcium 70mg; Fibre 1.2g; Sodium 1315mg.

Angels on horseback

This 19th-century recipe still makes a luxurious addition to an afternoon tea table.

SERVES 4

16 oysters, removed from
their shells
fresh lemon juice
8 rindless rashers (strips) of
streaky bacon

8 small slices of bread
butter, for spreading
paprika (optional)

1 Preheat the oven to 200°C/400°F/Gas 6. Sprinkle the oysters with a little lemon juice.

2 Lay the bacon rashers on a board, slide the back of a knife along each one to stretch it and then cut it in half crosswise. Wrap a rasher around each oyster, secure with a cocktail stick and lay them on a baking sheet.

3 Cook the oysters and bacon for 8–10 minutes, until the bacon is just cooked through.

4 Meanwhile, toast the bread, then butter it and serve the bacon-wrapped oysters on top. Sprinkle with paprika.

Devils on horseback

Another classic from Victorian times, these combine sweet and savoury in a dainty package.

SERVES 4

16 stoned prunes
fruity chutney, such as Apple &
Sultana Chutney (see page 264)
8 rindless rashers (strips) of
streaky bacon

8 small slices of bread
butter, for spreading

1 Preheat the oven to 200°C/400°F/Gas 6. Ease open the prunes with a small sharp knife and spoon a small amount of chutney into each.

2 Lay the bacon rashers on a board, slide the back of a knife along each one to stretch it and then cut in half crosswise. Wrap a piece of bacon around each prune.

3 Lay them close together on a baking sheet. Cook for 8–10 minutes until the bacon is just cooked through.

4 Meanwhile, toast the bread, then butter it and serve the bacon-wrapped prunes alongside.

Angels: Energy 326kcal/1365kJ; Protein 20.3g; Carbohydrate 26.4g, of which sugars 1.4g; Fat 16.2g, of which saturates 6.9g; Cholesterol 79mg; Calcium 147mg; Fibre 0.8g; Sodium 1483mg.
Devils: Energy 309kcal/1303kJ; Protein 14.7g; Carbohydrate 41.7g, of which sugars 18.3g; Fat 10.4g, of which saturates 3.5g; Cholesterol 30mg; Calcium 75mg; Fibre 3.6g; Sodium 1132mg.

Danish 'caviar' toasts

Using lightly salted lumpfish roe as a substitute for the real thing, these deceptively economical little morsels bring sophistication and elegance to a special teatime spread.

MAKES 24

6 slices good white bread, crusts removed

115g/4oz lumpfish caviar

100ml/3½fl oz/scant ½ cup crème fraîche

½ red onion, thinly sliced

50g/2oz/4 tbsp chopped fresh dill

Cook's tip
Substitute red lumpfish caviar for the black variety, sour cream for the crème fraîche, and chopped fresh basil leaves for the dill.

1 Lightly toast the bread and cut each slice into four triangles. Spread each toast with a spoon of lumpfish caviar. Top with a blob of crème fraîche and slices of red onion, and sprinkle with dill. Arrange on a serving plate.

2 Alternatively, spoon the lumpfish caviar, crème fraîche, dill and onion into separate small bowls alongside a plate of the toasts, for guests to assemble at the table.

Energy 37kcal/153kJ; Protein 1.2g; Carbohydrate 3.7g, of which sugars 0.4g; Fat 2g, of which saturates 1.2g; Cholesterol 17mg; Calcium 11mg; Fibre 0.2g; Sodium 124mg.

Mushroom tapenade

A flavourful savoury dip with crackers is welcome at any tea table. This tasty tapenade blends both wild and cultivated mushrooms to offer a delicious umami hit.

SERVES 4

60ml/4 tbsp olive oil
4 garlic cloves, peeled and bruised
50g/2oz chestnut mushrooms, chopped
50g/2oz shiitake, chopped
50g/2oz ceps, chopped

10g/2 tsp capers
2 anchovies
zest and juice of 1 lemon
black pepper
flatbreads or water biscuits, to serve

1 In a large frying pan, heat 15ml/1 tbsp of the oil and add the garlic, sautéing for 2 minutes. Stir in all the mushrooms and cook, stirring, for 10 minutes. Season with pepper and allow to cool.

2 Transfer the garlic and mushrooms to a food processor, then blend with the capers, anchovies, lemon zest and juice, and remaining 45ml/3 tbsp oil. Transfer to a serving bowl and chill for 20 minutes.

Energy 115kcal/472kJ; Protein 1.8g; Carbohydrate 1.2g, of which sugars 0.2g; Fat 11.4g, of which saturates 1.7g; Cholesterol 1mg; Calcium 9mg; Fibre 1.1g; Sodium 62mg.

Parmesan thins

These crisp, light, savoury crackers are very moreish and provide the perfect crunchy bite at teatime – they are also very quick to make.

MAKES 16–20

50g/2oz/½ cup plain
(all-purpose) flour
40g/1½oz/3 tbsp butter, softened
1 egg yolk

40g/1½oz Parmesan cheese,
freshly grated
pinch of salt
pinch of mustard powder

1 Rub together the flour and the butter in a bowl, then work in the egg yolk, the cheese, salt and mustard.

2 Mix with a wooden spoon to bring the dough together into a ball. Shape into a log, then wrap in foil or clear film (plastic wrap) and chill for at least 10 minutes.

3 Preheat the oven to 200°C/400°F/Gas 6. Cut the dough log into thin slices, about 3–6mm/⅛–¼in, and arrange on a well-greased baking sheet.

4 Flatten with a fork to give a pretty ridged pattern. Bake for 10 minutes or until crisp. Cool on a wire rack.

Variations
• You can use any strong hard cheese, such as mature (sharp) Cheddar or Grana Padano.
• You could also form the dough into cheese straws rather than rounds. Chill it for 30 minutes, roll it into a square, slice it into narrow strips and bake for 12 minutes.

Energy 36kcal/148kJ; Protein 1.2g; Carbohydrate 2g, of which sugars 0.1g; Fat 2.6g, of which saturates 1.5g; Cholesterol 16mg; Calcium 29mg; Fibre 0.1g; Sodium 34mg.

Three-cheese crumbles

A delicious combination of cheeses and the fresh taste of pesto make these cookies totally irresistible. The addition of chopped nuts adds texture.

MAKES 10

225g/8oz/2 cups self-raising (self-rising) flour
50g/2oz/4 tbsp butter, diced
50g/2oz mozzarella cheese, diced
50g/2oz Red Leicester cheese, diced

15ml/1 tbsp pesto
1 egg
60ml/4 tbsp milk
15g/½oz/2 tbsp Parmesan cheese, freshly grated
15ml/1 tbsp mixed chopped nuts

1 Preheat the oven to 200°C/400°F/Gas 6. Put the flour in a bowl and rub in the butter until the mixture resembles fine breadcrumbs.

2 Add the diced mozzarella and Red Leicester cheeses to the bowl and stir well. In a separate bowl, beat together the pesto, egg and milk, then pour into the flour and cheese mixture. Stir together quickly until well combined.

3 Using a tablespoon, place in rocky piles on non-stick baking sheets. Sprinkle over the Parmesan cheese and chopped nuts.

4 Bake for 12–15 minutes until well risen and golden brown. Transfer to a wire rack to cool.

Energy 182kcal/760kJ; Protein 6.6g; Carbohydrate 17.9g, of which sugars 0.7g; Fat 9.7g, of which saturates 5.3g; Cholesterol 41mg; Calcium 135mg; Fibre 0.8g; Sodium 129mg.

Gouda-filled puffs

These light choux-pastry cheese puffs make a welcome savoury alternative to éclairs or profiteroles at the tea table, while still being elegant. They are best served warm.

MAKES ABOUT 25

100g/3½oz/scant ½ cup butter
250ml/8½fl oz/1 cup water
150g/5oz/1¼ cups plain
(all-purpose) flour
4 eggs

150g/5oz/1 cup grated extra-
mature (sharp) Gouda cheese
freshly grated nutmeg
salt and ground black pepper

1 Preheat the oven to 220°C/425°F/Gas 7. Line two baking sheets with baking parchment.

2 Heat the butter, water and a pinch of salt in a small covered pan over a low heat until the butter has melted. Bring to the boil, remove from the heat and add in all the flour immediately.

3 Return to the heat and cook, stirring constantly, until the mixture comes away from the side of the pan and forms a ball. This may take a few minutes.

4 Transfer the dough to a bowl and beat in the eggs, one at a time, with a hand-held mixer fitted with dough hooks. Continue beating until the dough is smooth and glossy.

5 Add a third of the cheese and season with nutmeg, salt and pepper to taste. Stir to mix.

6 Using two teaspoons, place 25 walnut-size mounds of the mixture on the prepared baking sheets, spacing them about 5cm/2in apart. Bake for about 20 minutes, until puffed up and light golden brown.

7 Remove from the oven and leave to cool. Cut the puffs open with scissors and fill with the remaining cheese using a teaspoon.

8 Just before serving, heat through in a hot oven for a few minutes to melt the cheese.

Energy 285kcal/1183kJ; Protein 12.6g; Carbohydrate 5.8g, of which sugars 3.2g; Fat 22.7g, of which saturates 8.7g; Cholesterol 57mg; Calcium 73mg; Fibre 0.2g; Sodium 103mg.

Cheese & dill pastries

These little cheese pastries are best served hot so that the cheese is still soft and light and the pastry melts in the mouth. They make ideal snacks for a teatime spread.

MAKES 16

225g/8oz feta cheese, rinsed and drained

225g/8oz mozzarella or halloumi cheese

small bunch of fresh dill, chopped

2 eggs, lightly beaten, plus 2 egg yolks, mixed with water, for brushing

450g/1lb puff pastry, thawed if frozen

flour, for dusting

salt and ground black pepper

1 Preheat the oven to 200°C/400°F/Gas 6. In a bowl, mash the feta with a fork.

2 Grate the mozzarella or halloumi, or whizz to a paste in a blender or food processor, and add it to the feta.

3 Mix in the dill and beaten eggs, season with salt and pepper and mix together. Set aside while you prepare the pastry.

4 Dust the work surface with flour and roll out the pastry thinly. Using a round cutter, or the rim of a cup, cut out as many 10cm/4in circles as you can, then gather up the trimmings, reroll and cut out further rounds. Dust the pastry circles lightly with flour before stacking them.

5 Place 10ml/2 tsp of the cheese mixture just off-centre on each pastry round. Lift the other side and bring it up over the filling until the edges touch each other to make a half-moon shape.

6 Use your finger to dampen the edges with a little water and pinch them together to seal. You can press along the edges with the back of a fork to make a pattern, if you like.

7 Line several baking trays with baking parchment and arrange the pastries on them. Brush the top of each pastry with a little of the beaten egg yolk mixture.

8 Bake for about 20 minutes, until the pastries are puffed up and golden brown. Serve immediately, while the cheese filling is still warm.

Energy 526kcal/2192kJ; Protein 20.6g; Carbohydrate 30.5g, of which sugars 1.8g; Fat 37.4g, of which saturates 11.3g; Cholesterol 179mg; Calcium 352mg; Fibre 0.5g; Sodium 950mg.

Chorizo pastry puffs

These flaky pastry puffs are a lively update on sausage rolls, for a teatime table with a difference. For best results, choose a mild cheese, as the chorizo has plenty of flavour.

MAKES 16

225g/8oz puff pastry, thawed if frozen
flour, for dusting
50g/2oz/½ cup grated cheese
115g/4oz cured chorizo sausage, finely chopped
1 small egg, beaten
5ml/1 tsp paprika

1 Roll out the pastry thinly on a floured work surface. Using a 7.5cm/3in cutter, stamp out 16 rounds.

2 Preheat the oven to 230°C/450°F/Gas 8. Put the grated cheese and chopped chorizo sausage in a bowl and toss together lightly.

3 Lay one of the pastry rounds in the palm of your hand and place a little of the chorizo mixture across the centre. Using your other hand, pinch together the edges of the pastry along the top to seal. Repeat the process with the remaining rounds to make 16 puffs in all.

4 Place the pastries on a non-stick baking sheet and brush lightly with the beaten egg. Dust the tops of the pastries lightly with a little paprika.

5 Bake the pastries in the oven for 10–12 minutes, until puffed and golden. Serve warm, dusted with the remaining paprika.

Per 2 puffs: Energy 183kcal/763kJ; Protein 5.4g; Carbohydrate 12.1g, of which sugars 0.6g; Fat 13.1g, of which saturates 3g; Cholesterol 36mg; Calcium 73mg; Fibre 0.1g; Sodium 258mg.

Pimiento tartlets

These pretty little tartlets are filled with strips of roasted sweet peppers and a deliciously creamy, cheesy custard, and are dainty enough to grace any teatime spread.

MAKES 12

1 red (bell) pepper
1 yellow (bell) pepper
175g/6oz/1½ cups plain (all-purpose) flour, plus extra for dusting
75g/2½oz/6 tbsp chilled butter, diced

30–45ml/2–3 tbsp cold water
60ml/4 tbsp double (heavy) cream
1 egg
15ml/1 tbsp grated fresh Parmesan cheese
salt and ground black pepper, to taste

1, Heat the grill or broiler. Place the peppers on a baking sheet and grill for 10 minutes, turning occasionally, until blackened all over.

2 Cover the baking sheet with a clean dish towel, or put the peppers into a plastic bag and seal the top, and leave to steam for 5 minutes.

3 Peel away the skin from the peppers, then discard the seeds and cut the flesh into very thin strips.

4 Preheat the oven to 200°C/400°F/Gas 6. Sift the flour and a little salt into a bowl. Add the butter and rub it in until the mixture resembles breadcrumbs. Stir in enough water to make a firm dough.

5 Roll the dough out thinly on a lightly floured surface and stamp out rounds that can be used to line 12 individual moulds or a 12-hole tartlet tin or muffin pan.

6 Prick the bases with a fork and fill the pastry cases with crumpled foil and baking beans. Bake in the preheated oven for 10 minutes.

7 Remove the foil and baking beans from the pastry cases and divide the pepper strips among them.

8 Whisk the cream and egg in a bowl. Season well and pour over the peppers.

9 Sprinkle each tartlet with Parmesan cheese and bake for 15–20 minutes, until the filling is firm and set.

10 Leave to cool in the moulds or tin for 2 minutes, then gently ease them out and transfer to a wire rack.

Per 3 tartlets: Energy 427kcal/1778kJ; Protein 8.4g; Carbohydrate 40g, of which sugars 6.4g; Fat 27g, of which saturates 16.1g; Cholesterol 112mg; Calcium 131mg; Fibre 2.8g; Sodium 180mg.

Quiche Lorraine

This classic quiche has very thin flaky pastry, a creamy and light egg-rich filling, and smoked bacon. Ever-popular, it makes a tasty start to an afternoon tea.

SERVES 6–8
For the pastry
175g/6oz/1½ cups plain (all-purpose) flour, sifted, plus extra for dusting
pinch of salt
1 egg yolk
115g/4oz/½ cup unsalted butter, at room temperature, diced

For the filling
6 rashers (strips) of smoked streaky bacon, rinds removed
300ml/½ pint/1¼ cups double (heavy) cream
3 eggs, plus 3 yolks
25g/1oz/2 tbsp unsalted butter
salt and ground black pepper

1 To make the pastry, put the flour, salt, yolk and butter in a food processor and process until blended. Turn on to a lightly floured surface and bring the mixture together into a ball. Leave to rest for 20 minutes.

2 Lightly flour a deep 20cm/8in round flan tin (pan), and place it on a baking tray.

3 Roll out the pastry and use to line the tin. Trim off the excess. Gently press the pastry into the corners of the tin. If the pastry breaks up, just push it into shape. Chill for 20 minutes. Preheat the oven to 200°C/400°F/Gas 6.

4 Meanwhile, cut the bacon rashers into thin pieces and grill until the fat runs. Arrange the bacon in the pastry case. Beat together the cream, the whole eggs and yolks and seasoning. Carefully pour into the pastry case.

5 Bake for 15 minutes, then reduce the heat to 180°C/350°F/Gas 4 and bake for a further 15–20 minutes, until the filling is puffed up and golden brown, and the pastry edge crisp.

6 Remove from the oven and top with little pieces of butter. Leave to stand and cool a little for 5 minutes before serving.

Energy 976kcal/4043kJ; Protein 18.1g; Carbohydrate 35.5g, of which sugars 2.2g; Fat 85.8g, of which saturates 48.4g; Cholesterol 519mg; Calcium 149mg; Fibre 1.4g; Sodium 678mg.

Herbed mini tarts

These little savoury tarts are ideal for teatime, being small enough to eat daintily with your fingers, but large enough to be satisfying. They are packed with fresh herby flavour.

MAKES 8

For the pastry
115g/4oz/1 cup plain (all-purpose) flour, plus extra for dusting
pinch of salt
50g/2oz/4 tbsp butter, chilled and diced
30ml/2 tbsp chilled water

For the filling
45–60ml/3–4 tbsp tapenade or sun-dried tomato paste
1 large egg
100ml/3½fl oz/scant ½ cup Greek (strained) yogurt
90ml/6 tbsp milk
1 garlic clove, crushed
30ml/2 tbsp chopped mixed herbs, such as thyme, marjoram, basil and parsley
salt and ground black pepper

1 To make the pastry, sift the flour and salt into a large bowl. Rub or cut in the butter until the mixture resembles fine breadcrumbs. Sprinkle over the water and mix to a dough.

2 Knead briefly, then wrap and chill for 20 minutes.

3 Roll out the pastry and cut out 8 rounds. Use to line deep tartlet tins or muffin pans. Chill the pastry cases for 30 minutes. Preheat the oven to 190°C/375°F/Gas 5.

4 Line each pastry case with a small piece of foil. Bake for about 15 minutes. Remove the foil and bake for a further 5 minutes, until crisp. Set aside to cool.

5 Spread a little tapenade or tomato paste in the base of each pastry case.

6 Whisk together the egg, yogurt, milk, garlic, herbs and seasoning in a bowl and spoon into the pastry cases.

7 Bake for about 30 minutes, or until the filling is just firm to the touch and the pastry golden.

8 Allow the pies to cool slightly before carefully removing them from the tins. Serve warm or cold.

Energy 133Kcal/555kJ; Protein 4g; Carbohydrate 13g, of which sugars 2g; Fat 7.7g, of which saturates 4.3g; Cholesterol 43mg; Calcium 74mg; Fibre 1g; Sodium 78mg.

Leek, saffron & mussel tarts

Serve these colourful pastries as a treat for a special occasion – they look wonderful as part of a spread and are the perfect way to begin a teatime feast.

MAKES 12
For the pastry
450g/1lb/4 cups plain (all-purpose) flour, plus extra for dusting
5ml/1 tsp salt
225g/8oz/1 cup butter, diced
30–45ml/2–3 tbsp water

For the filling
4 large yellow (bell) peppers, halved
large pinch of saffron threads

30ml/2 tbsp hot water
4 large leeks, sliced
60ml/4 tbsp olive oil
2kg/4½lb mussels, scrubbed and beards removed
4 large eggs
600ml/1 pint/2½ cups single (light) cream
60ml/4 tbsp chopped fresh parsley
salt and ground black pepper, to taste

1 To make the pastry, mix together the flour and salt and rub in the butter. Mix in the water and knead lightly. Wrap the dough in clear film (plastic wrap) and chill for 30 minutes.

2 Grill or broil the pepper halves, skin sides uppermost, until blackened. Place them in a plastic bag and leave for 10 minutes, then peel and cut the flesh into thin strips.

3 Preheat the oven to 190°C/375°F/Gas 5. Use the pastry to line twelve 10cm/4in tartlet tins or muffin pans, 2.5cm/1in deep. Prick the bases and line with foil. Bake for 10 minutes, then remove the foil and bake for another 5–8 minutes, or until lightly coloured. Reduce the oven temperature to 180°C/350°F/Gas 4.

4 Soak the saffron in the hot water for 10 minutes. Meanwhile, fry the leeks in the oil for 6–8 minutes until beginning to brown. Add the pepper strips and cook for another 2 minutes.

5 Put the mussels in a large pan, discarding any that do not shut when tapped sharply. Cover and cook, shaking the pan occasionally, for 3–4 minutes, or until the mussels open. Shell, discarding any that do not open.

6 Beat the eggs, cream, saffron liquid and parsley together and season. Arrange the leeks, peppers and mussels in the pastry, add the egg mixture and bake for 20–25 minutes, until just firm. Serve warm or cold.

Energy 506kcal/2112kJ; Protein 17.2g; Carbohydrate 35.1g, of which sugars 6.1g; Fat 34.1g, of which saturates 18.3g; Cholesterol 155mg; Calcium 221mg; Fibre 2.8g; Sodium 273mg.

Smoked trout filo tarts

Crisp, golden filo pastry contrasts with a creamy trout and three-cheese filling in these pretty little tartlets. Emmenthal or Jarlsberg cheese can be used instead of Gruyère, if you prefer.

MAKES 8

2 sheets of filo pastry, thawed if frozen
50g/2oz/4 tbsp butter, melted
50g/2oz/½ cup Gruyère cheese, grated
115g/4oz/1 cup mascarpone cheese
50g/2oz/½ cup Parmesan cheese, grated
45ml/3 tbsp milk
75g/2½oz smoked trout
8 cherry tomatoes, halved
salt and ground black pepper

1 Preheat the oven to 180°C/350°F/Gas 4. Cut the filo into sixteen 15cm/6in squares. Lightly butter eight 10cm/4in tartlet pans.

2 Brushing the pastry squares with melted butter, for each tartlet, place two squares of filo pastry on top of each other at angles to form a star shape.

3 Support the pans on a baking sheet and brush the pastry with a little more butter. Bake for 5 minutes or until crisp and light golden brown. Remove the tartlets from the oven but leave the oven on.

4 In a large bowl, combine the three cheeses and milk. Season generously with salt and pepper and mix well.

5 Cut the smoked trout into bitesize pieces using kitchen scissors or a knife. Arrange the halved tomatoes and trout in the pastry cases.

6 Spoon the mixture into the cases, pressing it down with the back of a spoon. Return to the oven and bake for 10–15 minutes until the cheese is bubbling and golden brown. Remove carefully and serve warm.

Energy 469kcal/1953kJ; Protein 17g; Carbohydrate 25g, of which sugars 4g; Fat 33g, of which saturates 21g; Cholesterol 94mg; Calcium 298mg; Fibre 0g; Sodium 515mg.

Mini sausage rolls

Small sausage rolls rank high in the league of popular teatime foods. They are delicious when homemade, particularly if good-quality butcher's sausage meat is used to fill them.

MAKES 16

For the pastry
175g/6oz/1½ cups plain (all-purpose) flour, plus extra for dusting
pinch of salt
40g/1½oz/3 tbsp lard or white vegetable fat, diced
40g/1½oz/3 tbsp butter, chilled and diced
45ml/3 tbsp iced water

For the filling
250g/9oz pork sausage meat (bulk sausage), or meat squeezed from your favourite sausages
beaten egg, to glaze

1 To make the pastry, sift the flour and salt and add the lard and butter. Rub the fats into the flour until the mixture resembles fine breadcrumbs.

2 Stir in enough of the ice-cold water until the mixture can be gathered into a smooth ball of dough. Wrap the dough in clear film (plastic wrap) and chill for 30 minutes.

3 Preheat the oven to 190°C/375°F/Gas 5. Roll out the pastry on a lightly floured surface to make a rectangle about 30cm/12in long. Cut the rectangle lengthways into two long strips.

4 Divide the sausage meat into two pieces and, on a lightly floured surface, shape each into a long roll the same length as the pastry.

5 Lay a roll on each strip of pastry. Brush the pastry edges with a little water and fold them over the meat, pressing the edges together to seal them well.

6 Turn the rolls over and, with the seam side down, brush with beaten egg. Cut each roll into 8 and place on a baking sheet.

7 Bake in the hot oven for 30 minutes, until crisp and golden brown. Cool on a wire rack.

Variation
Add 2.5ml/½ tsp English (hot) mustard powder with the flour for an extra little bite to your sausage rolls.

Energy 469kcal/1953kJ; Protein 17g; Carbohydrate 25g, of which sugars 4g; Fat 33g, of which saturates 21g; Cholesterol 94mg; Calcium 298mg; Fibre 0g; Sodium 515mg.

Mini pork & bacon pies

These little pies with a hot water crust pastry require a little bit of effort and need to be made in advance, but the results are well worth it as they taste as wonderful as they look.

MAKES 12

450g/1lb/4 cups plain (all-purpose) flour, plus extra for dusting
salt and ground black pepper
115g/4oz/½ cup lard or white vegetable fat
275ml/9fl oz/generous 1 cup water

For the filling

10ml/2 tsp sunflower oil
1 onion, chopped
225g/8oz pork, coarsely chopped
115g/4oz cooked bacon, diced
45ml/3 tbsp chopped fresh herbs
6 eggs, hard-boiled and halved
1 egg yolk, beaten
20g/¾oz packet powdered aspic
300ml/½ pint/1¼ cups water
salt and ground black pepper

1 To make the pastry, sift the flour into a bowl and add a pinch of seasoning. Gently heat the fat and water in a pan until the fat has melted. Increase the heat and bring to the boil. Pour the liquid into the flour, stirring constantly. Press the mixture into a ball of dough using a spoon. When the dough is smooth, cover the bowl and set aside.

2 Preheat the oven to 200°C/400°F/Gas 6. Heat the oil in a pan, add the onion and cook until soft. Stir in the pork and bacon and cook until just brown, then stir in the herbs and season well.

3 Roll out two-thirds of the pastry on a floured surface. Use a 12cm/4½in fluted cutter to stamp out rounds. Line 12 tartlet tins or muffin pans with the rounds and place some meat mixture in each. Add half an egg and top with the remaining mix.

4 Roll out the remaining pastry and use a 7.5cm/3in fluted cutter to stamp out lids. Dampen the rim of each pastry base and press a lid in place. Brush with egg yolk and make a small steam hole in the top of each pie.

5 Bake for 30–35 minutes. Leave to cool for 15 minutes, then place on a wire rack to cool completely.

6 Meanwhile, add the aspic powder to 300ml/½ pint boiling water and stir until dissolved. Shape a piece of foil into a small funnel and use this to guide a little aspic through the hole in the top of each pie. Chill for up to 24 hours before serving at room temperature.

Energy 164kcal/682kJ; Protein 10g; Carbohydrate 5g, of which sugars 2g; Fat 12g, of which saturates 3g; Cholesterol 40mg; Calcium 5mg; Fibre 1g; Sodium 92mg.

Oven-baked potato cakes

Potato cakes come in a variety of forms, but they're all at their best if made with freshly cooked potatoes, preferably while still warm. Serve fresh from the oven, split open and buttered.

MAKES ABOUT 12

225g/8oz/2 cups self-raising (self-rising) flour, plus extra for dusting
2.5ml/½ tsp baking powder
50g/2oz/4 tbsp butter

pinch of salt
175g/6oz mashed potato
15ml/1 tbsp chopped fresh chives
200ml/7fl oz/scant 1 cup buttermilk

1 Preheat the oven to 220°C/425°F/Gas 7 and lightly grease a baking tray with butter.

2 Sift the flour and baking powder into a bowl and rub in the butter. Season with salt.

3 Add the mashed potato and chives. Mix well, and then incorporate enough buttermilk to make a soft dough. Turn on to a floured work surface, knead lightly into shape then quickly roll out.

4 Cut the dough into squares with a sharp floured knife or stamp out into rounds with a 5cm/2in cutter.

5 Place the squares or rounds on the greased baking tray and bake in the preheated oven for about 20 minutes or until well risen, golden brown and crisp. Remove to a wire rack to cool slightly, then serve warm.

Energy 108Kcal/455kJ; Protein 2g; Carbohydrate 16.5g, of which sugars 0.4g; Fat 4.3g, of which saturates 2.6g; Cholesterol 11mg; Calcium 68mg; Fibre 0.7g; Sodium 99mg.

Walnut & caramelized onion scones

These savoury scones are delicious served warm with butter, good cheese and fruity chutney (see page 264). They can also be made as bite-sized scones and topped with cheese or ham.

MAKES 10–12

90g/3oz/7 tbsp butter
15ml/1 tbsp olive oil
1 onion, chopped
5ml/1 tsp cumin seeds, lightly crushed
200g/7oz/1¾ cups self-raising (self-rising) flour, plus extra for dusting
5ml/1 tsp baking powder
25g/1oz/¼ cup fine oatmeal
5ml/1 tsp light unrefined muscovado (brown) sugar
90g/3oz/scant 1 cup chopped walnuts
5ml/1 tsp chopped fresh thyme
120–150ml/4–5fl oz/½–⅔ cup buttermilk
salt and ground black pepper
a little milk or soya milk, to glaze

1 Melt 15g/½oz/1 tbsp of the butter with the oil in a small pan and cook the onion gently, covered, for 10–12 minutes. Uncover, then continue to cook gently until it begins to brown.

2 Add half the cumin seeds and increase the heat slightly. Continue to cook, stirring occasionally, until the onion begins to caramelize. Remove from the heat and leave to cool. Preheat the oven to 200°C/400°F/Gas 6.

3 Sift the flour and baking powder into a large bowl and add the oatmeal, sugar, 2.5ml/½ tsp salt and a pinch of black pepper.

4 Add the remaining butter and rub in until the mixture resembles fine breadcrumbs.

5 Add the cooked onion and cumin mixture, chopped walnuts and fresh thyme, then bind to make a soft, but not sticky, dough with the buttermilk.

6 Roll or pat out the mixture on a floured surface to an even thickness of just over 1cm/½in. Stamp out 10–12 scones using a floured 5–6cm/2–2½in round cutter.

7 Place the scones on a floured baking tray, glaze with the milk or soya milk and sprinkle with a little salt and the remaining cumin seeds.

8 Bake the scones for 12–15 minutes until risen and golden brown. Cool for a few minutes on a wire rack and serve warm.

Energy 131kcal/543kJ; Protein 1.8g; Carbohydrate 3g, of which sugars 1.3g; Fat 12.6g, of which saturates 4.6g; Cholesterol 17mg; Calcium 23mg; Fibre 0.5g; Sodium 51mg.

Savoury cheese muffins

Puffed up and golden with their yummy cheese filling and the merest hint of hot spice, these savoury muffins are a real crowd-pleaser. Serve them warm and freshly baked, to accompany light sandwiches over a pot or two of tea.

MAKES 9

175g/6oz/1½ cups plain (all-purpose) flour
10ml/2 tsp baking powder
30ml/2 tbsp caster (superfine) sugar
5ml/1 tsp paprika

2 eggs
120ml/4fl oz/½ cup milk
50g/2oz/4 tbsp butter, melted
5ml/1 tsp dried thyme
50g/2oz mature (sharp) Cheddar cheese, diced

1 Preheat the oven to 190°C/375°F/Gas 5. Lightly grease 9 cups of a muffin tin (pan) or line them with paper muffin cases.

2 Sift together the flour, baking powder, sugar and paprika into a large bowl. Make a well in the centre. Set aside.

3 Combine the eggs, milk, melted butter and dried thyme in another bowl and beat lightly with a whisk until thoroughly blended.

4 Add the milk mixture to the dry ingredients and stir lightly with a wooden spoon until just combined. Do not overmix.

5 Place a heaped tablespoonful of the mixture in each of the prepared paper cases. Divide the pieces of cheese equally among the paper cases, then top with another spoonful of the batter, ensuring that the cheese is completely covered.

6 Bake for about 25 minutes, until puffed and golden. Leave to stand for 5 minutes before transferring to a wire rack to cool slightly before serving.

Energy 166kcal/698kJ; Protein 5.1g; Carbohydrate 19.3g, of which sugars 4.4g; Fat 8.1g, of which saturates 4.6g; Cholesterol 60mg; Calcium 93mg; Fibre 0.6g; Sodium 96mg.

Wild mushroom & pine nut muffins

These light savoury muffins make attractive additions to a high tea. The pine nuts are decorative as well as adding texture and crunch, and a delicious warm nutty flavour. Serve them freshly baked and warm to enjoy them at their best.

MAKES 6–7

250g/9oz/2¼ cups self-raising (self-rising) flour

11.5ml/2¼ tsp baking powder

150g/5oz mixture of wild mushrooms

165g/5½oz/scant ¾ cup butter

large pinch of cayenne pepper

large pinch of mace

50–75g/2–2½oz/½–¾ cup pine nuts

30ml/2 tbsp olive oil

90ml/3fl oz/6 tbsp buttermilk

2 eggs

1 Preheat the oven to 180°C/350°F/Gas 4. Lightly grease the cups of a muffin tin (pan).

2 Sift the flour and baking powder into a large bowl and set aside.

3 Clean and slice the mushrooms. In a frying pan, heat about half butter over medium heat. When it is foaming, add the mushrooms. Season with cayenne pepper and mace. Fry gently, stirring, until just softened. Scrape into a bowl and set aside to cool.

4 Fry the pine nuts in 15g/1 tbsp more butter and the olive oil for 30 seconds, until just golden, then add them to the mushrooms.

5 Melt the remaining butter. Beat together the buttermilk, melted butter and eggs in a bowl, then stir into the dry ingredients along with the mushrooms and pine nuts.

6 Spoon the batter into the muffin tins and bake for 25 minutes, until the tops are golden and firm.

Energy 399kcal/1660kJ; Protein 6.9g; Carbohydrate 28g, of which sugars 1.4g; Fat 29.6g, of which saturates 14.2g; Cholesterol 109mg; Calcium 154mg; Fibre 1.5g; Sodium 334mg.

Shallot, thyme & garlic cheese muffins

These light muffins are best served warm, fresh from the oven, when the cream cheese and the caramelized flavour complement each other perfectly. Spread them with soft cheese for an unusual, but tempting, addition to the afternoon tea table.

MAKES 10

225g/8oz shallots, peeled
25ml/1½ tbsp olive oil, for frying
90g/3oz/7 tbsp unsalted butter, melted
10ml/2 tsp fresh thyme, plus a few sprigs for garnishing
225g/8oz/2 cups self-raising (self-rising) flour
10ml/2 tsp baking powder
10ml/2 tsp caster (superfine) sugar
115g/4oz soft herb and garlic cream cheese
175ml/6fl oz/¾ cup milk
2 eggs
salt and ground black pepper

1 Preheat the oven to 180°C/350°F/Gas 4. Lightly grease and line 10 dariole moulds with baking parchment.

2 Drop the peeled shallots into a pan of boiling water and blanch them for 2 minutes. Drain thoroughly, then leave to stand on kitchen paper. When the shallots are cool enough to handle, slice them into quarters.

3 In a frying pan, heat the oil and 15ml/1 tbsp of the butter over medium heat. Add the shallots and sauté them, until caramelized on all sides.

4 Stir in the thyme and seasoning, then remove from the heat and leave to cool.

5 In a large bowl, sift together the flour, a pinch of salt, baking powder and sugar.

6 In another bowl, beat together the cream cheese, milk, eggs and the remaining melted butter. Pour into a well in the centre of the dry ingredients and blend until partly mixed.

7 Scrape the shallots and any liquid into the batter (reserving a few shallots for garnishing) and stir lightly to just combine. Do not overmix.

8 Divide the batter between the moulds and dot with the reserved shallots and a few thyme sprigs.

9 Bake for 25–30 minutes or until the tops are firm to the touch. Leave to cool slightly then transfer to a wire rack. Serve warm.

Energy 236kcal/984kJ; Protein 4.5g; Carbohydrate 20.7g, of which sugars 3.5g; Fat 15.6g, of which saturates 9g; Cholesterol 71mg; Calcium 124mg; Fibre 1g; Sodium 207mg.

Vegetable muffins

Onions, courgettes, cream cheese and herbs have a healthy appeal. When combined in these muffins, they impart a sharp and tangy flavour and a moist texture. Serve them warm as part of a teatime spread.

MAKES 8

150g/5oz courgettes (zucchini)
250g/9oz/2¼ cups self-raising (self-rising) flour
pinch of celery salt or salt
12.5ml/2½ tsp baking powder
5ml/1 tsp caster (superfine) sugar
3.5ml/¾ tsp cayenne pepper
8 spring onions (scallions)
30ml/2 tbsp grated red onion
10ml/2 tsp malt vinegar
115g/4oz soft herb and garlic cream cheese
60ml/4 tbsp sour cream
75g/2½oz/6 tbsp butter, melted
2 eggs
15ml/1 tbsp finely chopped mixed fresh parsley and thyme
15g/½oz Parmesan cheese
ground black pepper
olive oil, to drizzle

1 Preheat the oven to 180°C/350°F/Gas 4. Lightly grease and line 8 dariole moulds with baking parchment.

2 Coarsely grate the courgettes into a bowl.

3 In a large bowl, sift together the flour, salt, baking powder, sugar and cayenne pepper and set aside.

4 Slice the white parts of the spring onions into thin discs and add to the courgettes with the grated red onion. Sprinkle with the vinegar. Season and set aside to marinate.

5 In a small bowl, whisk the cheese into the sour cream, then whisk in the melted butter, eggs and herbs, until smooth and combined.

6 Pour the egg mixture into the dry ingredients with the Parmesan and grated vegetables and any juices from the bowl. Stir to mix until just combined.

7 Fill the prepared paper cases three-quarters full. Drizzle lightly with olive oil. Add a few twists of black pepper and a sprinkle of cayenne, and then bake for 25–30 minutes, until risen and golden.

8 Leave to cool slightly, then serve warm.

Energy 291kcal/1215kJ; Protein 6.8g; Carbohydrate 25.8g, of which sugars 1.9g; Fat 18.6g, of which saturates 11.1g; Cholesterol 126mg; Calcium 109mg; Fibre 1.4g; Sodium 154mg.

Bacon, brie & date savouries

The strong flavours of bacon and fresh dates make a wonderful marriage, set off by the creamy brie. These delicious little savouries are made in miniature form for the tea table, but the batter will make 12–14 standard-size muffins, if you prefer.

MAKES 24–28

225g/8oz/2 cups plain (all-purpose) flour
pinch of salt
10ml/2 tsp baking powder
10ml/2 tsp caster (superfine) sugar
12 fresh dates, pitted
30ml/2 tbsp olive oil, for frying

65g/2¼oz/5 tbsp butter, melted
12 rashers (strips) smoked, streaky bacon
75g/2½oz brie, diced
150ml/5fl oz/⅔ cup milk
2 eggs, beaten

1 Preheat the oven to 180°C/350°F/Gas 5. Lightly grease the cups of a mini muffin tin (pan) or line them with mini paper cases.

2 In a large bowl, sift together the flour, salt, baking powder and sugar and set aside. Using a knife dusted with flour, chop the dates into pieces. Separate out any clumps and add to the flour.

3 In a frying pan, heat the oil and 15ml/1 tbsp of the butter, and fry the bacon for 4 minutes or until crisp.

4 When cool enough to handle, cut the warm bacon into small pieces and stir back into the warm juices in the pan. Cover with foil and set aside.

5 Mash the brie as well as you can into the milk, then mix it into the dry ingredients along with the melted butter, eggs, fried bacon and any juices from the pan. Mix lightly together until just combined.

6 Fill the prepared paper cases three-quarters full. Bake for 18–20 minutes, until risen and golden.

7 Leave to stand and set for 5 minutes before turning out on to a wire rack. Serve warm. These will store for up to 3 days in an airtight container, just warm up in a microwave before serving.

Energy 183kcal/724kJ; Protein 4.9g; Carbohydrate 12.2g, of which sugars 0.6g; Fat 11.9.6g, of which saturates 8.3g; Cholesterol 53mg; Calcium 99mg; Fibre 0.8g; Sodium 202mg.

Corn cakes with ham

These little savoury cakes are perfect to serve as a finger food at an afternoon tea buffet. If you like, serve them unfilled with a pot of herb butter. The quantity of batter will also make 6 larger muffin-sized cakes. Serve them freshly baked.

MAKES 12

50g/2oz/scant ½ cup yellow cornmeal

65g/2¼oz/generous ½ cup plain (all-purpose) flour, sifted

30ml/2 tbsp caster (superfine) sugar

7.5ml/1½ tsp baking powder

50g/2oz/4 tbsp butter, melted, plus extra for spreading

120ml/4fl oz/½ cup whipping cream

1 egg, beaten

1–2 jalapeño or other medium-hot chillies, seeded and finely chopped (optional)

pinch of cayenne pepper

grainy mustard, for spreading

50g/2oz oak-smoked ham, sliced, for filling

1 Preheat the oven to 200°C/400°F/Gas 6. Lightly grease the cups of a mini muffin tin (pan) or line them with mini paper cases.

2 In a large bowl, combine the cornmeal, sifted flour, sugar and baking powder.

3 In another bowl, whisk together the melted butter, cream, egg, chillies, if using, and the cayenne pepper.

4 Make a well in the cornmeal mixture, pour in the egg mixture and gently stir in just enough to blend (do not over-beat – the batter does not have to be smooth).

5 Drop a spoonful of batter into each paper case. Bake for 12–15 minutes, until golden. Leave to stand for a few minutes, then transfer to a wire rack to go cold.

6 To serve, split the muffins, spread with a little butter and mustard and sandwich with ham.

Energy 54kcal/227kJ; Protein 1.5g; Carbohydrate 6.8g, of which sugars 1.6g; Fat 2.5g, of which saturates 1.4g; Cholesterol 14mg; Calcium 13mg; Fibre 0.2g; Sodium 43mg.

Scones, crumpets & teabreads

From teacakes to teabreads, this chapter is packed with enticing classics that you will turn to again and again. Some, such as iconic scones, are best made fresh on the day, but others, such as fruit malt loaf or ginger loaf, actually improve with age and benefit from a day or two in the cake tin, meaning you can get organized in advance. Many freeze brilliantly, too, so it's worth doubling up and making twice the quantity so you have a stash to hand for when you want to lay on a more impromptu spread.

Left What could be better than a freshly baked scone with jam and clotted cream to accompany a pot of tea? An essential element of every proper afternoon tea.

Scones with jam & cream

The contrast of warm, buttered scone, homemade jam bursting with fruit, and thick cream, is the quintessential taste of English afternoon tea.

MAKES 12

450g/1lb/4 cups self-raising (self-rising) flour or 450g/1lb/ 4 cups plain (all-purpose) flour and 10ml/2 tsp baking powder, plus extra flour for dusting
pinch of salt
50g/2oz/4 tbsp butter, chilled and diced

15ml/1 tbsp lemon juice
about 400ml/14fl oz/1⅔ cups milk, plus extra to glaze
fruit jam (see pages 262–3) and whipped or clotted cream, to serve

1 Preheat the oven to 230°C/450°F/Gas 8.

2 Sift the flour, salt and baking powder, if using, into a mixing bowl. Rub in the butter with your fingertips until the mixture resembles fine breadcrumbs.

3 In a small bowl, whisk the lemon juice into the milk and leave for about 1 minute to thicken slightly, then pour into the flour and mix quickly to form a dough.

4 Knead the dough very lightly until it just comes together as a ball, then roll it out on a floured surface to a thickness of about 2.5cm/1in.

5 Using a 5cm/2in cutter and dipping it into flour each time, stamp out 12 scones, and place them on a well-floured baking sheet. Re-roll any trimmings and cut out more if you can.

6 Brush the tops of the scones lightly with a little milk and then bake for about 20 minutes, or until risen and golden brown.

7 Wrap the scones in a clean dish towel to keep them warm and soft until ready to serve.

8 Eat with your favourite fruit jam and a generous dollop of clotted cream, or whipped cream if you prefer.

Energy 177kcal/749kJ; Protein 4.7g; Carbohydrate 30.7g, of which sugars 2.2g; Fat 4.8g, of which saturates 2.8g; Cholesterol 12mg; Calcium 93mg; Fibre 1.2g; Sodium 43mg.

Caraway scones

These little scented seeds were once used in many breads, cakes and confections in northern Europe and give a wonderful, warm, old-fashioned aroma as they bake.

MAKES 12

350g/12oz/3 cups plain (all-purpose) flour, plus extra for dusting
115g/4oz/²⁄₃ cup ground rice or semolina
10ml/2 tsp baking powder
115g/4oz/½ cup butter, diced
75g/2½oz/½ cup caster (superfine) sugar, plus extra for dusting
30ml/2 tbsp caraway seeds
2 eggs
about 75ml/5 tbsp milk

1 Preheat the oven to 200°C/400°F/Gas 6. Line a baking sheet with baking parchment.

2 Sift the flour into a large mixing bowl, then add the ground rice and baking powder and mix to combine.

3 Add the butter to the flour and, with your fingertips, rub it into the flour until the mixture resembles fine breadcrumbs. Stir in the sugar and caraway seeds.

4 Lightly beat the eggs and stir them into the flour mixture, together with sufficient milk to enable you to gather the mixture into a ball of soft dough. Transfer to a lightly floured surface.

5 Roll out to about 2.5cm/1in thick. Using a 5cm/2in cutter, cut into rounds, gathering up the offcuts and re-rolling to make more.

6 Arrange the rounds on the lined baking sheet, setting them quite close together so they support each other as they rise.

7 Put into the hot oven and cook for 15–20 minutes until risen and golden brown.

8 Transfer to a wire rack and dust with caster sugar. Leave to cool slightly, then serve with butter.

Energy 128kcal/540kJ; Protein 4.1g; Carbohydrate 22.8g, of which sugars 1.3g; Fat 2.9g, of which saturates 1.4g; Cholesterol 29mg; Calcium 66mg; Fibre 0.9g; Sodium 29mg.

Brown soda scones

These unusually light scones are virtually fat-free, so they must be eaten very fresh – warm from the oven if possible, but definitely on the day of baking.

MAKES 16

oil, for greasing
225g/8oz/2 cups plain
(all-purpose) flour, plus extra for
dusting
2.5ml/½ tsp bicarbonate of soda
(baking soda)
2.5ml/½ tsp salt

225g/8oz/2 cups wholemeal
(wholewheat) flour
about 350ml/12fl oz/1½ cups
buttermilk or sour cream and
milk mixed
egg wash (1 egg yolk mixed with
15ml/1 tbsp water) or grated
cheese

1 Preheat the oven to 220°C/425°F/Gas 7.

2 Sift the plain flour, bicarbonate of soda and salt in a bowl, add the wheaten flour and mix.

3 Make a well in the centre, pour in almost all the liquid and mix, adding the remaining liquid as needed to make a soft, moist dough. Do not overmix.

4 Lightly dust a work surface with flour, turn out the dough and dust the top with flour; press out evenly to a thickness of 4cm/1½in.

5 Cut out about 16 scones with a 5cm/2in fluted cutter. Place on the prepared baking tray and brush the tops with egg wash, or sprinkle with a little grated cheese.

6 Oil and flour a baking tray. Place on the scones and bake for about 12 minutes until well risen and golden brown. Serve warm.

Cook's tip

For a more traditional scone mixture that keeps longer, rub 50g/2oz/4 tbsp butter into the dry ingredients, and increase the proportion of the bicarbonate of soda (baking soda) to 5ml/1 tsp, as the scones will not be as light.

Energy 117Kcal/493kJ; Protein 3.8g; Carbohydrate 20.9g, of which sugars 1.5g; Fat 2.6g, of which saturates 1.4g; Cholesterol 6mg; Calcium 49mg; Fibre 1.7g; Sodium 72mg.

Drop scones

Variously known as girdle cakes, griddlecakes and Scotch pancakes, these make a quick and easy teatime snack. Serve warm with butter and honey, maple syrup or golden syrup.

MAKES 8–10

115g/4oz/1 cup plain (all-purpose) flour
5ml/1 tsp bicarbonate of soda (baking soda)
5ml/1 tsp cream of tartar
25g/1oz/2 tbsp butter, diced
1 egg, beaten
about 150ml/5fl oz/⅔ cup milk
butter and honey or maple syrup, to serve

1 Lightly grease a griddle pan or heavy frying pan, then preheat it over medium heat.

2 Meanwhile, sift the flour, bicarbonate of soda and cream of tartar together into a mixing bowl.

3 Add the diced butter and rub it into the flour with your fingertips until the mixture resembles fine, evenly sized breadcrumbs.

4 Make a well in the centre of the flour mixture, then stir in the egg. Add the milk a little at a time, stirring well after each addition. Add enough milk to give a thick creamy consistency.

5 Cook the batter in batches. Drop three or four evenly sized spoonfuls of the mixture, spaced slightly apart, on the griddle or frying pan. Cook over medium heat for 2–3 minutes, until bubbles rise to the surface and burst.

6 Turn the scones over and cook for a further 2–3 minutes, until golden underneath.

7 Place the cooked scones between the folds of a clean dish towel while cooking the remaining batter. Serve warm.

Energy 59kcal/249kJ; Protein 2g; Carbohydrate 10.9g, of which sugars 1.8g; Fat 1.1g, of which saturates 0.2g; Cholesterol 11mg; Calcium 65mg; Fibre 0.4g; Sodium 56mg.

Crumpets

Made with a yeast batter and cooked quickly in metal rings on a griddle, crumpets are a particularly traditional English teatime food with an unusual dense and spongy texture. They are best served fresh and hot, with plenty of good butter and perhaps some jam.

MAKES ABOUT 10

225g/8oz/2 cups plain
(all-purpose) flour
pinch of salt
2.5ml/½ tsp bicarbonate of soda
(baking soda)

5ml/1 tsp easy-blend (rapid-rise)
dried yeast
150ml/5fl oz/⅔ cup milk
200ml/7fl oz/scant 1 cup
lukewarm water

1 Sift the flour, salt and bicarbonate of soda into a bowl and stir in the yeast. Make a well in the centre.

2 Heat the milk with the measured water in a small pan or in the microwave until lukewarm. Pour the milk into the well and beat or whisk vigorously to make a thick, smooth batter.

3 Cover the bowl with a clean dish towel and leave in a warm place for about 1 hour, until the mixture has a spongy texture.

4 Heat a griddle or heavy frying pan. Lightly oil the hot surface and the inside of three or four metal rings, each measuring about 8cm/3½in in diameter. Place the rings on the hot surface and leave for 1–2 minutes until hot.

5 Spoon the batter into the rings to a depth of about 1cm/½in. Cook over medium-high heat for 6 minutes, until the surface is set and holes have appeared.

6 When set, carefully lift off the metal rings and flip the crumpets over, cooking the second side for just 1 minute until lightly browned.

7 Lift off the griddle and leave to cool on a wire rack. Repeat with the remaining crumpet mixture.

8 Just before serving, toast the crumpets on both sides so that the surface is quite hard. Butter and serve as they are or top with a spread or jam of your choice.

Cook's tip
Crumpets, like muffins and teacakes, freeze beautifully, and if you aren't going to eat them on the day of making it is a good idea to freeze them as soon as they are cool and then toast them straight from the freezer on a defrost setting. To make life easier, slice the muffins and teacakes in half before freezing, so they can easily be separated into two halves while frozen and will fit into the toaster. This isn't necessary for crumpets.

Energy 93kcal/393kJ; Protein 3g; Carbohydrate 16.5g, of which sugars 1g; Fat 2.1g, of which saturates 1g; Cholesterol 21mg; Calcium 48mg; Fibre 0.6g; Sodium 21mg.

English muffins

English muffins are circles of bread cooked on a griddle, which are made for toasting. They have a bland flavour so are perfect served warm, split open and spread with butter, accompanied by a cup of strong tea and perhaps some jam or citrus curd.

MAKES 9

450g/1lb/4 cups strong white bread flour
7.5ml/1½ tsp salt
350–375ml/12–13fl oz/1½–1⅔ cups lukewarm milk

pinch of caster (superfine) sugar
15g/½oz fresh yeast
15ml/1 tbsp melted butter or olive oil
rice flour or semolina, for dusting

1 Flour a non-stick baking sheet and grease a griddle pan.

2 Sift the flour and salt into a bowl and make a well in the centre.

3 In another bowl, blend 150ml/5fl oz/⅔ cup of the milk, sugar and yeast. Stir in the remaining milk and butter or oil.

4 Add the yeast mixture to the well and beat for 4–5 minutes, until smooth and elastic. The dough will be soft but just hold its shape.

5 Cover with lightly oiled clear film (plastic wrap) and leave to rise in a warm place for 45–60 minutes, or until doubled in bulk.

6 Turn out the dough on to a floured surface and knock back (punch down). Roll out to 1cm/¼in thick. Stamp out 7.5cm/3in rounds.

7 Dust the dough rounds with rice flour or semolina and place on the prepared baking sheet. Cover and leave to rise, in a warm place, for about 20–30 minutes.

8 Warm the griddle over medium heat. Carefully transfer the muffins in batches to the griddle. Cook slowly for about 7 minutes on each side or until golden brown. Transfer to a wire rack to cool.

9 When cold, toast like bread, and serve.

Energy 201kcal/852kJ; Protein 6g; Carbohydrate 40.7g, of which sugars 2.6g; Fat 2.7g, of which saturates 1.4g; Cholesterol 6mg; Calcium 117mg; Fibre 1.6g; Sodium 356mg.

Teacakes

These fruit-filled teatime treats are thought to be a refinement of the original 'handbread':
a shaped roll made on a flat tin. You can add a teaspoon of allspice to the flour, if you like.
Serve them split and buttered, either warm from the oven or toasted.

MAKES 8–10

450g/1lb/4 cups strong white
bread flour, plus extra for dusting
5ml/1 tsp salt
5ml/1 tsp easy-blend (rapid-rise)
dried yeast
40g/1½oz/3 tbsp caster
(superfine) sugar

300ml/½ pint/1¼ cups lukewarm
milk, plus extra for glazing
40g/1½oz/3 tbsp butter, diced
50g/2oz/⅓ cup currants
50g/2oz/⅓ cup sultanas
(golden raisins)

1 Sift the flour and salt into a bowl.

2 In a jug or bowl mix the yeast, 5ml/1 tsp of the sugar and the lukewarm milk and leave to stand for 5 minutes.

3 Add the remaining sugar to the flour and make a well in the centre. Pour in the milk a little at a time and mix well, adding just enough to make a dry dough. Add the butter and knead briefly, to bring it together.

4 Turn the dough out on to a lightly floured surface and knead for at least 15 minutes, until the dough is no longer sticky and full of little bubbles, adding a little extra milk if necessary. You can also do this in a food processor using the hook attachment, for 10 minutes.

5 Shape the dough into a ball, place in a clean bowl and cover with a dampened dish towel. Leave at room temperature for 1 hour, until it has doubled in bulk.

6 Generously grease two baking sheets. Turn out the dough and knead in the dried fruit until it is evenly distributed. Divide the dough into eight to ten portions, and shape into balls. Flatten each one into a disc about 1cm/½in thick.

7 Place the discs on the baking sheets, 2.5cm/1in apart. Cover with oiled clear film (plastic wrap) and leave in a warm place for 30–45 minutes, or until they have almost doubled in size. Preheat the oven to 200°C/400°F/Gas 6.

8 Brush the top of each teacake with milk, then bake for 15–18 minutes, or until golden. Turn out on to a wire rack to cool slightly.

9 To serve, split open the teacakes while warm and spread generously with butter, or let the teacakes cool, then split and toast them.

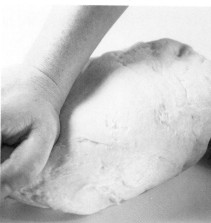

Energy 285kcal/1183kJ; Protein 12.6g; Carbohydrate 5.8g, of which sugars 3.2g; Fat 22.7g, of which saturates 8.7g; Cholesterol 57mg; Calcium 73mg; Fibre 0.2g; Sodium 103mg.

Saffron teabread

The beautiful yellow colour and distinctive flavour of this teabread comes from saffron, transforming a simple fruit loaf into a special treat. Serve sliced, spread with butter.

MAKES 1 LOAF

good pinch of saffron threads
450g/1lb/4 cups plain (all-purpose) flour
2.5ml/½ tsp salt
50g/2oz/4 tbsp butter, diced
50g/2oz/4 tbsp lard or vegetable fat, diced
10ml/2 tsp easy-blend (rapid-rise) yeast
50g/2oz/¼ cup caster (superfine) sugar
115g/4oz/⅔ cup currants, raisins or sultanas (golden raisins), or a mixture
50g/2oz/⅓ cup chopped mixed candied peel
150ml/5fl oz/⅔ cup milk
beaten egg, to glaze

1 Put the saffron in a bowl and add 150ml/5fl oz/⅔ cup boiling water. Cover and leave for several hours to allow the colour and flavour to develop.

2 Sift the flour and salt into a large bowl. Add the butter and lard and rub them into the flour until the mixture resembles fine breadcrumbs. Stir in the yeast, sugar, dried fruit and chopped mixed peel.

3 Make a well in the centre of the ingredients. Add the milk to the saffron water and heat gently. Pour into the flour and stir until it can be gathered into a ball.

4 Cover with oiled cling film (plastic wrap) and leave in a warm place for 1 hour, until doubled in size. Grease and line a 900g/2lb loaf tin (pan) with baking parchment.

5 Turn the dough on to a lightly floured surface and knead gently and briefly. Put the dough in the prepared tin, cover and leave in a warm place for 30 minutes until nearly doubled in size. Preheat the oven to 200°C/400°F/Gas 6.

6 Brush the top of the loaf with beaten egg and cook for 40 minutes or until risen and cooked through; cover with foil if it starts to brown too much.

7 Leave in the tin for about 15 minutes before turning out on to a wire rack to cool.

Energy 3041kcal/12821kJ; Protein 50.7g; Carbohydrate 516.8g, of which sugars 173.9g; Fat 99.9g, of which saturates 48.7g; Cholesterol 162mg; Calcium 1018mg; Fibre 18.5g; Sodium 541mg.

Cardamom loaf

This is a traditional teabread of Scandinavia, where the warm-flavoured cardamom is a much-loved spice. A lovely fruit cakey loaf that tastes good without being too rich.

MAKES 1 LOAF

375g/13oz/3¼ cups plain (all-purpose) flour
45ml/3 tbsp baking powder
10 cardamom pods, seeds removed and finely crushed
250g/9oz/generous 1 cup butter, plus extra for greasing
250g/9oz/1¼ cups caster (superfine) sugar

3 eggs, lightly beaten
150ml/5fl oz/⅔ cup milk
45ml/3 tbsp raisins
45ml/3 tbsp candied peel
15ml/1 tbsp flaked or sliced almonds

1 Preheat the oven to 190°C/ 375°F/Gas 5. Grease and line a 900g/2lb loaf tin (pan) with baking parchment.

2 Sift the flour, baking powder and crushed cardamom seeds together.

3 In a large bowl, cream together the butter and sugar until light and fluffy. Beat in the eggs, one at a time, adding a teaspoon of the flour with each egg. Fold in the remaining flour.

4 Add the milk, a little at a time, folding in well after each addition.

5 Add the raisins, candied peel and flaked almonds, and fold in well. Turn the mixture into the tin and smooth the top level.

6 Bake for 50 minutes, or until risen and firm to the touch. Turn out and cool on a wire rack. Remove the lining paper. Slice to serve, perhaps with butter; this loaf will make about 10 slices.

Energy 4594kcal/19277kJ; Protein 64.2g; Carbohydrate 624.9g, of which sugars 338.7g; Fat 221.5g, of which saturates 133.3g; Cholesterol 544mg; Calcium 894mg; Fibre 17.9g; Sodium 2012mg.

Fruit malt loaf

Malt extract gives this traditional fruity loaf its wonderful chewy consistency, and wholemeal flour adds depth of flavour. Cut in slices and spread with butter, it's just right for hungry guests with afternoon tea. Keep for up to 5 days in an airtight container.

MAKES 1 LOAF

250g/9oz/2¼ cups wholemeal (wholewheat) self-raising (self-rising) flour
pinch of salt
2.5ml/½ tsp bicarbonate of soda (baking soda)
175g/6oz/1 cup mixed dried fruit
15ml/1 tbsp malt extract
250ml/8½fl oz/1 cup milk

Cook's tip
Malt extract can sometimes be hard to find in standard supermarkets, but it is usually stocked in health-food stores. You could try using black treacle (molasses) instead, although the flavour will be different.

1 Preheat the oven to 160°C/325°F/Gas 3. Grease and line a 900g/2lb loaf tin (pan) with baking parchment.

2 Put the dry ingredients and dried fruit in a bowl and stir to combine. Make a well in the middle

3 Heat the malt extract and milk in a small pan, stirring until dissolved.

4 Mix the malt and milk mixture into the dry ingredients until well combined. Spoon into the tin.

5 Bake for 45 minutes, or until a skewer inserted into the loaf comes out clean.

6 Leave to stand for a few minutes, then turn out on to a wire rack to go cold.

7 Remove the lining paper and serve sliced, generously spread with butter.

Energy 1403kcal/5971kJ; Protein 44.3g; Carbohydrate 302.3g, of which sugars 147.9g; Fat 10.4g, of which saturates 3.4g; Cholesterol 15mg; Calcium 525mg; Fibre 35.1g; Sodium 923mg.

Date & walnut loaf

This fruit loaf is lower in sugar than some cakes but the dates and bananas add sweetness. As they also make the loaf very moist, it's great for keeping for an unexpected tea party. Keep for a week in an airtight container or freeze for up to 2 months.

MAKES 1 LOAF

150g/5oz/scant 1 cup dried dates, stoned (pitted) and chopped
finely grated rind and juice of 1 lemon
5ml/1 tsp bicarbonate of soda (baking soda)
75g/2½oz/6 tbsp butter, softened
50g/2oz/¼ cup soft light brown sugar

2 eggs, beaten
150g/5oz/½ cup sweetened condensed milk
150g/5oz ripe bananas, peeled and mashed
225g/8oz/2 cups self-raising (self-rising) flour
5ml/1 tsp baking powder
75g/2½oz/¾ cup chopped walnuts

1 Preheat the oven to 160°C/325°F/Gas 3. Grease and line a 900g/2lb loaf tin (pan) with baking parchment.

2 Put the dates in a bowl with the lemon rind and juice, and 30ml/2 tbsp boiling water. Stir in the bicarbonate of soda. Leave to cool.

3 Put the butter, sugar and condensed milk in a bowl and beat until smooth. Gradually beat in the eggs. Stir in the bananas and the date mixture.

4 Sift the flour and baking powder into the bowl, then add the chopped nuts and stir together until smooth.

5 Spoon the mixture into the tin and smooth the top level. Bake for about 1 hour 10–15 minutes, or until a skewer inserted into the middle comes out clean.

6 Leave for 10 minutes, then turn on to a wire rack to cool. Remove the lining paper. Serve sliced and buttered.

Energy 3153kcal/13263kJ; Protein 62.7g; Carbohydrate 457.5g, of which sugars 286.4g; Fat 131.7g, of which saturates 54.9g; Cholesterol 214mg; Calcium 1412mg; Fibre 24.1g; Sodium 1728mg.

Ginger loaf

Cinnamon as well as ginger gives gingerbread its familiar warm flavouring, which wouldn't be achieved by using ginger alone. Treacle and golden syrup ensure the finished cake is soft and sticky. Store, foil-wrapped, for 5 days in an airtight container.

MAKES 1 LOAF

115g/4oz/½ cup soft light brown sugar
75g/2½oz/6 tbsp butter
75g/2½oz/¼ cup golden (light corn) syrup
75g/2½oz/¼ cup treacle (molasses)
100ml/3½fl oz/scant ½ cup milk

1 egg, beaten
175g/6oz/1½ cups plain (all-purpose) flour
50g/2oz/½ cup gram flour
pinch of salt
10ml/2 tsp ground ginger
5ml/1 tsp ground cinnamon
7.5ml/1½ tsp baking powder

1 Preheat the oven to 160°C/325°F/Gas 3. Grease and line a 900g/2lb loaf tin (pan) with baking parchment.

2 Put the sugar, butter, golden syrup and treacle in a pan and heat gently until melted, stirring occasionally.

3 Remove the pan and leave to cool slightly. Mix in the milk and egg.

4 Sift the flours, salt, spices and baking powder into a large bowl. Make a well in the centre and pour in the liquid mixture. Beat well.

5 Pour the batter into the tin. Bake for 1–1¼ hours, or until firm.

6 Turn out on to a wire rack to go cold. Peel off the lining and serve in slices.

Energy 2241kcal/9458kJ; Protein 26.6g; Carbohydrate 410g, of which sugars 238.2g; Fat 66.2g, of which saturates 40.6g; Cholesterol 167mg; Calcium 896mg; Fibre 9.3g; Sodium 854mg.

Banana bread

When you have some bananas that have become over-ripe in the fruit bowl, use them for this delicious teatime cake. They need to be very ripe and will give the bread a lovely sweetness and fragrance as well as making it wonderfully moist.

MAKES 1 LOAF

115g/4oz/½ cup butter
5ml/1 tsp bicarbonate of soda (baking soda)
225g/8oz/2 cups wholemeal (whole-wheat) flour
2 eggs, beaten
3 very ripe bananas
30–45ml/2–3 tbsp coconut milk

Cook's tip
This comforting bread contains very little fat, which gives it a slightly chewy texture.

1 Preheat the oven to 180°C/350°F/Gas 4. Grease and line a 900g/2lb loaf tin (pan) with baking parchment.

2 In a large bowl, cream the butter until it is fluffy.

3 Sift the bicarbonate of soda with the flour, then add to the butter, alternating with the eggs.

4 Peel the bananas and slice them on to a plate. Mash them well, using the back of a fork, then stir them into the cake mixture. Mix in the coconut milk and stir together until just combined.

5 Spoon the batter into the tin and smooth the top level. Bake for 1¼ hours, or until firm to touch and golden.

6 Cool on a wire rack. Remove the lining paper and serve in slices. This bread will keep for about 5 days.

Energy 2033kcal/8503kJ; Protein 48.9g; Carbohydrate 215.5g, of which sugars 69.5g; Fat 114.3g, of which saturates 65g; Cholesterol 709mg; Calcium 229mg; Fibre 31.4g; Sodium 2257mg.

Pineapple & carrot loaf

This is one of the most irresistible loaf cakes. The poppy seeds and walnut pieces add crunch, the pineapple and carrot give moisture, and a tangy citrus mascarpone icing makes a delicious topping. Keep for up to 4 days in an airtight container.

MAKES 1 LOAF

250g/9oz/2¼ cups plain
(all-purpose) flour
10ml/2 tsp baking powder
5ml/1 tsp bicarbonate of soda
(baking soda)
pinch of salt
5ml/1 tsp ground cinnamon
45ml/3 tbsp poppy seeds
225g/8oz/1 cup soft light
brown sugar
3 eggs, beaten
finely grated rind of 1 orange
225g/8oz raw carrots,
finely grated

75g/2½oz fresh or canned
pineapple, drained and
roughly chopped
75g/2½oz/¾ cup walnut pieces,
roughly chopped
115g/4oz/½ cup butter, melted
and cooled

For the icing

150g/5oz/1 cup mascarpone
30ml/2 tbsp icing (confectioners')
sugar, sifted
finely grated rind of 1 orange

1 Preheat the oven to 180°C/350°F/Gas 4. Grease and line a 900g/2lb loaf tin (pan) with baking parchment.

2 Sift the flour, baking powder, bicarbonate of soda, salt and cinnamon into a bowl. Stir in the poppy seeds. In another bowl, beat the sugar, eggs and orange rind.

3 Squeeze the excess moisture from the carrots and stir into the egg mixture with the pineapple and walnuts.

4 Stir in the flour, until it is all incorporated, then gently fold in the butter.

5 Spoon the batter into the prepared tin and smooth the top level. Bake for 1–1¼ hours, until risen.

6 Leave to cool for 10 minutes, then turn out on a wire rack. Remove the paper when cold.

7 To make the icing, beat the mascarpone with the icing sugar and orange rind until smooth.

8 Spread the icing thickly over the top of the cake. Store in the fridge.

Energy 3914kcal/16407kJ; Protein 85.4g; Carbohydrate 494g, of which sugars 293g; Fat 216.2g, of which saturates 91g; Cholesterol 1010mg; Calcium 1680mg; Fibre 22.2g; Sodium 2774mg.

Courgette & double ginger loaf

Both fresh and preserved ginger are used to flavour this teabread, which is made with oil rather than butter. Courgettes, like several other vegetables, bring moisture to a cake mix, making it soft and tasty. Keep for up to 5 days in an airtight container or freeze for 2 months.

MAKES 1 LOAF

3 eggs

225g/8oz/1 cup caster (superfine) sugar

250ml/8½fl oz/1 cup sunflower oil

5ml/1 tsp vanilla extract

15ml/1 tbsp syrup from a jar of preserved stem ginger

225g/8oz courgettes (zucchini), grated, drained

2.5cm/1in piece fresh root ginger, peeled and grated

350g/12oz/3 cups plain (all-purpose) flour

5ml/1 tsp baking powder

5ml/1 tsp ground cinnamon

pinch of salt

2 pieces preserved stem ginger, chopped

15ml/1 tbsp demerara (raw) sugar

1 Preheat the oven to 190°C/325°F/Gas 5. Grease and line a 900g/2lb loaf tin (pan) with baking parchment.

2 In a large bowl, beat together the eggs and sugar until light and fluffy.

3 Slowly beat in the oil until a batter forms. Mix in the vanilla extract and ginger syrup, then stir in the grated courgettes and fresh ginger.

4 Sift the flour, baking powder, cinnamon and salt over the batter and stir in.

5 Pour into the prepared tin and smooth level. Sprinkle the chopped ginger and demerara sugar on top.

6 Bake for 1 hour, or until a skewer inserted into the centre comes out clean.

7 Leave to cool for 20 minutes, then turn out to cool on a wire rack.

Energy 2496kcal/10595kJ; Protein 60.7g; Carbohydrate 538.7g, of which sugars 271.7g; Fat 25.6g, of which saturates 6.6g; Cholesterol 693mg; Calcium 721mg; Fibre 17.2g; Sodium 317mg.

Lemon & walnut loaf

The unusual combination of earthy walnuts and zesty lemons tastes so good in this recipe, and makes a change from the more common pairing of lemon and almond. Unusually for a teabread, whisked egg whites are added to the batter, making it light and airy.

MAKES 1 LOAF

115g/4oz/½ cup butter, softened
100g/3½oz/generous ½ cup caster (superfine) sugar
2 eggs, separated
finely grated rind of 2 lemons
30ml/2 tbsp freshly squeezed lemon juice

200g/7oz/1¾ cups plain (all-purpose) flour
10ml/2 tsp baking powder
120ml/4fl oz/½ cup milk
50g/2oz/¾ cup walnuts, chopped

1 Preheat the oven to 180°C/350°F/Gas 4. Grease and line a 900g/2lb loaf tin (pan) with baking parchment.

2 Beat the butter with the sugar. Beat in the egg yolks, lemon rind and juice. Set aside.

3 Sift the flour and baking powder over the butter mixture in batches, and stir well, alternating with the milk. Fold in the walnuts.

4 Put the egg whites into a clean, grease-free bowl and whisk until they form stiff peaks.

5 Fold a large tablespoon of the egg whites into the walnut mixture to lighten it. Fold in the remaining egg whites until just blended.

6 Pour the batter into the tin and smooth the top level. Bake for 45–50 minutes, or until a skewer inserted into the centre comes out clean.

7 Leave to stand in the tin for 5 minutes then turn out on to a wire rack to go cold. Peel off the lining paper.

Variation
This works equally well with orange and blanched or flaked almonds, in place of the lemon and walnuts.

Energy 2512kcal/10503kJ; Protein 46.3g; Carbohydrate 268.1g, of which sugars 115.4g; Fat 146.7g, of which saturates 69.1g; Cholesterol 716mg; Calcium 577mg; Fibre 10.6g; Sodium 939mg.

Peanut butter loaf

Peanut butter gives this teabread richness and sweetness, which is balanced by the topping of salted peanuts. It makes a substantial teatime treat and is a real crowd-pleaser This cake will keep for 2 days in an airtight container.

MAKES 1 LOAF

225g/8oz/2 cups plain (all-purpose) flour

7.5ml/1½ tsp baking powder

2.5ml/½ tsp bicarbonate of soda (baking soda)

50g/2oz/4 tbsp butter, softened

175g/6oz/½ cup peanut butter

50g/2oz/¼ cup caster (superfine) sugar

2 eggs, beaten

250ml/8½fl oz/1 cup milk

25g/1oz/¼ cup roasted salted peanuts

1 Preheat the oven to 180°C/350°F/Gas 4. Grease and line a 900g/2lb loaf tin (pan) with baking parchment.

2 Sift the flour, baking powder and bicarbonate of soda together into a large bowl.

3 Put the butter and peanut butter in a large bowl and beat together with a wooden spoon to soften. Beat in the caster sugar until light and fluffy and the sugar grains have disintegrated.

4 Gradually whisk in the eggs a little at a time, then beat in the milk with the sifted flour and mix until smooth.

5 Pour the mixture into the prepared tin, smooth the top and sprinkle the roasted salted peanuts evenly on top.

6 Bake for 1 hour or until a skewer inserted into the centre comes out clean.

7 Cool in the tin for 5 minutes, then turn out on to a wire rack. Remove the lining paper.

Variation

You can substitute peanut butter with any nut butter, and the roasted salted peanuts with other nuts.

Energy 2845kcal/11893kJ; Protein 91g; Carbohydrate 264.3g, of which sugars 80.8g; Fat 165.4g, of which saturates 57.8g; Cholesterol 586mg; Calcium 756mg; Fibre 11.3g; Sodium 1318mg.

Sour cherry coffee loaf

Dried sour cherries have a wonderfully concentrated fruit flavour that makes them just right for adding to cakes. Here they are partnered with coffee, both in the cake and in the delicious icing. This teabread will keep for up to 4 days in an airtight container.

MAKES 1 LOAF

175g/6oz/¾ cup butter, softened, plus extra for greasing

175g/6oz/scant 1 cup caster (superfine) sugar

5ml/1 tsp vanilla extract

2 eggs, beaten

225g/8oz/2 cups plain (all-purpose) flour

1.5ml/¼ tsp baking powder

75ml/5 tbsp strong brewed coffee

175g/6oz/1 cup dried sour cherries

For the icing

50g/2oz/½ cup icing (confectioners') sugar

20ml/4 tsp strong brewed coffee

1 Preheat the oven to 180°C/350°F/Gas 4. Grease and line a 900g/2lb loaf tin (pan) with baking parchment.

2 Cream the butter, sugar and vanilla until pale and fluffy, then add the eggs, beating after each addition. Add a teaspoon of flour if the mix curdles.

3 Fold in the flour and baking powder then the coffee and two-thirds of the sour cherries.

4 Spoon into the tin. Bake for just over 1 hour, or until firm to the touch. Cool in the tin for 5 minutes, then turn out on to a wire rack. Peel off the lining paper.

5 Mix together the icing sugar and coffee, and the remaining cherries. Spoon over the top of the cake and leave to set before cutting into 8–10 slices.

Energy 5662kcal/23929kJ; Protein 36g; Carbohydrate 1063.4g, of which sugars 1055.2g; Fat 170.4g, of which saturates 98.2g; Cholesterol 1239mg; Calcium 288mg; Fibre 17g; Sodium 1485mg.

Raspberry & almond teabread

Fresh raspberries and almonds combine perfectly in this mouthwatering loaf with its crunchy, toasted nutty topping. Serve warm with a spoonful of crème fraîche as part of a tea table buffet. Eat on the day of making or store in the fridge for up to 3 days.

MAKES 1 LOAF

175g/6oz/1½ cups self-raising (self-rising) flour
90g/3oz/7 tbsp butter
90g/3oz/scant ½ cup caster (superfine) sugar
40g/1½oz/scant ½ cup ground almonds

2 eggs, beaten
30ml/2 tbsp milk
115g/4oz/1 cup fresh raspberries or partly thawed frozen raspberries
30ml/2 tbsp toasted flaked (sliced) almonds

1 Preheat the oven to 180°C/350°F/Gas 4. Grease and line a 450g/1lb loaf tin (pan) with baking parchment.

2 Sift the flour into a large bowl or the bowl of a food processor. Add the butter and rub in, or process, until the mixture resembles fine breadcrumbs.

3 Stir in the sugar and ground almonds, then gradually mix in the eggs and milk, and beat until smooth.

4 Gently fold in the raspberries, being careful not to crush them.

5 Spoon into the prepared tin and sprinkle over the flaked almonds.

6 Bake for about 55 minutes, or until a skewer inserted into the centre comes out clean.

7 Cool in the tin for 5 minutes, then turn out on to a wire rack to go cold. Remove the lining paper.

Variation

You can swap in blueberries or blackberries in place of the raspberries in this cake, or for a decadent version, add some chocolate chips in place of some or all of the raspberries, and use ground hazelnuts and chopped roasted hazelnuts instead of the almonds.

Energy 2229kcal/9329kJ; Protein 47.5g; Carbohydrate 233.9g, of which sugars 102g; Fat 129.1g, of which saturates 54.5g; Cholesterol 656mg; Calcium 928mg; Fibre 7.7g; Sodium 1373mg.

Brownies, bars & slices

A treat for any time of day, all of the brownies, bars, squares and slices in this chapter have one thing in common: they are easy to make in bulk, and are simple to plate up and serve. The range of goodies on offer is broad, though – from wholesome favourites such as oaty apricot slices, parkin, and banana sheet cake, to fancier fare for more special occasions, such as lamingtons, pistachio & white chocolate blondies, and hazelnut praline slices. Some don't even require you to switch on the oven, and many consist of a simple batter to which various flavours are added, to be later crowned, or not, with icing or some other topping. Truly scrumptious.

Left Flapjack and brownies are universally popular traybakes, and you can make them as simple or as fancy as you like by adding fruits or nuts to the basic mix.

Parkin

From the north of England, parkin contains oatmeal and lots of syrup and treacle. This exceptionally moist ginger cake improves in flavour and texture when stored in a tin for several days. It is just the thing for autumnal tea parties.

MAKES 16–20

300ml/½ pint/1¼ cups milk
225g/8oz/⅔ cup golden (light corn) syrup
225g/8oz/⅔ cup treacle (molasses)
115g/4oz/½ cup butter
50g/2oz/¼ cup dark brown sugar
450g/1lb/4 cups plain (all-purpose) flour
2.5ml/½ tsp bicarbonate of soda (baking soda)
7.5ml/1½ tsp ground ginger
350g/12oz/3 cups medium oatmeal
1 egg, beaten
icing (confectioners') sugar, for dusting

1 Preheat the oven to 180°C/350°F/Gas 4. Grease and line a 20cm/8in square deep cake tin (pan).

2 In a pan, gently heat together the milk, syrup, treacle, butter and sugar, stirring until smooth; do not boil.

3 Sift the flour into a bowl, add the bicarbonate of soda, ginger and oatmeal. Make a well in the centre.

4 Allow the treacle mixture to cool in the pan slightly so that it is just warm. Add the mixture to the bowl with the egg, stirring to make a smooth batter.

5 Pour the batter into the tin and bake for 45 minutes, or until firm to the touch.

6 Cool slightly in the tin, then turn out on to a wire rack to go cold. Remove the lining paper. Dust with icing sugar and cut into squares.

Cook's tip

This keeps for up to 5 days in an airtight container. Parkin also freezes well, wrapped in foil for up to 3 months. After this the spices lose their power.

Energy 273kcal/1152kJ; Protein 5.3g; Carbohydrate 50g, of which sugars 20.1g; Fat 7.1g, of which saturates 3.3g; Cholesterol 23mg; Calcium 127mg; Fibre 1.9g; Sodium 102mg.

Blueberry traybake

This cake is studded with blueberries, giving it a lovely fruity flavour and texture, and topped with a sweet icing drizzle. It is the perfect accompaniment to a cup of tea (or coffee). Keep for up to 2 days in an airtight container.

MAKES 10–12

225g/8oz/2 cups plain (all-purpose) flour
15ml/1 tbsp baking powder
5ml/1 tsp salt
65g/2½oz/5 tbsp butter, at room temperature
150g/5oz/¾ cup caster (superfine) sugar
1 egg

250ml/8½fl oz/1 cup milk
2.5ml/½ tsp grated lemon rind
225g/8oz/2 cups fresh or frozen blueberries, well drained
115g/4oz/1 cup icing (confectioners') sugar
30ml/2 tbsp fresh lemon juice

1 Preheat the oven to 180°C/350°F/Gas 4. Grease and line a 33 × 9cm/13 × 9in shallow tin (pan).

2 Sift the flour with the baking powder and salt.

3 In a large bowl, beat the butter and sugar until light and fluffy. Beat in the egg and milk. Fold in the flour mixture, then mix in the lemon rind.

4 Scrape half of the batter into the cake tin, spreading it to the edges.

5 Sprinkle with half the blueberries. Top with the remaining batter and then the remaining blueberries.

6 Bake for 35–45 minutes, or until golden brown and a skewer inserted into the centre comes out clean.

7 Allow to stand for 5 minutes in the tin, then turn out on to a wire rack to go cold. Remove the lining.

8 To make the topping, mix the icing sugar with the lemon juice to make a glaze with a pouring consistency.

9 Drizzle the glaze over the top of the warm cake. Allow to set before cutting into slices and serving.

Energy 217kcal/918kJ; Protein 3.3g; Carbohydrate 41.3g, of which sugars 26.3g; Fat 5.5g, of which saturates 3.3g; Cholesterol 30mg; Calcium 66mg; Fibre 1g; Sodium 60mg.

Mini Victoria sponges

These dainty little cakes are simplicity itself to make, yet pretty enough for a special afternoon tea table. This recipe has been adapted to give you a lower-fat and egg-free sponge, with air and lightness added by the bicarbonate of soda and baking powder, and moisture by the yogurt.

MAKES 24

225g/8oz/1 cup low-fat
baking spread
225g/8oz/1 cup caster
(superfine) sugar
300g/10oz/2½ cups self-raising
(self-rising) flour
2.5ml/½ tsp bicarbonate of soda
(baking soda)
5ml/1 tsp baking powder

5ml/1 tsp vanilla extract
120ml/4fl oz/½ cup skimmed milk
250ml/8½fl oz/1¼ cup fat-free
natural (plain) yogurt
60ml/4 tbsp raspberry, strawberry
or cherry jam
icing (confectioners') sugar,
for dusting

1 Preheat the oven to 180°C/350°F/Gas 4. Grease a 35 x 25cm/14 x 10in deep baking tin (pan), then line it with baking parchment.

2 Whisk the low-fat baking spread and sugar for about 5 minutes until very light and creamy. It is important to whisk in as much air as possible as this will give lightness to the cake.

3 Sift together the flour, bicarbonate of soda and baking powder and then whisk into the creamed butter mixture. Add the vanilla, milk and yogurt and whisk in.

4 Spoon the mixture into the prepared tin and bake for 40–50 minutes until the cake is firm and springs back to your touch and a knife comes out clean when inserted into the middle of the cake.

5 Remove from the oven, leave it for 5 minutes, then lift out the cake using the paper and place it on a wire rack to cool.

6 Carefully split the cake in half using a serrated knife so that you have two large rectangles, and spread the jam over one of the halves. Place the second rectangle on top and cut into 24 squares.

7 Dust with a little icing sugar to serve. This cake will keep for up to 2 days in an airtight container.

Variation
If you want to vary the flavour of this cake, you can add chocolate chips, citrus zest or substitute 30g/1¼oz of the flour with sifted unsweetened cocoa powder.

Energy 126kcal/534kJ; Protein 2.5g; Carbohydrate 22.2g, of which sugars 12.8g; Fat 3.7g, of which saturates 0.8g; Cholesterol 1mg; Calcium 72mg; Fibre 0.5g; Sodium 117mg.

Banana sheet cake squares

Everyone likes banana cake – this one is rich and dense and has a lovely oaty topping and juicy sultanas. It is important that the bananas are very ripe, with skins beginning to turn black.

MAKES 24

3 ripe bananas
350g/12oz/1½ cups caster (superfine) sugar
350g/12oz/1½ cups butter or margarine, softened
6 eggs
175ml/6fl oz/¾ cup low-fat Greek (strained) yogurt
400g/14oz/3½ cups self-raising (self-rising flour), sifted
10ml/2 tsp ground cinnamon
175g/6oz/1 cup sultanas (golden raisins)
35g/1¼oz/⅓ cup rolled oats
15ml/1 tbsp caster (superfine) sugar
5ml/1 tsp mixed (apple pie) spice

1 Preheat the oven to 180°C/350°F/Gas 4. Grease a 35 x 25cm/14 x 10in deep baking tin (pan), then line it with baking parchment.

2 Crush the bananas with a fork until they are soft.

3 To prepare the sponge, whisk together the sugar, butter and banana in a bowl using a mixer or whisk until light and creamy. Add the eggs and whisk again.

4 Fold in the yogurt, sifted flour and ground cinnamon, then fold in the sultanas. Pour the batter into the lined tin and level with a spatula.

5 Mix together the oats, caster sugar and mixed spice and sprinkle over the top of the cake.

6 Bake for 35–40 minutes until the cake is firm and springs back to your touch.

7 Remove from the oven and leave to cool for a few minutes, then turn out on to a rack to cool completely.

8 When you are ready to serve, cut the cooled cake into 24 pieces. This cake will keep for up to 3 days in an airtight container.

Energy 274kcal/1147kJ; Protein 4.1g; Carbohydrate 35.5g, of which sugars 23.8g; Fat 13.7g, of which saturates 7.9g; Cholesterol 88mg; Calcium 83mg; Fibre 1.1g; Sodium 165mg.

American apple-sauce squares

When apples are plentiful, cook them into a purée and add to this cake mixture to make it wonderfully moist. Top with vanilla frosting and decorate with walnuts for a moreish treat.

MAKES 15

450g/1lb dessert apples, peeled, cored and sliced

75g/2½oz/6 tbsp butter, plus extra for greasing

115g/4oz/generous ½ cup golden caster (superfine) sugar

2 eggs

175g/6oz/1½ cups plain (all-purpose) flour

10ml/2 tsp baking powder

5ml/1 tsp mixed (apple pie) spice

50g/2oz/½ cup walnut pieces

115g/4oz/²⁄₃ cup raisins

For the frosting

175g/6oz/1½ cups icing (confectioners') sugar

75g/2½oz/6 tbsp unsalted butter, softened

1 egg white

few drops of vanilla extract

15 walnut halves, to decorate

1 Put the sliced apples into a pan with 15ml/1 tbsp water. Cook until thick and pulpy, stirring, then pour into a bowl and leave to cool.

2 Preheat the oven to 180°C/350°F/Gas 4. Grease and line a 28 × 18cm/11 × 7in shallow tin (pan) with baking parchment.

3 In a large bowl, beat the butter and sugar together until light and fluffy. Gradually beat in the eggs.

4 Stir in the cold apple purée and mix well. Sift the flour, baking powder and mixed spice into the bowl, then add the walnuts and raisins. Mix well.

5 Spoon into the tin and smooth the top level. Bake for 45 minutes, or until a skewer inserted into the centre comes out clean. Cool for 5 minutes, then turn out on to a wire rack. Peel away the lining paper.

6 Put all the frosting ingredients except the walnuts into a bowl, and beat together until fluffy. Spread on top of the cooled cake and leave to set.

7 Cut into squares and decorate each with a walnut. This cake will keep for 2–3 days in an airtight container.

Energy 255kcal/1070kJ; Protein 3g; Carbohydrate 37.4g, of which sugars 28.4g; Fat 11.4g, of which saturates 5.8g; Cholesterol 48mg; Calcium 40mg; Fibre 1.1g; Sodium 95mg.

Glazed cinnamon apple slices

Cinnamon and apple is a classic flavour combination that works wonderfully well in this moist traybake, which is decorated with attractive fans of finely sliced apple.

MAKES 24

350g/12oz/1½ cups dark brown sugar
350g/12oz/1½ cups butter or margarine, softened
6 eggs
250g/9oz/1 cup ricotta
300g/10oz/2½ cups self-raising (self-rising) flour, sifted
200g/7oz/2 cups ground almonds
10ml/2 tsp ground cinnamon
5ml/1 tsp mixed (apple pie) spice
115g/4oz/⅔ cup raisins

600g/1lb5oz baking apples (approx. 4–5)
juice of 1 lemon
15ml/1 tbsp caster (superfine) sugar, to sprinkle

For the glaze

90g/3oz apricot glaze or apricot jam
juice of 1 lemon

1 Preheat the oven to 180°C/350°F/Gas 4. Grease a 35 x 25cm/14 x 10in deep baking tin (pan), then line it with baking parchment.

2 To prepare the sponge, whisk together the sugar and the butter in a bowl until light and creamy. Add the eggs and whisk again. Whisk in the ricotta.

3 Fold in the flour and almonds. Add the cinnamon and mixed spice and the raisins and stir in gently. Grate two of the apples. It is fine to leave the skins on but do not grate the core. Stir the apple into the cake mixture.

4 Spoon the mixture into the prepared cake tin and smooth out level using a spatula.

5 To prepare the topping, peel and core the remaining apples and cut into thin slices. Place the slices in a bowl and toss with the lemon juice to prevent the apple from browning. It is important to cut the apple thinly so that you have enough slices to cover the top of the cake. Arrange the apple slices over the top of the cake in decorative patterns. Sprinkle with the caster sugar.

6 Bake in the preheated oven for 40–50 minutes until the cake is firm and springs back to your touch. Remove from the oven.

7 For the glaze, place the apricot glaze or jam in a pan with the lemon juice and simmer over a gentle heat until the mixture is runny and the glaze/jam has dissolved. If using jam which contains pieces of fruit, pass the mixture through a sieve or strainer to remove them. Brush the glaze over the top of the apples using a pastry brush. Leave the cake to cool.

8 To serve, cut the cake into 24 slices. This cake will keep for up to 3 days in an airtight container but is best eaten on the day it is made.

Energy 327kcal/1366kJ; Protein 6.3g; Carbohydrate 32.7g, of which sugars 21.6g; Fat 19.9g, of which saturates 9.4g; Cholesterol 93mg; Calcium 99mg; Fibre 1.2g; Sodium 199mg.

Blackberry & passion fruit slice

Blackberry and passion fruit are not commonly paired in a cake but they are truly delicious together – the tang of the passion fruit curd balances the sweet blackberries perfectly.

MAKES 24
225g/8oz/1 cup butter or margarine, softened
225g/8oz/1 cup caster (superfine) sugar
4 eggs
250g/9oz/2¼ cups self-raising (self-rising) flour, sifted
60ml/4 tbsp passion fruit curd
150ml/5fl oz/¼ cup low-fat natural (plain) yogurt
600g/1lb5oz blackberries
175g/6oz/¾ cup cream cheese

For the topping
100g/3½oz/¾ cup self-raising (self-rising) flour
75g/2½oz/⅓ cup caster (superfine) sugar
75g/2½oz/6 tbsp butter, chilled

Variation
To make a lower-fat version of this fruity cake you can use low-fat cream cheese and low-fat baking spread.

1 Preheat the oven to 180°C/350°F/Gas 4. Grease a 35 x 25cm/14 x 10in deep baking tin (pan), then line it with baking parchment.

2 To prepare the sponge, whisk together the butter and caster sugar in a bowl using a mixer, until light and creamy. Add the eggs and whisk again. Whisk in the flour, 30ml/2 tbsp of the passion fruit curd and the yogurt, gently, until everything is incorporated.

3 Spoon the batter into the prepared tin and spread into an even layer using a spatula. Sprinkle the blackberries evenly over the top of the cake mixture.

4 In a separate bowl, whisk together the cream cheese and the remaining 30ml/2 tbsp of the passion fruit curd. Place small spoonfuls of the cream cheese/passion fruit curd mixture over the top of the cake mixture in between the blackberries.

5 For the crumble topping, sift the flour into a bowl and stir in the sugar. Cut the butter into cubes and rub into the flour mixture with your fingertips until the mixture comes together into large crumbs.

6 Sprinkle the crumbs over the top of the cake and bake in the oven for 45–50 minutes until the cake is firm and springs back to your touch. If the crumble starts to brown too much, cover the top of the cake loosely with a sheet of foil.

7 Allow the cake to cool completely in the tin and then cut into 24 squares.

8 As with most cakes, this cake is best eaten on the day it is made but can be stored in an airtight container in the refrigerator for up to 3 days. It needs to be stored in the refrigerator due to the cream cheese.

Energy 260kcal/1086kJ; Protein 3.5g; Carbohydrate 27.9g, of which sugars 16.5g; Fat 15.7g, of which saturates 9.4g; Cholesterol 74mg; Calcium 91mg; Fibre 1.6g; Sodium 174mg.

Frosted red velvet squares

Red velvet cake is always a hit – it has such a vibrant shade, created by the dark cocoa and red food colouring. This cake is topped with a classic cream cheese frosting, which is a perfect foil for the deep rich cake.

MAKES 24

350g/12oz/1½ cups caster (superfine) sugar

350g/12oz/1½ cups butter or margarine, softened

6 eggs

350g/12oz/3 cups self-raising (self-rising) flour, sifted

50g/2oz/½ cup unsweetened cocoa powder, sifted

150ml/5fl oz/⅔ cup sour cream

5ml/1 tsp red food colouring paste or gel

For the frosting

600g/1lb5oz/5⅓ cups icing (confectioners') sugar, sifted

100g/3½oz/scant ½ cup low-fat cream cheese

50g/2oz/4 tbsp butter, softened

juice of 1 lemon

unsweetened cocoa powder, for dusting

red sugar sprinkles

1 Preheat the oven to 180°C/350°F/Gas 4. Grease a 35 x 25cm/14 x 10in deep baking tin (pan), then line it with baking parchment.

2 To prepare the sponge, whisk together the caster sugar and the butter in a mixing bowl using a mixer or whisk until light and creamy. Add the eggs and whisk again.

3 Fold in the sifted flour and cocoa. Add the sour cream and food colouring and whisk gently so that the cake has an even deep red-brown colour.

4 Spoon the mixture into the prepared cake tin and smooth out level using a spatula.

5 Bake in the preheated oven for 25–30 minutes, until the cake is firm and springs back to your touch.

6 Remove from the oven and leave to cool for a few minutes in the tin, then turn out the cake on to a rack to cool completely.

7 For the frosting, place the sifted icing sugar, cream cheese, butter and lemon juice into a mixing bowl and whisk together until thick and creamy. If the frosting is too stiff add a little more lemon juice and if it is too runny add a little more icing sugar. The consistency of the icing will depend on how soft your butter and cream cheese are.

8 Cut the cake into 24 pieces. Spoon the frosting into the piping bag and pipe a swirl of icing on to each piece of cake. Dust with a little cocoa powder and decorate with the sugar sprinkles.

9 Transfer to the refrigerator for an hour or so for the icing to set. This cake will keep for up to 2 days in an airtight container.

Variation
For a lower fat version 1) use low-fat yogurt in place of the sour cream 2) make up half the icing quantity and just spread a thin layer of icing over the top of the cake rather than piping.

Energy 374kcal/1571kJ; Protein 4.6g; Carbohydrate 52.5g, of which sugars 41.4g; Fat 17.7g, of which saturates 10.5g; Cholesterol 98mg; Calcium 80mg; Fibre 1g; Sodium 221mg.

Lamingtons

Lamingtons are a popular Australian traybake – delicate vanilla sponge coated in a chocolate syrup and rolled in coconut. In a twist on the classic chocolate sauce, this version is made with a raspberry chocolate sauce, which gives these little cakes a lovely flavour.

MAKES 20

350g/12oz/1½ cups butter or
margarine, softened
350g/12oz/1½ cups caster
(superfine) sugar
6 eggs
350g/12oz/3 cups self-raising
(self-rising) flour, sifted
5ml/1 tsp vanilla extract

For the coconut icing

40g/1½oz/3 tbsp butter
300g/10oz raspberry jam
115g/4oz/1 cup icing
(confectioners') sugar
50g/2oz/½ cup unsweetened
cocoa powder
350g/12oz desiccated (dry
unsweetened shredded)
coconut

1 Preheat the oven to 180°C/350°F/Gas 4. Grease a 35 x 25cm/14 x 10in deep baking tin (pan), then line it with baking parchment.

2 To prepare the sponge, whisk together the butter and caster sugar in a bowl using a mixer until light and creamy. Add the eggs and whisk again.

3 Fold in the flour and vanilla extract gently. Spoon the cake batter into the tin and spread out evenly.

4 Bake in the oven for 35–40 minutes until the cake is firm to touch and a knife comes out clean when inserted into the centre of the cake. Turn out on to a rack and leave to cool. Remove the paper and cut the traybake into 20 rectangles.

5 In a pan, heat the butter and raspberry jam with 60ml/4 tbsp of water, then sift in the icing sugar and cocoa. Whisk together until you have a smooth syrup. Pass through a sieve or strainer to remove any lumps or seeds and leave to cool slightly.

6 Place a sheet of foil or a tray under a cooling rack to catch any drips. Place the coconut on a large plate or tray. One by one dip the cakes into the syrup, coating to ensure that all sides are covered. Roll the cake in the coconut until completely coated, and transfer to the rack to set. Repeat with all the remaining cakes.

7 Leave the cakes to set and then serve. These are best eaten on the day they are made but will store for up to 2 days in an airtight container.

Energy 489kcal/2041kJ; Protein 5g; Carbohydrate 48.5g, of which sugars 35.8g; Fat 31.9g, of which saturates 21.7g; Cholesterol 110mg; Calcium 84mg; Fibre 3.9g; Sodium 214mg.

Walnut & date bars

These wonderfully rich, moist cake bars are perfect for afternoon tea. The dates are first soaked before being added to the batter, giving this sweet treat a lovely texture.

MAKES 24

225g/8oz/1⅓ cups chopped dates
225ml/8fl oz/1 cup boiling water
5ml/1 tsp bicarbonate of soda (baking soda)
225g/8oz/1 cup caster (superfine) sugar
1 egg, beaten

300g/10oz/2½ cups plain (all-purpose) flour
pinch of salt
75g/2½oz/6 tbsp butter, softened
5ml/1 tsp vanilla extract
5ml/1 tsp baking powder
50g/2oz/½ cup chopped walnuts

1 Put the chopped dates into a warm bowl and pour the boiling water over the top; it should just cover the dates. Add the bicarbonate of soda and mix well. Leave to stand for 5–10 minutes.

2 Preheat the oven to 180°C/350°F/Gas 4. Lightly grease a 23 x 30cm/9 x 12in cake tin (pan) and line with baking parchment.

3 Combine all the remaining ingredients in a separate mixing bowl.

4 Mix in the dates, along with the soaking water until you have a thick batter. You may find it necessary to add a little more boiling water to help the consistency.

5 Pour the batter into the tin and bake for 45 minutes until firm.

6 Leave to cool slightly in the tin, then turn out on to a wire rack and cut into bars.

Energy 111kcal/468kJ; Protein 2.5g; Carbohydrate 17.9g, of which sugars 10.2g; Fat 3.75g, of which saturates 0.5g; Cholesterol 0.75mg; Calcium 27mg; Fibre 1.45g; Sodium 6.8mg.

Chocolate brownies

This classic recipe is popular with lovers of all things sweet and chocolatey.
The double dose of chocolate makes them a rich and intense indulgence at teatime.

MAKES 15

90g/3oz dark (bittersweet) chocolate
115g/4oz/½ cup butter, plus extra
for greasing
4 eggs, beaten
10ml/2 tsp vanilla extract
400g/14oz/2 cups caster
(superfine) sugar

115g/4oz/1 cup plain
(all-purpose) flour
25g/1oz/¼ cup unsweetened
cocoa powder
115g/4oz dark (bittersweet)
chocolate chips
115g/4oz/1 cup chopped walnuts

1 Preheat the oven to 190°C/375°F/Gas 5. Liberally grease an 18 x 28cm/7 x 11in shallow baking tin (pan) and line the base with baking parchment.

2 Break the dark chocolate into pieces and put it in a heatproof bowl with the butter. Place the bowl over a pan of barely simmering water until the chocolate and butter have melted.

3 Remove from the heat and stir in the beaten eggs, vanilla and sugar. Mix all the ingredients well together.

4 Sift the flour with the cocoa powder into the chocolate mixture. Gently stir these in along with the chocolate chips and walnuts. Pour the mixture into the tin and level the surface.

5 Bake for about 35 minutes. To test if the brownies are fully cooked, gently shake the tin. The cakes should be set but moist. Leave to cool in the tin. Cut into bars when cold.

Energy 285kcal/1190kJ; Protein 3.1g; Carbohydrate 29.6g, of which sugars 25.9g; Fat 18g, of which saturates 10.7g; Cholesterol 61mg; Calcium 37mg; Fibre 0.9g; Sodium 98mg.

Chocolate cherry brownies

These squidgy, fruity brownies are intensely chocolatey yet not oversweet, thanks to the tartness of the cherries, which also make these treats special enough for a teatime table.

MAKES 24

300g/10oz plain (semisweet) chocolate
250g/9oz/generous 1 cup butter or margarine
225g/8oz/generous 1 cup caster (superfine) sugar

200g/7oz/scant 1 cup dark brown sugar
5 large eggs
200g/7oz/1¾ cups plain (all-purpose) flour, sifted
150g/5oz dried cherries
400g/14oz/2 cups cherry compote

1 Preheat the oven to 180°C/350°F/Gas 4. Grease a 35 x 25cm/14 x 10in deep baking tin (pan), then line it with baking parchment.

2 Break the chocolate into small pieces and place in a heatproof bowl with the butter over a pan of simmering water and heat until the chocolate and butter have melted and you have a smooth glossy sauce. Remove from the heat and leave to cool whilst you make the brownie mixture. If you are short of time you can place the broken chocolate and butter in a microwave-proof bowl and microwave on high power for 1–2 minutes, stirring part-way through.

3 In a bowl, whisk the caster sugar and dark brown sugar with the eggs using a mixer or a whisk, until the mixture is very light and creamy and has doubled in size. Whilst still whisking, slowly pour in the melted chocolate and butter mixture.

4 Fold in the flour, then stir in the dried cherries. Pour half of the mixture into the prepared tin and spread out in an even layer.

5 Using a spoon, gently place spoonfuls of the cherry compote over the brownie mixture evenly. Pour over the remaining brownie mixture. It is best to do this very slowly so that all the cherry compote is covered.

6 Bake in the oven for 25–30 minutes until a crust has formed on top of the brownies but they still feel a little soft underneath.

7 Allow to cool completely before removing the lining paper and cutting into 24 squares. These brownies will store in an airtight container for at least 3 days.

Energy 288kcal/1206kJ; Protein 3.6g; Carbohydrate 39.4g, of which sugars 33g; Fat 13.9g, of which saturates 8g; Cholesterol 81mg; Calcium 36mg; Fibre 1.2g; Sodium 88mg.

Raspberry cheesecake blondies

Everyone loves raspberry cheesecake. These blondies – creamy with white chocolate – have a cheesecake layer and fresh berries and for extra crunch are topped with a biscuit crumb.

MAKES 24

250g/9oz/generous 1 cup butter or margarine
250g/9oz white chocolate, chopped
4 eggs
250g/9oz/1¼ cups caster (superfine) sugar
90g/3oz/½ cup dark brown sugar
pinch of salt
5ml/1 tsp vanilla extract
250g/9oz/2¼ cups plain (all-purpose) flour, sifted

For the cheesecake mixture

300g/10oz/1¼ cups low-fat cream cheese
30ml/2 tbsp icing (confectioners') sugar, sifted
2 egg yolks
400g/14oz raspberries
3 digestive biscuits (graham crackers)

1 Preheat the oven to 180°C/350°F/Gas 4. Grease a 35 x 25cm/14 x 10in deep baking tin (pan), then line it with baking parchment.

2 Melt the butter in a pan over a gentle heat. Remove from the heat and add the white chocolate to the butter and stir occasionally, so that the white chocolate melts.

3 Whisk together in a bowl the eggs and the caster sugar and brown sugar with the salt and vanilla until the mixture is thick and creamy and the mixture has doubled in size.

4 Fold in the flour and the chocolate mixture and then pour the batter into the prepared tin.

5 In a separate bowl, whisk together the cream cheese, icing sugar and egg yolks until smooth. Sprinkle the raspberries over the top of the blondie mixture and then place spoonfuls of the cream cheese mixture between the raspberries.

6 Crush the digestives into small pieces with your hands and sprinkle over the raspberries and cream cheese. Bake for 30–40 minutes, then remove from the oven and leave to cool in the tin completely.

7 Remove the lining paper and cut the blondies into 24 squares to serve. Store in an airtight container for up to 3 days.

Energy 240kcal/1000kJ; Protein 5.6g; Carbohydrate 22.2g, of which sugars 13.4g; Fat 14.9g, of which saturates 8.6g; Cholesterol 81mg; Calcium 74mg; Fibre 1g; Sodium 155mg.

Pistachio & white chocolate blondies

Pistachios are a vibrant nut and give such a wonderful flavour to this rich and indulgent traybake. Sprinkling chopped white chocolate and pistachio nuts on top makes these blondies look even more pretty and appealing.

MAKES 24

200g/7oz/2 cups pistachio nuts
60ml/4 tbsp sunflower or other flavourless oil
30ml/2 tbsp icing (confectioners') sugar
250g/9oz/generous 1 cup butter or margarine

4 eggs
400g/14oz/2 cups caster (superfine) sugar
250g/9oz/2¼ cups plain (all-purpose) flour
250g/9oz white chocolate, chopped

1 Preheat the oven to 180°C/350°F/Gas 4. Grease a 35 x 25cm/14 x 10in deep baking tin (pan), then line it with baking parchment.

2 Blitz the pistachio nuts to fine crumbs in a food processor and reserve a few tablespoons for the top of the blondies. Add the oil and icing sugar to the remaining pistachio nuts and blitz to a smooth paste. Melt the butter in a pan and leave to cool.

3 Whisk together the eggs and caster sugar. Stir the pistachio paste into the melted butter and add to the egg mixture and whisk well until incorporated. Sift in the flour and whisk in gently until just incorporated – do not over-mix.

4 Pour the mixture into the lined tin. Sprinkle the chopped chocolate over the top of the mixture along with the reserved chopped pistachio nuts.

5 Bake for 25–30 minutes until a crust has formed on top but the blondie is still soft underneath.

6 Leave to cool in the tin completely. When you are ready to serve, remove the lining paper and cut the blondie into 24 squares. These blondies will store well for up to 3 days in an airtight container.

Cook's tip

For best results use bright green pistachios – Iranian and Turkish supermarkets usually have a good choice. You can substitute other nuts in place of the pistachios, such as hazelnuts or walnuts if you prefer.

Energy 312kcal/1303kJ; Protein 4.4g; Carbohydrate 33.5g, of which sugars 25.4g; Fat 18.7g, of which saturates 8.4g; Cholesterol 61mg; Calcium 63mg; Fibre 1g; Sodium 126mg.

Cherry flapjack squares

Flapjacks are always popular, and a staple treat in many households, but the addition of sweet and tart cherry compote makes these ones a little bit different and special for an afternoon tea. Serving them in paper cakes is a good way to make them look the part, too.

MAKES 24

250g/9oz/generous 1 cup butter or margarine

90ml/6 tbsp golden (light corn) syrup

250g/9oz/1¼ cups caster (superfine) sugar

seeds of 1 vanilla pod (bean)

500g/1lb2oz/5 cups rolled oats

150g/5oz/scant 1 cup dried cherries

a pinch of salt

400g/14oz/1 heaped cup cherry compote

1 Preheat the oven to 180°C/350°F/Gas 4. Grease a 35 x 25cm/14 x 10in deep baking tin (pan), then line it with baking parchment.

2 Place the butter, syrup and caster sugar in a large heavy pan and simmer over a gentle heat until the butter and sugar have melted. Add the vanilla seeds, oats, dried cherries and salt to the pan and stir well so that all the oats are coated in the syrup.

3 Tip half of the oat mixture into the lined pan and spread out in an even layer using a spatula or the back of a large spoon. Spoon over the cherry compote in an even layer. If the cherry compote is very runny, remove some of the liquid before you spoon them over as it will make the flapjack soggy.

4 Top the cherries with the remaining flapjack mixture and spread out into a layer so that all of the cherry compote is covered.

5 Bake in the oven for 15–20 minutes until the top of the flapjack is golden brown. Remove from the oven and leave to cool completely.

6 When cool remove the lining paper and cut the flapjack into 24 squares. Store in an airtight container until needed. The flapjack will store for at least 5 days.

Variations

• If you wish you can replace the vanilla extract with a little almond extract, which will also go well with the cherries.
• To make plain flapjack (as pictured on page 107) simply leave out the cherries and compote.

Energy 243kcal/1021kJ; Protein 2.9g; Carbohydrate 36.6g, of which sugars 21.4g; Fat 10.4g, of which saturates 5.4g; Cholesterol 22mg; Calcium 22mg; Fibre 2.3g; Sodium 83mg.

Oaty apricot slices

This slice is more delicate and light than standard flapjack but still with the same oaty goodness. If you are short of time replace the fresh apricots with about 30 dried apricots, though roasting gives fresh ones a sweet sherbet taste and make this slice so much nicer – so worth the effort.

MAKES 24

450g/1lb fresh apricots
200g/7oz/scant 1 cup butter or margarine, plus extra for greasing
350g/12oz/3 cups plain (all-purpose) flour, sifted
225g/8oz/2½ cups rolled oats

175g/6oz/scant 1 cup caster (superfine) sugar
30ml/2 tbsp golden (light corn) syrup
1 egg, beaten
zest of 1 lemon

1 Preheat the oven to 140°C/275°F/Gas 1. Grease a 35 x 25cm/14 x 10in deep baking tin (pan), then line it with baking parchment.

2 Cut the apricots in half and remove the stones/pits. Lay the apricots in a roasting dish, cut side up and bake in the oven for about an hour until the fruit is soft. Leave to cool.

3 Turn the oven temperature up to 180°C/350°F/Gas 4. Melt the butter in a pan and leave to cool.

4 Place the flour, oats and sugar in a mixing bowl and stir together to mix everything. Pour in the cooled melted butter, golden syrup and the beaten egg and whisk in. The dough should be loose and crumbly but should hold together when you press it gently with your fingers.

5 Spoon just over half of the mixture into the prepared tin and press down flat with your clean fingertips so that the whole base is covered.

6 Roughly chop the cooled apricots into small pieces and mix with the lemon zest. Sprinkle over the oaty base mixture so that the apricots are evenly distributed.

7 Sprinkle the remaining oat mixture on top of the apricots and press down. Bake for 25–30 minutes until the top of the slice is golden brown.

8 Leave to cool in the tin, then remove the lining paper and cut into 24 slices to serve. This slice will keep for up to 3 days stored in an airtight container.

Energy 215kcal/902kJ; Protein 4.3g; Carbohydrate 24.1g, of which sugars 10.5g; Fat 12g, of which saturates 5.3g; Cholesterol 44mg; Calcium 59mg; Fibre 1.4g; Sodium 79mg.

Strawberry crumble squares

The base of this traybake is a buttery shortcake, topped with ripe berries and cheesecake cream and then finally sprinkled with a pine nut crumble layer. The smell of sweet strawberries when you take this from the oven will get your tastebuds tingling.

MAKES 24

300g/10oz/2½ cups plain (all-purpose) flour
5ml/1 tsp baking powder
175g/6oz/scant 1 cup dark brown sugar
175g/6oz/¾ cup butter or margarine, chilled
1 egg
50g/2oz/½ cup pine nuts

For the strawberry layer

300g/10oz/1¼ cups low-fat cream cheese
115g/4oz/generous ½ cup caster (superfine) sugar
2 eggs
500g/1lb2oz ripe strawberries
30ml/2 tbsp cornflour (cornstarch)

1 Preheat the oven to 180°C/350°F/Gas 4. Grease a 35 x 25cm/14 x 10in deep baking tin (pan), then line it with baking parchment.

2 Sift the flour and baking powder into a bowl and stir in the sugar. Cut the butter into cubes and rub into the flour mixture with your fingertips until it resembles fine breadcrumbs. Beat the egg and mix into the crumbs which should come into larger clumps.

3 Reserve a quarter of the crumbs for the topping and press the rest firmly into the base of the lined tin in an even layer with your fingertips.

4 For the strawberry layer, in a mixing bowl, whisk together the cream cheese, half of the caster sugar and the eggs until you have a smooth mixture.

5 Hull and halve the strawberries. Place in a bowl and sift over the cornflour and the remaining caster sugar and leave for a few minutes. Stir the fruit to ensure that it is all coated in the cornflour and the sugar.

6 Sprinkle the strawberries over the shortcake base and spoon over the cream cheese mixture. Mix lightly together. Sprinkle over the remaining crumb mixture and the pine nuts.

7 Bake in the preheated oven for 35–40 minutes until the top is lightly golden brown then leave to cool completely in the tin before serving.

8 Remove the lining paper and cut into 24 squares to serve. Store any uneaten cakes in the refrigerator for up to 3 days but this is best eaten on the day it is made.

Energy 202kcal/846kJ; Protein 4.6g; Carbohydrate 25.1g, of which sugars 14.4g; Fat 9.9g, of which saturates 4.9g; Cholesterol 48mg; Calcium 45mg; Fibre 0.9g; Sodium 114mg.

Sticky treacle squares

This three-layered treat of buttery cookie base, covered with a jam-like dried fruit filling, followed by an oaty flapjack-style topping, is utterly delicious. It's perfect to serve for afternoon tea, with its complex flavours, sticky texture and zesty combination.

MAKES 12

175g/6oz/1½ cups plain (all-purpose) flour
90g/3oz/7 tbsp butter, diced
50g/2oz/¼ cup caster (superfine) sugar

For the filling

250g/9oz/1 cup mixed dried fruit, such as prunes, apricots, peaches, pears and apples
300ml/½ pint/1¼ cups apple or orange juice

For the topping

225g/8oz/⅔ cup golden (light corn) syrup
finely grated rind of 1 small orange, plus 45ml/3 tbsp juice
90g/3oz/1 cup rolled oats

Variation

For a darker, sweeter twist, dried dates or figs can be used in place of the suggested fruits.

1 Preheat the oven to 180°C/350°F/Gas 4. Lightly grease a 28 x 18cm/11 x 7in shallow baking tin (pan) and line it with baking parchment.

2 Put the flour and butter in a food processor and process until the mixture begins to resemble fine breadcrumbs. Add the sugar and mix until the dough starts to cling together in a ball.

3 Transfer the mixture to the baking tin and press down in an even layer with the back of a fork. Bake for about 15 minutes, until the surface just begins to colour.

4 Meanwhile prepare the filling. Remove the stones from any of the dried fruits. Chop the fruit fairly finely and put in a pan with the fruit juice.

5 Bring to the boil, reduce the heat and cover with a lid. Simmer gently for about 15 minutes, or until all the juice has been absorbed.

6 Now spoon the dried fruit filling on top of the base in the tin, and spread out in an even layer with the back of a spoon.

7 Put the golden syrup in a bowl with the orange rind and juice and oats and mix together. Spoon over the fruits, spreading it out evenly. Return to the oven for 25 minutes, until golden.

8 Remove from the oven and leave to cool slightly in the tin, then lift it out using the baking parchment and leave to cool completely on a wire rack.

9 Once cool, peel off the baking parchment, cut into 12 squares and serve. Store in an airtight container for 2–3 days.

Energy 213kcal/898kJ; Protein 2.6g; Carbohydrate 39.3g, of which sugars 25.1g; Fat 6.1g, of which saturates 3.4g; Cholesterol 14mg; Calcium 35mg; Fibre 1.8g; Sodium 88mg.

Luscious lemon bars

A crisp shortbread cookie base is drenched with a light and tangy lemon topping to make a sweet citrus confection. These bars make a wonderful addition to the summer tea table. Try exchanging the lemon for orange to give a new twist to this recipe.

MAKES 12

150g/5oz/1¼ cups plain (all-purpose) flour

90g/3oz/7 tbsp unsalted butter, chilled and diced

50g/2oz/½ cup icing (confectioners') sugar, sifted, plus extra for dusting

For the topping

2 eggs

175g/6oz/scant 1 cup caster (superfine) sugar

finely grated rind and juice of 1 large lemon

15ml/1 tbsp plain (all-purpose) flour

2.5ml/½ tsp bicarbonate of soda (baking soda)

Variation

You can use other citrus fruits to make these bars. Orange will give a sweeter result, whereas lime or grapefruit are tart and tangy.

1 Preheat the oven to 180°C/350°F/Gas 4. Grease and line a 20cm/8in square shallow cake tin (pan) with baking parchment.

2 Blend the flour, butter and icing sugar in a food processor until the mixture comes together as a firm dough. Press into the base of the tin and spread smooth using the back of a spoon. Bake for 12–15 minutes.

3 To make the topping, whisk the eggs in a bowl until frothy. Add the caster sugar, a little at a time, whisking between each addition. Whisk in the lemon rind and juice, flour and bicarbonate of soda.

4 Pour the lemon mixture over the cookie base. Bake for 20–25 minutes, until set and golden.

5 Leave to cool slightly in the tin, then remove from the tin and leave to cool completely on a wire rack. Once cool, peel off the baking parchment, cut into bars and dust with icing sugar. Store in an airtight container for 2–3 days.

Energy 189kcal/795kJ; Protein 2.5g; Carbohydrate 30.3g, of which sugars 19.8g; Fat 7.3g, of which saturates 4.2g; Cholesterol 48mg; Calcium 35mg; Fibre 0.4g; Sodium 59mg.

Apple shortcake squares

Viennese pastry forms the base of this apple shortbread-style traybake. With a delectable sweet apple layer and a buttery crumble top, it is sure to be popular at any teatime table.

MAKES 24

1kg/2lb3oz cooking apples
100g/3½oz/generous ½ cup caster (superfine) sugar
5ml/1 tsp ground cinnamon
250g/9oz/generous 1 cup butter or margarine, softened
100g/3½oz/¾ cup icing (confectioners') sugar, sifted
250g/9oz/2¼ cups plain (all-purpose flour), sifted, plus extra for dusting

For the crumble topping

150g/5oz/1¼ cups self-raising (self-rising) flour
75g/2½oz/scant ½ cup caster (superfine) sugar
5ml/1 tsp vanilla extract
90g/3oz/7 tbsp butter, chilled

1 Preheat the oven to 180°C/350°F/Gas 4. Grease and line a 35 x 25cm/14 x 10in deep baking tin (pan).

2 Peel and core the apples, then chop them into small pieces and place in a pan over a gentle heat with the caster sugar, ground cinnamon and 75ml/5 tbsp of water.

3 Simmer until the apple is soft, adding a splash more water if necessary. Leave to cool completely.

4 Cream together butter and icing sugar until light and creamy. Whisk in the flour to make a soft dough. Dust your hands with flour, then press the dough into the tin in an even layer. Chill for 30 minutes.

5 For the crumble topping, sift the flour into a bowl and stir in the sugar and vanilla. Cut the chilled butter into cubes and rub into the flour with your fingertips until the mixtures resembles large breadcrumbs.

6 Spread the cooled apple over the shortbread base and then sprinkle over the crumble in a thin layer.

7 Bake for 25–30 minutes until the crumble is golden brown. Leave to cool in the tin, then cut into 24 squares. This will store for up to 3 days in an airtight container.

Energy 225kcal/942kJ; Protein 1.8g; Carbohydrate 28.7g, of which sugars 16.4g; Fat 12.2g, of which saturates 7.6g; Cholesterol 31mg; Calcium 43mg; Fibre 1.6g; Sodium 111mg.

Hazelnut praline slices

These scrumptious no-bake crispy squares are perfect for anyone who loves Nutella as they are topped with a generous chocolate layer of hazelnut ganache.

MAKES 16

For the praline
50g/2oz/¼ cup caster (superfine) sugar
50g/2oz/½ cup blanched hazelnuts

For the caramel
15ml/1 tbsp golden (light corn) syrup
15ml/1 tbsp glucose
100g/3½oz/2½–3 cups marshmallows
80g/3¼oz/6½ tbsp butter

115g/4oz/4 cups rice crispies
50g/2oz/½ cup chopped roasted hazelnuts

For the topping
90g/3oz plain (semisweet) chocolate
15ml/1 tbsp butter
30ml/2 tbsp chocolate hazelnut spread, such as Nutella
40g/1½oz/2 tbsp chopped roasted hazelnuts

1 Grease a 20cm/8in square cake tin (pan), then line it with baking parchment.

2 To prepare the hazelnut praline, heat the sugar in a pan until melted. Do not stir the pan as the sugar is cooking but swirl it to ensure that the sugar does not burn. Cook until golden brown in colour.

3 Spread the hazelnuts out on a silicone mat or greased baking sheet and pour over the syrup. Leave to cool, then blitz in a food processor or blender to fine crumbs.

4 For the caramel, place the golden syrup, glucose, marshmallows and butter in a pan and heat gently until melted. Stir in the hazelnut praline powder, then add the rice crispies and hazelnuts and stir to combine.

5 Spoon the mixture into the tin and press out with the back of a spoon into an even layer. Leave to cool.

6 Place a heatproof bowl over a pan of simmering water and add the plain chocolate broken into pieces, and then the butter. Stir until melted and combined. Stir in the chocolate hazelnut spread. The mixture will thicken.

7 Spread the chocolate mixture over the top of the crispy cake and sprinkle with the chopped hazelnuts. Leave in the refrigerator to set for 3 hours then cut into squares. Store in an airtight container for up to 3 days.

Energy 206kcal/863kJ; Protein 2.3g; Carbohydrate 22.6g, of which sugars 14.6g; Fat 12.5g, of which saturates 4.7g; Cholesterol 13mg; Calcium 52mg; Fibre 1g; Sodium 92mg.

Millionaire's shortbread

The combination of rich shortbread, sweet sticky caramel, and marbled milk, plain and white chocolate makes this a truly luxurious teatime treat.

MAKES ABOUT 24

250g/9oz/2¼ cups plain (all-purpose) flour

75g/2½oz/scant ½ cup caster (superfine) sugar

175g/6oz/¾ cup unsalted butter, softened

For the filling

90g/3oz/7 tbsp unsalted butter, diced

90g/3oz/½ cup light muscovado (brown) sugar

2 x 400g/14oz cans sweetened condensed milk

For the topping

90g/3oz plain (semisweet) chocolate

90g/3oz milk chocolate

50g/2oz white chocolate

1 Preheat the oven to 180°C/350°F/Gas 4. Lightly grease a 33 x 23cm/13 x 9in Swiss roll tin (jelly roll pan) and line with baking parchment.

2 Put the flour and caster sugar in a bowl and rub in the butter until the mixture resembles fine breadcrumbs. Work with your hands until the mixture forms a dough.

3 Put the dough into the prepared tin and press it out with the back of a spoon to cover the base. Smooth it evenly into the tin. Prick all over with a fork and bake for about 20 minutes, or until firm to the touch and very light brown. Leave in the tin to cool.

4 To make the filling, put the butter, muscovado sugar and condensed milk into a pan and heat gently, whisking, until the sugar has dissolved.

5 Bring the mixture to the boil, stirring constantly. Reduce the heat and simmer gently, still stirring constantly, for about 5–10 minutes, or until it has thickened and has turned a caramel colour. Remove from the heat.

6 Pour the caramel over the cookie base, spread evenly, then leave until cold.

7 To make the topping, melt each type of chocolate separately in heatproof bowls set over a pan of hot water or in a microwave in short bursts. Spoon lines of plain and milk chocolate over the set caramel.

8 Add small spoonfuls of white chocolate. Use a skewer to form a marbled effect on the topping. Leave to set, remove from the tin, then cut into bars.

Energy 305kcal/1281kJ; Protein 4.6g; Carbohydrate 39.6g, of which sugars 31.6g; Fat 15.4g, of which saturates 9.6g; Cholesterol 37mg; Calcium 132mg; Fibre 0.4g; Sodium 120mg.

Coconut mint slices

Coconut and mint are perhaps not a combination that you would often put together but they marry well in this rich and indulgent slice. It has pretty brown and white layers and will look elegant displayed on your tea table.

MAKES 20
For the coconut base
225g/8oz/1 cup butter or margarine
175g/6oz/¾ cup caster (superfine) sugar
225g/8oz/2 cups plain (all-purpose) flour
50g/2oz/½ cup unsweetened cocoa powder
100g/3½oz/generous 1 cup desiccated (dry unsweetened shredded) coconut

For the peppermint layer
350g/12oz/3 cups icing (confectioners') sugar, sifted
50g/2oz/4 tbsp butter, softened
5ml/1 tsp peppermint extract
15ml/1 tbsp cream cheese
15–30ml/1–2 tbsp milk

For the ganache
200g/7oz plain (semisweet) chocolate
30ml/2 tbsp butter
30ml/2 tbsp milk

1 Preheat the oven to 180°C/350°F/Gas 4. Grease a 35 x 25cm/14 x 10in deep baking tin (pan), then line it with baking parchment.

2 For the coconut base, cream together the butter and caster sugar until light and creamy. Sift in the flour and cocoa powder and whisk in with the desiccated coconut until you have a soft dough.

3 Spoon the dough into the tin and press it out flat using your fingertips, which you may need to lightly dust with flour, or a sheet of baking parchment.

4 Bake the coconut biscuit base in the preheated oven for 15–20 minutes until the coconut base is firm. Leave to cool completely.

5 For the peppermint layer, whisk together the sifted icing sugar, softened butter, peppermint extract, cream cheese and milk until very light and creamy. It is best to do this with an electric mixer.

6 Spread the peppermint icing over the coconut base and chill in the refrigerator for about an hour.

7 For the ganache, break the chocolate into pieces and place in a heatproof bowl over a pan of simmering water with the butter and milk. Stir until the butter and chocolate have melted and combined and you have a smooth, glossy mixture.

8 Leave the ganache until it is just cool and then spread over the peppermint icing. Return to the refrigerator and leave to set for at least 3 hours or overnight.

9 Lift out the slice, remove the lining paper, cut into about 20 slices using a sharp knife and serve. This slice will store in an airtight container in the refrigerator for up to 3 days.

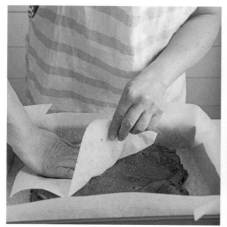  

Energy 202kcal/846kJ; Protein 4.6g; Carbohydrate 25.1g, of which sugars 14.4g; Fat 9.9g, of which saturates 4.9g; Cholesterol 48mg; Calcium 45mg; Fibre 0.9g; Sodium 114mg.

Large cakes & gâteaux

No afternoon tea table is complete without a stunning cake for a centrepiece. Here are light and airy recipes that are perfect for summer, such as cherry cake, or an easy all-in-one sponge that is delicious served with a flavourful berry compote. For cold winter days choose fruit cake, or apple & sultana cake, with their dense textures and complex flavours. Also included in the chapter are the special-occasion cakes such as rich Sachertorte, and the intriguing Battenberg, with its chequerboard marking.

Left Cherry cake, and lemon roulade with lemon curd cream, are showcase cakes perfect for serving for afternoon tea.

Classic fruit cake

The texture of this fruit cake is really special, with plump dried fruit made even more succulent by being heated gently with the butter, sugar and milk before baking. As with most fruit cakes, this keeps well and improves with age – ideal as a make-ahead cake for a tea party.

SERVES 8

350g/12oz/2 cups mixed dried fruit

225g/8oz/1 cup butter

225g/8oz/1 cup soft dark brown sugar

450g/1lb/4 cups self-raising (self-rising) flour

5ml/1 tsp bicarbonate of soda (baking soda)

5ml/1 tsp mixed (apple pie) spice

400ml/14fl oz/1⅔ cup milk

2 eggs, beaten

1 Preheat the oven to 160°C/325°F/Gas 3. Lightly grease and line a 20cm/8in cake tin (pan).

2 Put the dried fruit in a large pan and add the butter and sugar. Bring slowly to boil, stirring occasionally.

3 When the butter has melted and the sugar has dissolved, let the mixture bubble gently for about 2 minutes. Remove from the heat and cool slightly.

4 Sift the flour with the bicarbonate of soda and mixed spice. Add this, the milk and the eggs to the fruit mixture and mix together well.

5 Pour the mixture into the tin and smooth the surface. Bake for about 1½ hours or until firm to the touch and the cake is cooked through – a skewer inserted in the centre should come out free of sticky mixture.

6 Leave in the tin to cool for 20–30 minutes, then turn out and cool completely on a wire rack.

Energy 643.7kcal/2711kJ; Protein 9g; Carbohydrate 99g, of which sugars 62g; Fat 26.1g, of which saturates 15.7g; Cholesterol 110mg; Calcium 294mg; Fibre 2.5g; Sodium 412.1mg.

Caraway seed cake

Just a few caraway seeds give this cake a delicately warm and spicy flavour that blends well with the tang of the citrus peel. It's a simple and traditional teatime cake, ideal with a cup of something hot on a chilly afternoon. It will keep for up to 2 days in an airtight container.

SERVES 8

175g/6oz/¾ cup butter, softened
175g/6oz/scant 1 cup caster
    (superfine) sugar
3 eggs
225g/8oz/2 cups plain
    (all-purpose) flour

5ml/1 tsp baking powder
10ml/2 tsp caraway seeds
30ml/2 tbsp milk or buttermilk
50g/2oz/⅓ cup finely chopped
    mixed (candied) peel

1 Preheat the oven to 180°C/350°F/Gas 4. Grease a 20cm/8in round deep cake tin (pan) and line the bottom and sides with baking parchment.

2 Beat the butter and sugar with an electric mixer until fluffy, then beat in the eggs one at a time, adding a spoonful of flour each time. Sift the remaining flour with the baking powder into the bowl. Add the caraway seeds and milk. Beat well.

3 Fold in the candied peel and mix until combined. Spoon into the tin and smooth the top. Bake for 1–1¼ hours, or until a skewer comes out clean when inserted.

4 Cool for 15 minutes in the tin, then turn out on to a wire rack to go cold. Remove the lining paper.

Energy 281kcal/1181kJ; Protein 4.6g; Carbohydrate 36.9g, of which sugars 15.5g; Fat 13.8g, of which saturates 8g; Cholesterol 87mg; Calcium 58mg; Fibre 0.8g; Sodium 109mg.

Classic Victoria sandwich

Serve this richly flavoured sponge cake sandwiched together with your favourite jam or preserve. For special occasions, fill the cake with prepared fresh fruit, such as raspberries or sliced peaches and whipped cream or some fromage frais.

SERVES 8–10

175g/6oz/¾ cup butter, softened

175g/6oz/scant 1 cup caster (superfine) sugar, plus extra for dusting

3 eggs beaten

175g/6oz/1½ cups self-raising (superfine) flour, sifted

60ml/4 tbsp jam

150ml/5fl oz/⅔ cup whipped cream or fromage frais

Cook's tip

The traditional way to make a Victoria sponge is to weigh the whole eggs and use exactly the same weight of fat, flour and sugar.

1 Preheat the oven to 180°C/350°F/Gas 4. Lightly grease and line the bases of two 18cm/7in sandwich tins (pans).

2 Place the butter and caster sugar in a bowl and cream together until pale and fluffy.

3 Add the eggs, a little at a time, and beat in. Fold in half the flour, using a metal spoon, then fold in the rest.

4 Divide the mixture between the two sandwich tins and level the surfaces with the back of a spoon.

5 Bake for 25–30 minutes, until the cakes have risen, feel just firm to the touch and are golden brown. Turn out, peel off the baking parchment and leave to cool on a wire rack.

6 When the cakes are cool, sandwich them with the jam and whipped cream or fromage frais. Dust the top of the cake with sifted icing sugar and serve cut into slices.

7 Store the cake in the refrigerator in an airtight container or wrapped in foil.

Energy 355.3Kcal/1484.5kJ; Protein 4.2g; Carbohydrate 36.3g, of which sugars 23.2g; Fat 22.5g, of which saturates 4.4g; Cholesterol 84.2mg; Calcium 90.8mg; Fibre 0.5g; Sodium 235.8mg.

Easy all-in-one sponge

This strawberry and 'cream' cake is so quick and easy to make. You'll find this simple cream cheese topping handy for other cakes too. Store for up to 3 days in an airtight container, or you can freeze the basic cakes undecorated for up to 2 months.

SERVES 8–10

175g/6oz/1½ cups self-raising (self-rising) flour
5ml/1 tsp baking powder
175g/6oz/¾ cup soft margarine
175g/6oz/scant 1 cup caster (superfine) sugar
3 eggs
15ml/1 tbsp milk
5ml/1 tsp vanilla extract

For the filling & topping

150g/5oz white chocolate
200g/7oz/scant 1 cup cream cheese
25g/1oz/¼ cup icing (confectioners') sugar
30ml/2 tbsp strawberry jam
12 strawberries

1 Preheat the oven to 180°C/350°F/Gas 4. Grease and line two 20cm/8in round shallow cake tins (pans) with baking parchment.

2 Sift the flour and baking powder into a large bowl, then add all the remaining cake ingredients. Beat until just smooth and combined – do not over-mix.

3 Divide the mixture between the tins and smooth the tops level.

4 Bake for 20 minutes, or until the cakes spring back when pressed. Allow to stand in the tin for 5 minutes, then turn out on to a wire rack to go cold. Remove the lining papers.

5 To make the icing, break the chocolate into squares and melt in a heatproof bowl over a pan of gently simmering water. Remove from the heat and cool slightly, then beat in the cream cheese and icing sugar.

6 Spread the top of one sponge with jam. Carefully spread one-third of the icing on top.

7 Slice 4 strawberries, then sprinkle the slices over the jam. Put the cakes together. Spread the remaining icing over the cake top. Decorate with the whole strawberries.

Energy 395kcal/1648kJ; Protein 4.7g; Carbohydrate 39.6g, of which sugars 28.5g; Fat 25.3g, of which saturates 15.2g; Cholesterol 94mg; Calcium 90mg; Fibre 0.5g; Sodium 173mg.

Lemon drizzle cake

Wonderfully moist and lemony, this cake is a favourite at coffee mornings and afternoon tea. A lemon and sugar syrup is poured over the cooked cake and allowed to soak through, so that the whole cake is sweet and tangy. Store in an airtight container for up to 5 days.

SERVES 6–8

finely grated rind of 2 lemons
175g/6oz/scant 1 cup caster (superfine) sugar, plus extra for sprinkling
225g/8oz/1 cup unsalted butter, softened
4 eggs
225g/8oz/2 cups self-raising (self-rising) flour
5ml/1 tsp baking powder
shredded rind of 1 lemon, to decorate

For the syrup

juice of 1 lemon
150g/5oz/¾ cup caster (superfine) sugar

Variations

• You can make this cake using oranges and/or limes instead of lemons.
• You can use the lemon icing opposite in place of the syrup and sugar.

1 Preheat the oven to 160°C/325°F/Gas 3. Grease and line the base and sides of an 18–20cm/7–8in round deep cake tin (pan) with baking parchment.

2 Mix the lemon rind and sugar together in a bowl.

3 In a large bowl, beat the butter with the lemon and sugar mixture until light and fluffy, then beat in the eggs one at a time.

4 Sift the flour and baking powder into the mixture in three batches and beat well.

5 Turn the batter into the prepared tin and smooth the top level. Bake for 1½ hours, or until golden brown and springy to the touch.

6 To make the syrup, slowly heat the juice with the sugar until dissolved.

7 Prick the cake top with a skewer and pour over the syrup. Sprinkle over the shredded lemon rind and a teaspoon of sugar, then leave to cool. Remove the lining paper and serve.

Energy 659kcal/2765kJ; Protein 8g; Carbohydrate 84.1g, of which sugars 56.2g; Fat 34.8g, of which saturates 21.4g; Cholesterol 213mg; Calcium 184mg; Fibre 1.2g; Sodium 466mg.

Cherry cake

Both dried and glacé cherries are used in this elegant cake, partnered with the delicate flavour of almonds and decorated with a drizzle of icing. It is a combination that is perfect for a summer tea party. Store in an airtight container for up to 5 days. Freeze undecorated for 2 months.

SERVES 8–10

175g/6oz/¾ cup butter, softened

175g/6oz/scant 1 cup caster (superfine) sugar

3 eggs, beaten

150g/5oz/1¼ cups self-raising (self-rising) flour

50g/2oz/½ cup plain (all-purpose) flour

75g/2½oz/¾ cup ground almonds

75g/2½oz/½ cup glacé (candied) cherries, washed, dried and halved

25g/1oz dried cherries

a few drops of almond extract

For the decoration

115g/4oz/1 cup icing (confectioners') sugar, sifted

5ml/1 tsp lemon juice

50g/2oz/½ cup flaked (sliced) almonds, toasted

10 natural glacé (candied) cherries

1 Preheat the oven to 160°C/325°F/Gas 3. Grease and line a 20cm/8in round deep cake tin (pan).

2 In a bowl, beat the butter with the sugar until light and fluffy, using an electric whisk, if possible. Add the eggs a little at a time, including 5ml/1 tsp of flour with each addition.

3 In another bowl, sift in the flours, then add the ground almonds and both cherries. Stir well.

4 Add the flour and cherry mixture to the butter and sugar and fold together with the almond extract until smooth. Spoon into the cake tin and smooth level.

5 Bake for 45–50 minutes, or until a skewer inserted into the centre comes out clean. Cool slightly, then turn on to a wire rack to go cold. Remove the lining paper.

6 In a bowl, mix the icing sugar with the lemon juice, and 10–15ml/2–3 tsp water, to make a soft icing. Drizzle half over the cake top. Sprinkle the almonds into the centre. Place the cherries around the edge. Drizzle over the remaining icing and serve.

Energy 367kcal/1535kJ; Protein 5g; Carbohydrate 43.7g, of which sugars 26.6g; Fat 20.4g, of which saturates 12g; Cholesterol 118mg; Calcium 75mg; Fibre 0.9g; Sodium 309mg.

Apple & sultana cake

This traditional, simple, farmhouse cake has a sweet, crispy top, a lovely moist texture and a spicy apple flavour – it makes an ideal teatime treat.

SERVES 8–10

175g/6oz/¾ cup softened butter, plus extra for greasing

175g/6oz/¾ cup soft light brown sugar

3 eggs

225g/8oz/2 cups self-raising (self-rising) flour, sifted

5ml/1 tsp baking powder, sifted

10ml/2 tsp mixed (apple pie) spice

350g/12oz cooking apples, peeled, cored and diced

175g/6oz/1 cup sultanas (golden raisins)

75ml/5 tbsp milk

30ml/2 tbsp demerara (raw) sugar

1 Preheat the oven to 160°C/325°F/Gas 3. Grease a 20cm/8in round deep cake tin (pan) and line the base and sides with baking parchment.

2 Put the butter in a large bowl with the sugar. Beat together until light and fluffy. Beat in the eggs. Sift in the flour, baking powder and spice, then beat until thoroughly mixed.

3 Fold in the apples, sultanas and sufficient milk to make a soft dropping consistency.

4 Spoon the batter into the prepared tin. Wet a metal spoon by running it under the tap and use the back of the wet spoon to smooth the cake top level. Sprinkle with demerara sugar.

5 Bake for about 1½ hours, or until risen, golden brown and firm to the touch.

6 Cool in the tin for 5 minutes, then turn out on to a wire rack. Keep this cake for 2 days in an airtight container in a cool place.

Energy 310kcal/1305kJ; Protein 4.2g; Carbohydrate 45.5g, of which sugars 31.2g; Fat 13.7g, of which saturates 8.4g; Cholesterol 81mg; Calcium 63mg; Fibre 1.3g; Sodium 135mg.

Gooseberry cake

Gooseberries can be slightly acidic, so here they are sweetened with sugar and elderflower before they are added to the cake batter. The elderflower infuses the cake with a light, sweet flavour.

SERVES 10

150g/5oz gooseberries
150g/5oz/¾ cup, plus 22.5ml/
4½ tsp, golden caster (superfine)
sugar
15ml/1 tbsp elderflower cordial,
plus extra for brushing
225g/8oz/2 cups plain
(all-purpose) flour
10ml/2 tsp baking powder

75g/2½oz/6 tbsp butter, melted,
plus extra for greasing
2.5ml/½ tsp vanilla extract
1 egg, lightly beaten
250ml/8½fl oz/1 cup buttermilk
icing (confectioners') sugar,
for dusting

1 Preheat the oven to 180°C/350°F/Gas 4. Grease a 23cm/9in round loose-based cake tin (pan) with butter.

2 Arrange the fruit in a single layer on a plate and sprinkle evenly with the 22.5ml/4½ tsp of the sugar and the elderflower cordial. Leave to stand for 30 minutes.

3 Sift the flour, baking powder and sugar into a large bowl and stir in the 150g/5oz sugar. Make a well in the centre.

4 In a separate bowl, lightly whisk together the melted butter, vanilla extract, egg and buttermilk. Pour into the dry ingredients and fold partly together.

5 Lightly combine half the reserved gooseberries and all of the syrupy juices into the batter, then fold together with a metal spoon.

6 Spoon the mixture into the tin and sprinkle the remaining fruit on top.

7 Bake for 30 minutes, but check after 25 minutes. If the centre of the cake is springy to the touch, it is ready.

8 Lightly brush the surface of the warm cake with elderflower cordial, if you like, and serve, dusted with icing sugar.

Energy 273kcal/1144kJ; Protein 3.9g; Carbohydrate 34.6g, of which sugars 18.1g; Fat 14.2g, of which saturates 8.3g; Cholesterol 82mg; Calcium 51mg; Fibre 1g; Sodium 112mg.

Angel food cake

The texture of this American teatime classic is springy but slightly sticky, and the colour is snowy white. The cream of tartar helps to aerate the egg whites, and the addition of sugar creates a light meringue mixture.

SERVES 10–12

65g/2¼oz/generous ½ cup plain (all-purpose) flour

15ml/1 tbsp cornflour (cornstarch)

225g/8oz/1 cup caster (superfine) sugar

10 egg whites

5ml/1 tsp cream of tartar

7.5ml/1½ tsp vanilla extract

For the frosting

2 egg whites

115g/4oz/generous ½ cup caster (superfine) sugar

10ml/2 tsp golden (light corn) syrup

2.5ml/½ tsp vanilla extract

rind of 1 orange, to decorate

1 Preheat the oven to 180°C/350°F/Gas 4.

2 In a large bowl, sift together the flour, cornflour, and 50g/2oz of the sugar three times, so that the texture is very, very light.

3 Put the egg whites and cream of tartar into a clean, grease-free bowl and whisk together until they form stiff peaks.

4 Gradually whisk in the remaining sugar, 15ml/1 tbsp at a time, until the mixture becomes thick and glossy.

5 Using a metal spoon, gently fold the sifted flour and vanilla extract into the whisked egg whites until combined.

6 Transfer the mixture to a 25cm/10in non-stick ring mould and smooth out the batter so it is level. Bake for 35–40 minutes, or until risen and golden.

7 Remove from the oven, invert the cake in its mould onto a wire rack, and leave to go cold.

8 To make the meringue frosting, put the egg whites into a clean, grease-free bowl and whisk until stiff and dry. Set aside.

9 Heat the sugar and 60ml/4 tbsp water in a small pan, stirring constantly until the sugar dissolves. Increase the heat and boil until it reaches 115°C/240°F on a sugar thermometer. As soon as this temperature is reached, remove the pan from the heat.

10 Pour the sugar liquid into the egg whites, whisking constantly, until the mixture is thick and glossy.

11 Beat in the golden syrup and vanilla, beating for 5 minutes.

12 Lift the mould off the cake and put the cake on a serving plate. Quickly spread the frosting over the cake. Sprinkle with orange rind to decorate. This cake will keep refrigerated for up to 5 days.

Energy 177kcal/500kJ; Protein 3.1g; Carbohydrate 27.7g, of which sugars 21.4g; Fat 0.1g, of which saturates 0g; Cholesterol 0mg; Calcium 24mg; Fibre 0.3g; Sodium 49mg.

Frosted carrot & parsnip cake

The grated carrots and parsnips in this light and crumbly cake help to keep it moist and account for its very good keeping qualities. The creamy sweetness of the cooked meringue topping gives a wonderful contrast to the cake's light crumb.

SERVES 8–10

oil, for greasing
zest of 1 lemon
zest and juice of 1 orange
15ml/1 tbsp caster
(superfine) sugar
225g/8oz/1 cup butter
225g/8oz/1 cup soft light
brown sugar
4 eggs
225g/8oz mixed carrots and
parsnips, peeled and grated
115g/4oz/⅔ cups sultanas (golden
raisins)

225g/8oz/2 cups self-raising
(self-rising) wholemeal
(wholewheat) flour
5ml/1 tsp baking powder

For the topping
50g/2oz/¼ cup caster
(superfine) sugar
1 egg white
pinch of salt

1 Preheat the oven to 180°C/350°F/Gas 4. Lightly grease a 20cm/8in loose-based cake tin (pan) and line the base with a circle of baking parchment.

2 Finely grate the lemon and orange. Put about half of the rind, selecting the longest shreds, in a bowl and mix with the caster sugar. Arrange the sugar-coated rind on a sheet of greaseproof paper and leave in a warm place, to dry thoroughly.

3 Cream the butter and sugar until pale and fluffy. Add the eggs gradually, then beat well.

4 Stir in the unsugared rinds, the grated carrots and parsnips, 30ml/2 tbsp orange juice and the sultanas.

5 Gradually fold in the flour and baking powder, and tip into the prepared tin. Bake for 1½ hours until risen, golden and just firm.

6 Leave the cake to cool slightly in the tin, then turn out on to a serving plate.

7 To make the topping, place the caster sugar in a bowl over boiling water with 30ml/2 tbsp of the remaining orange juice. Stir over the heat until the sugar begins to dissolve. Remove from the heat, add the egg white and salt, and whisk for 1 minute with an electric beater.

8 Return the pan to the heat and whisk the mixture for about 6 minutes until the mixture becomes stiff and glossy, holding a good shape. Allow to cool slightly, whisking frequently.

9 Swirl the cooked meringue topping evenly over the top of the cake and leave to firm up in the refrigerator for about 1 hour.

10 To serve, sprinkle the top of the cake with the sugared lemon and orange rind, which should now be dry and crumbly.

Energy 395kcal/1648kJ; Protein 4.7g; Carbohydrate 39.6g, of which sugars 28.5g; Fat 25.3g, of which saturates 15.2g; Cholesterol 94mg; Calcium 90mg; Fibre 0.5g; Sodium 173mg.

Raspberry & custard layer cake

Three light cakes enclose a crushed raspberry layer and another of custard, all covered with vanilla-flavoured cream. It is an ideal teatime cake for when raspberries are at their sweetest. Bake the cake layers the day before for the best flavour, then assemble the cake and eat fresh.

SERVES 10–12

115g/4oz/½ cup unsalted butter
200g/7oz/1 cup caster (superfine) sugar
4 eggs, separated
45ml/3 tbsp milk
175g/6oz/1½ cups plain (all-purpose) flour
25ml/1½ tbsp cornflour (cornstarch)
7.5ml/1½ tsp baking powder
5ml/1 tsp vanilla sugar
fresh raspberries, to decorate

For the custard filling
2 eggs
90g/3oz/½ cup caster (superfine) sugar
15ml/1 tbsp cornflour (cornstarch)
350ml/12fl oz/1½ cups milk

For the topping
475ml/16fl oz/2 cups double (heavy) cream or whipping cream
25g/1oz/¼ cup icing (confectioners') sugar
5ml/1 tsp vanilla sugar

For the raspberry filling
375g/13oz/3 cups raspberries
sugar, to taste

1 Preheat the oven to 230°C/450°F/Gas 8. Lightly grease and flour three 23cm/9in shallow cake tins (pans).

2 Cream the butter with the sugar in a large bowl until light and fluffy. Beat in the egg yolks, one at a time. Stir in the milk until blended.

3 In a separate bowl, sift together the flour, cornflour, baking powder and vanilla sugar. Beat the flour mixture into the egg mixture.

4 Put the egg whites into a clean, grease-free bowl and whisk until they form stiff peaks. Gently fold the egg whites into the cake mixture.

5 Divide the batter evenly among the tins and smooth to the edges. Bake for 12 minutes. Leave the cakes to cool for 10 minutes, then turn out to cool on a wire rack.

6 To make the custard filling, whisk together the eggs and sugar in a pan. Whisk in the cornflour and the milk. Cook over a low heat, stirring, for 6 minutes or until thickened, then remove the pan from the heat and leave to cool.

7 To make the topping, beat the cream in a bowl until soft peaks form. Stir in the icing sugar and vanilla sugar and beat until stiff.

8 To make the raspberry filling, crush the raspberries in a bowl and add a little sugar to taste.

9 To assemble the cake, place one layer on a serving plate and spread with the raspberry filling. Place a second cake layer over the first and spread with the cooled custard. Top with the final layer.

10 Spread the sweet whipped cream over the sides and top of the cake. Chill the cake until ready to serve, and decorate with raspberries.

Energy 433kcal/1811kJ; Protein 6.1g; Carbohydrate 44.6g, of which sugars 30.4g; Fat 27g, of which saturates 15.9g; Cholesterol 157mg; Calcium 86mg; Fibre 1.2g; Sodium 109mg.

Frosted walnut layer cake

Walnuts go very well in rich cakes, especially when combined with a sweet filling. This moist and nutty cake is layered with vanilla buttercream and then topped with swirls of a super-light and fluffy frosting. It is ideal for a special tea party. Keep for 5 days in an airtight container.

1 Preheat the oven to 160°C/325°F/Gas 3. Grease and line two 20cm/8in round shallow cake tins (pans) with baking parchment.

2 Sift the flour and baking powder into a large bowl, then add all the remaining cake ingredients.

3 Beat together for 2 minutes, or until smooth, then divide between the tins and spread level.

4 Bake for 25 minutes, or until golden and springy to the touch in the centre.

5 Allow the cakes to stand for 5 minutes, then turn out on to a wire rack to go cold. Remove the lining papers. Carefully cut each cake in half horizontally using a long-bladed sharp knife.

6 To make the buttercream, in a large bowl, beat the butter, vanilla extract and icing sugar together until light and fluffy.

7 Spread a third thinly over one sponge half and place a sponge layer on top, then continue layering the sponges with the buttercream. Put the cake on to a serving plate.

8 To make the frosting, put the egg whites in a large heatproof bowl and add the caster sugar, salt, cream of tartar and water. Put the bowl over a pan of hot water and whisk with an electric mixer for 7 minutes, or until the mixture is thick and stands in peaks.

9 Immediately, use a metal spatula to swirl the frosting over the top and sides of the cake.

10 Arrange the walnut halves on top and leave to set for 10 minutes before serving.

SERVES 10–12
225g/8oz/2 cups self-raising (self-rising) flour
5ml/1 tsp baking powder
225g/8oz/1 cup butter, softened
225g/8oz/1 cup soft light brown sugar
75g/2½oz/¾ cup walnuts, chopped
4 eggs, beaten
15ml/1 tbsp treacle (molasses

For the buttercream
75g/2½oz/6 tbsp unsalted butter
5ml/1 tsp vanilla extract
175g/6oz/1½ cups icing (confectioners') sugar

For the frosting
2 large egg whites
350g/12oz/1½ cups golden caster (superfine) sugar
pinch of salt
pinch of cream of tartar
15ml/1 tbsp warm water
walnut halves, to decorate

Variation
Pecan nuts work really well in this cake, too, being similar in texture and with a sweet, slightly caramel flavour.

Energy 563kcal/2349kJ; Protein 8.5g; Carbohydrate 50.6g, of which sugars 39.2g; Fat 35.3g, of which saturates 10.1g; Cholesterol 108mg; Calcium 114mg; Fibre 1.5g; Sodium 177mg.

Boston cream pie

Created by chef M. Sanzian at the Parker House Hotel in Boston in the 1850s, this famous 'pie' is unusual, because sandwiched between the two cake layers is a rich custard. With its chocolate glaze it is a very appealing addition to the tea table. Keep refrigerated for up to 3 days.

SERVES 10–12

225g/8oz/2 cups plain (all-purpose) flour
15ml/1 tbsp baking powder
pinch of salt
115g/4oz/½ cup butter, softened
200g/7oz/1 cup caster (superfine) sugar
2 eggs
5ml/1 tsp vanilla extract
175m/6fl oz/¾ cup milk

For the filling
250ml/8½fl oz/1 cup milk
3 egg yolks

90g/3oz/½ cup caster (superfine) sugar
25g/1oz/¼ cup plain (all-purpose) flour
15ml/1 tbsp butter
5ml/1 tsp vanilla extract

For the glaze
25g/1oz dark (bittersweet) chocolate
15g/½oz/1 tbsp butter
50g/2oz/½ cup icing (confectioners') sugar, plus extra for dusting
2.5ml/½ tsp vanilla extract
15ml/1 tbsp hot water

1 Preheat the oven to 190°C/375°F/Gas 5. Thoroughly grease and line two 20cm/8in round shallow cake tins (pans) with baking parchment.

2 Sift the flour, baking powder and salt into a bowl.

3 Beat the butter and sugar together until light and fluffy in another bowl. Beat in the eggs one at a time, beating well after each addition. Stir in the vanilla extract. Add the milk and the dry ingredients, alternating the batches and mixing only enough to blend.

4 Divide the cake batter between the prepared tins and spread it out evenly. Bake for 25 minutes, or until a skewer inserted into the centre comes out clean. Allow to stand in the tins for 5 minutes before turning out on to a wire rack to cool completely. Remove the lining.

5 To make the filling, in a small pan, heat the milk to boiling point and remove from the heat.

6 In a heatproof bowl, beat the egg yolks until smooth. Gradually add the sugar and continue beating until pale yellow, then beat in the flour. Pour the hot milk into the egg yolk mixture while beating.

7 When all the milk has been added, put the bowl over a pan of boiling water. Heat, stirring constantly, until thickened. Cook for 2 minutes more, then remove from the heat. Stir in the butter and vanilla. Leave to cool.

8 Slice off the top of each cake to create a flat surface. Put one cake on a plate and spread on the filling. Set the other cake on top, cut side down. Smooth the edge of the filling so it is flush with the sides of the cake layers.

9 To make the glaze, melt the chocolate and butter in a heatproof bowl set over a pan of simmering water. Stir well. When smooth, remove from the heat and beat in the icing sugar. Add the vanilla extract, then beat in a little hot water to give a spreadable consistency. Spread evenly over the top of the cake. When it is set dust the top with icing sugar.

Energy 499kcal/2100kJ; Protein 6g; Carbohydrate 77.1g, of which sugars 53.1g; Fat 20.3g, of which saturates 12.1g; Cholesterol 146mg; Calcium 112mg; Fibre 1g; Sodium 297mg.

Battenberg

Immediately identifiable, Battenberg cake has a characteristic light sponge that is set in a chequerboard arrangement of pink and yellow cake. It is encased in a smooth cover of marzipan and served in dainty slices – a perfect addition to the tea table.

SERVES 12

175g/6oz/¾ cup butter, softened
175g/6oz/scant 1 cup caster (superfine) sugar
3 large eggs, lightly beaten
175g/6oz/1½ cups self-raising (self-rising) flour, sifted
pinch of salt
2.5ml/½ tsp red food colouring

2.5ml/½ tsp rosewater
2.5ml/½ tsp orange flower water, or almond extract
90ml/6 tbsp apricot jam
30ml/2 tbsp sugar
450g/1lb marzipan
icing (confectioners') sugar, for dusting

1 Preheat the oven to 190°C/375°F/Gas 5. Lightly grease a Swiss roll tin (jelly roll pan), 30 x 20 x 2.5cm (12 x 8 x 1in). Line the tin with baking parchment.

2 Cut a strip of cardboard to fit the inside length of the tin. Cover with foil, lightly grease and wedge in place along the middle of the tin.

3 In a large bowl, beat the butter with the caster sugar until creamy. Add the eggs and beat well. Lightly fold in the flour and salt.

4 Put half the mixture in a clean bowl and mix in the red food colouring and rosewater until evenly tinted. Turn into one side of the tin.

5 Mix the orange flower water or almond extract into the remaining batter and turn into the empty side of the tin. Smooth into the corners.

6 Bake for 20 minutes until risen and firm to the touch. Remove from the oven and leave to stand in the tin for 5 minutes.

7 Slide the blade of a knife between cake, tin and foil strip, and turn out the cake on to a wire rack. Remove the lining paper. Leave the cake to go cold.

8 Trim the cake so that each half measures 28 x 9cm (11 x 3½in). Cut each slab in half lengthways so there are four equal pieces.

9 In a pan, bring the jam and sugar slowly to the boil, stirring constantly, until smooth. Boil for 30–60 seconds. Remove from the heat.

10 To assemble the cake, brush the top of each plain cake strip with the syrup and press a pink strip on top. Brush one side of each cake stack with syrup and press them together to make a chequerboard pattern and glue the sponges together in a block.

11 Roll out the marzipan on a surface dusted with plenty of icing sugar using a well-dusted rolling pin to 28cm/11in square. Brush the cake top with syrup, and place the cake syrup-side down 1cm/½in from one edge of the marzipan.

12 Brush the rest of the cake with syrup. Wrap the marzipan over and around the cake, smoothing it firmly with your hand. Press firmly at the join to seal. Trim away any excess marzipan and the cake is ready to serve, sliced in all its chequerboard glory.

Energy 355kcal/1492kJ; Protein 4.4g; Carbohydrate 51.2g, of which sugars 41.7g; Fat 15.7g, of which saturates 7.5g; Cholesterol 70mg; Calcium 55mg; Fibre 1g; Sodium 117mg.

Lemon roulade with lemon curd cream

This featherlight roulade is flavoured with almonds and filled with a rich lemon-curd cream. It makes a marvellous dessert or a teatime treat. Use best-quality or homemade lemon curd if you can. Eat this roulade fresh for the best taste, but it will store chilled for up to 2 days.

SERVES 10–12

4 eggs, separated

115g/4oz/generous ½ cup caster (superfine) sugar

finely grated rind of 2 lemons, plus extra to decorate

5ml/1 tsp vanilla extract

40g/1½oz/⅓ cup plain (all-purpose) flour

25g/1oz/¼ cup ground almonds

For the lemon cream

300ml/½ pint/1¼ cups double (heavy) cream

60ml/4 tbsp lemon curd (see page 264)

45ml/3 tbsp icing (confectioners') sugar, for dusting

1 Preheat the oven to 190°C/375°F/Gas 5. Grease and line a 33 × 23cm/13 × 9in Swiss roll tin (jelly roll pan) with baking parchment.

2 In a large bowl, beat the egg yolks with half the sugar until foamy. Beat in the lemon rind and vanilla extract.

3 Sift the flour over the egg mixture and lightly fold in with the ground almonds, using a metal spoon.

4 Put the egg whites into a clean, grease-free bowl and whisk until they form stiff, glossy peaks. Gradually whisk in the remaining sugar to form a stiff meringue.

5 Stir half the meringue into the egg yolk mixture to slacken it, then fold in the remainder of the mixture. Pour the batter into the prepared tin and smooth level.

6 Bake for 10 minutes, or until risen and spongy to the touch. Put the tin on a wire rack and cover loosely with a sheet of baking parchment and a damp dish towel. Leave to cool.

7 To make the lemon cream, whip the cream until it holds its shape, then fold in the lemon curd.

8 Sift the icing sugar over a piece of baking parchment. Turn the sponge out on to it. Peel off the lining paper and spread over the lemon cream.

9 Using the paper, roll up the sponge from one long side. Sprinkle with lemon rind and serve.

Energy 395kcal/1648kJ; Protein 4.7g; Carbohydrate 39.6g, of which sugars 28.5g; Fat 25.3g, of which saturates 15.2g; Cholesterol 94mg; Calcium 90mg; Fibre 0.5g; Sodium 173mg.

Double chocolate roulade

This decadent roulade can be made a day ahead and then filled and rolled before serving. The chocolate sponge has a rich brandy, chocolate and mascarpone filling and is decorated with chocolate-dipped strawberries. Once filled, keep refrigerated for up to 2 days.

SERVES 10–12

butter, for greasing
175g/6oz plain (semisweet) chocolate, broken into small pieces
4 eggs, separated
115g/4oz/½ cup caster (superfine) sugar
unsweetened cocoa powder, for dusting

For the filling & topping

225g/8oz plain (semisweet) chocolate, broken into pieces
45ml/3 tbsp brandy
2 eggs, separated
250g/9oz/1 cup mascarpone
chocolate-dipped strawberries (see Cook's tip)

1 Preheat the oven to 180°C/350°F/Gas 4. Grease and line a 33 × 23cm/13 × 9in Swiss roll tin (jelly roll pan) with baking parchment.

2 Melt the chocolate in a heatproof bowl over a pan of gently simmering water, or in short bursts in the microwave, then remove from the heat.

3 Whisk the egg yolks and sugar in a bowl until pale and thick, then stir in the melted chocolate.

4 Put the egg whites into a clean, grease-free bowl and whisk until they form soft peaks, then fold the whites lightly and evenly into the egg and chocolate mixture.

5 Pour the mixture into the prepared tin and smooth level. Bake for 15–20 minutes, or until well risen and firm to the touch.

6 Dust a sheet of baking parchment with cocoa. Turn the sponge out on to the paper, cover with a clean dish towel and leave to cool.

7 To make the filling, melt the chocolate with the brandy in a heatproof bowl set over a pan of gently simmering water. Remove from the heat.

8 Beat the egg yolks together, then beat into the warm chocolate mixture until smooth.

9 Put the egg whites into a clean, grease-free bowl and whisk until they form soft peaks.

10 Fold the egg whites lightly and evenly into the filling in three batches until the mixture is light and smooth. Cool completely.

11 Uncover the roulade, remove the lining paper and spread with most of the mascarpone. Spread the chocolate mixture over the top, then roll up from a long side to enclose the filling.

12 Transfer to a serving plate, top with mascarpone, fresh chocolate-dipped strawberries, and dust with cocoa powder.

Cook's tip

To make chocolate-dipped strawberries, dip the lower half of each strawberry into some good-quality melted chocolate. Leave to set on a baking sheet lined with baking parchment.

Energy 486kcal/2022kJ; Protein 10.2g; Carbohydrate 32.8g, of which sugars 32.4g; Fat 34.5g, of which saturates 19.9g; Cholesterol 189mg; Calcium 41mg; Fibre 1.3g; Sodium 143mg.

Chocolate sandwich cake

This light chocolate sponge cake has lots of appeal, filled and topped with a rich, chocolatey frosting. It also works as a celebration cake, when decorated with small squares of fudge and white chocolate buttons, or flaked chocolate. Keep it for up to 3 days in an airtight container.

SERVES 10–12

130g/4½oz/generous ½ cup butter, softened, plus extra for greasing
250g/9oz/1¼ cups caster (superfine) sugar
3 eggs, beaten
225g/8oz/2 cups plain (all-purpose) flour
5ml/1 tsp bicarbonate of soda (baking soda)
50g/2oz/½ cup unsweetened cocoa powder
250ml/8½fl oz/1 cup buttermilk

For the buttercream

50g/2oz dark (bittersweet) chocolate
175g/6oz/1½ cups icing (confectioners') sugar, sifted
115g/4oz/½ cup unsalted butter, softened
few drops of vanilla extract

1 Preheat the oven to 180°C/350°F/Gas 4. Grease and line two 20cm/8in round shallow cake tins (pans) with baking parchment.

2 In a mixing bowl, cream the butter and sugar until light and fluffy.

3 Gradually beat in the eggs. Sift the flour, bicarbonate of soda and cocoa over in batches and beat well to combine. Add the buttermilk and mix well.

4 Spoon the mixture into the prepared tins and bake for 30–35 minutes, or until firm to the touch.

5 Let stand for 5 minutes, then turn out of the tins, peel off the papers and leave on a wire rack to go cold.

6 To make the buttercream, melt the chocolate in a heatproof bowl set over a pan of gently simmering water. Stir occasionally. Allow to cool slightly.

7 In another bowl, beat the icing sugar with the butter and vanilla until creamy. Mix in the melted chocolate.

8 Use half of the buttercream to sandwich the cakes together, and spread the remainder on the top of the cake. Store refrigerated to keep the buttercream firm.

Energy 430kcal/1790kJ; Protein 7.8g; Carbohydrate 29.5g, of which sugars 28.8g; Fat 32.1g, of which saturates 13.6g; Cholesterol 96mg; Calcium 92mg; Fibre 1.9g; Sodium 125mg.

Cocoa, almond & coffee cake

This easy cake recipe is a favourite because it is so quick to make. Add a lovely coffee buttercream for the filling and topping, and the cake is transformed into something extra special. Keep this cake for up to 3 days, refrigerated, in an airtight container.

SERVES 8–10

175g/6oz/¾ cup unsalted butter, softened, plus extra for greasing
175g/6oz/¾ cup soft dark brown sugar
175g/6oz/1½ cups self-raising (self-rising) flour
25ml/1½ tbsp unsweetened cocoa powder
pinch of salt
50g/2oz/½ cup ground almonds
3 large eggs, lightly beaten

For the buttercream
175g/6oz/¾ cup unsalted butter
350g/12oz/3 cups icing (confectioners') sugar, sifted
30ml/2 tbsp coffee extract
whole hazelnuts or pecan nuts, to decorate (optional)

1 Preheat the oven to 180°C/350°F/Gas 4. Grease and line two 18cm/7in round shallow cake tins (pans).

2 In a large bowl, cream the butter with the sugar until light and fluffy.

3 Sift over the flour, cocoa and salt, then add the ground almonds and eggs, and beat well.

4 Divide the batter evenly between the tins. Bake for 25–30 minutes, or until firm to the touch.

5 Leave to stand for 5 minutes, then turn out of the tins, peel off the papers and leave on a wire rack to go cold.

6 To make the buttercream, beat the butter, then gradually beat in the icing sugar and coffee extract.

7 Put one quarter of the buttercream into a small piping or pastry bag fitted with a star nozzle.

8 Sandwich the cakes together with some of the buttercream. Cover the top and sides with the rest, smoothing it with a palette knife or spatula.

9 Pipe rosettes around the top of the cake and decorate with whole hazelnuts or pecan nuts, if you like.

Energy 240kcal/1000kJ; Protein 5.6g; Carbohydrate 22.2g, of which sugars 13.4g; Fat 14.9g, of which saturates 8.6g; Cholesterol 81mg; Calcium 74mg; Fibre 1g; Sodium 155mg.

Sachertorte

This glorious gâteau has a pedigree going back to 1832, when it was created by Franz Sacher, a chef of the royal household in Vienna. It is rich and dark, with a flavour that contrasts with the apricot glaze – and it's topped with a rich, glossy icing. Keep, refrigerated, for up to 3 days.

SERVES 10–12

225g/8oz dark (bittersweet) chocolate

150g/5oz/⅔ cup unsalted butter, plus extra for greasing

115g/4oz/generous ½ cup caster (superfine) sugar

8 eggs, separated

115g/4oz/1 cup plain (all-purpose) flour

For the glaze

225g/8oz apricot jam (see page 262)

15ml/1 tbsp lemon juice

For the icing

225g/8oz dark (bittersweet) chocolate, broken into pieces

200g/7oz/1 cup caster (superfine) sugar

15ml/1 tbsp golden (light corn) syrup

225ml/8fl oz/generous 1 cup double (heavy) cream

5ml/1 tsp vanilla extract

chocolate curls, to decorate (see page 162)

1 Preheat the oven to 180°C/350°F/Gas 4. Grease and line a 23cm/9in round deep cake tin (pan).

2 Melt the chocolate in a heatproof bowl set over a pan of just-simmering water, then leave to cool.

3 In a bowl, beat the butter and sugar until pale and fluffy, then add the egg yolks, one at a time, beating well.

4 Beat in the cooled melted chocolate, then sift the flour over the mixture and fold it in evenly and gently with a large metal spoon.

5 Put the egg whites into a clean, grease-free bowl and whisk until they form stiff peaks. Stir about a quarter of the whites into the chocolate mixture to lighten it, then fold in the remaining whites.

6 Pour the mixture into the prepared tin and smooth the top level. Bake for 50–55 minutes, or until firm.

7 Leave to stand in the tin for 5 minutes, then turn out on to a wire rack to go cold. Remove the lining paper. Slice in half across the middle to make two even layers.

8 To make the glaze, heat the apricot jam with the lemon juice in a small pan until melted, then strain through a sieve or strainer into a bowl.

9 Brush the top and sides of each layer with the glaze, then sandwich together. Put the cake on a wire rack.

10 To make the icing, put the chocolate, sugar, golden syrup, cream and vanilla in a pan. Heat gently, stirring constantly, until the mixture is thick and smooth.

11 Simmer gently for 3–4 minutes, without stirring, until it registers 95°C/200°F on a sugar thermometer.

12 Pour the icing quickly over the cake, spreading to cover the top and sides completely. Leave to set, then decorate with chocolate curls.

Energy 625kcal/2618kJ; Protein 7.6g; Carbohydrate 73.1g, of which sugars 65.5g; Fat 35.8g, of which saturates 20.8g; Cholesterol 184mg; Calcium 73mg; Fibre 1.2g; Sodium 143mg.

Black Forest gâteau

Perhaps the most famous chocolate cake of all, this Kirsch-flavoured gâteau is layered with fresh cream containing chopped black cherries, and is decorated with chocolate curls. It is the perfect cake for a special-occasion tea party. This will keep, refrigerated, for up to 3 days.

SERVES 10–12

5 eggs

175g/6oz/scant 1 cup caster (superfine) sugar

50g/2oz/½ cup plain (all-purpose) flour

50g/2oz/½ cup unsweetened cocoa powder

75g/2½oz/6 tbsp butter, melted, plus extra for greasing

For the filling & topping

75–90ml/5–6 tbsp Kirsch

600ml/1 pint/2½ cups double (heavy) cream

425g/15oz can black cherries, drained, pitted and chopped

For the decoration

225g/8oz plain (semisweet) chocolate, to make chocolate curls (see Cook's tip)

15–20 fresh cherries, preferably with stems

icing (confectioners') sugar, for dusting

Cook's tip

To make chocolate curls, scrape a sharp knife along the side of a bar of chocolate in one seamless movement, above a plate or board to catch the curls.

1 Preheat the oven to 180°C/350°F/Gas 4. Grease and line two 20cm/8in round deep cake tins (pans) with baking parchment.

2 Beat the eggs and sugar in a large bowl with an electric whisk for about 10 minutes, or until the mixture is thick and pale and leaves a trail when the beaters are lifted.

3 Sift together the flour and cocoa powder, then sift again into the whisked mixture.

4 Fold in gently using a metal spoon and a figure-of-eight motion. Slowly trickle in the cooled melted butter and fold in gently.

5 Divide the batter between the tins and smooth level. Bake for 30 minutes, until springy to the touch.

6 Leave in the tins for 5 minutes, then turn out on to a wire rack to cool. Peel off the lining papers.

7 Cut each cake in half horizontally. Sprinkle the four layers evenly with the Kirsch.

8 In a large bowl, whip the cream until it just holds soft peaks. Do not overwhip.

9 Transfer two-thirds of the cream to another bowl and stir in the chopped cherries for the filling.

10 Place a layer of cake on a serving plate and spread over one-third of the filling mixture. Top with another portion of cake and continue layering, finishing with the cake top.

11 Use the remaining whipped cream to cover the top and sides of the gâteau as evenly as you can. Decorate the top and sides with chocolate curls, pressing them lightly into the cream, and finish with fresh cherries and a dusting of icing sugar.

Energy 448kcal/1864kJ; Protein 4.8g; Carbohydrate 26.4g, of which sugars 22.7g; Fat 35.2g, of which saturates 21.1g; Cholesterol 161mg; Calcium 61.8mg; Fibre 0.8g; Sodium 121mg.

Coconut lime gâteau

American frosting is what makes this zesty lime and coconut gâteau so attractive. Made by whisking egg white and a sugar mixture over heat, the frosting is like a soft meringue icing. It tastes divine scattered with toasted coconut. Eat fresh or refrigerate for up to 2 days.

SERVES 10–12

225g/8oz/2 cups plain (all-purpose) flour
12.5ml/2½ tsp baking powder
225g/8oz/1 cup butter, at room temperature
225g/8oz/generous 1 cup caster (superfine) sugar
grated rind and juice of 2 limes
4 eggs
75g/2½oz/1 cup desiccated (dry unsweetened) coconut

For the frosting

275g/9½oz/1½ cups caster (superfine) sugar
2.5ml/½ tsp cream of tartar
2 egg whites
60ml/4 tbsp cold water
15ml/1 tbsp liquid glucose
10ml/2 tsp vanilla extract

1 Preheat the oven to 180°C/350°F/Gas 4. Grease and line two 23cm/9in cake tins (pans) with baking parchment.

2 Sift together the flour and baking powder into a bowl.

3 In another large bowl, beat the butter until soft. Add the sugar and lime rind, then beat until pale and fluffy.

4 Beat in the eggs, one at a time, adding 5ml/1 tsp of the flour mixture with each egg addition to stop the batter from curdling. Beat the mixture well between each addition.

5 Gently fold in the flour mixture in batches using a metal spoon, alternating with the lime juice. Stir in two-thirds of the coconut.

6 Divide the batter between the tins and spread it evenly to the sides. Bake for 30–35 minutes, or until a skewer inserted into the centre comes out clean.

7 Leave to cool in the tins for 10 minutes, then turn out to cool on a wire rack. Remove the lining papers. Leave to go cold.

8 Spread the remaining coconut on a baking tray Bake until golden brown, stirring occasionally. Watch carefully so that the coconut does not get too dark. Leave to cool in the tin.

9 To make the frosting, put the sugar in a large heatproof bowl and add the cream of tartar, egg whites, water and glucose. Stir to mix.

10 Set the bowl over a pan of boiling water. Beat the frosting with an electric whisk at high speed for 7 minutes or until thick and stiff peaks form. Remove from the heat.

11 Add the vanilla and beat for 3 minutes or until the frosting has cooled slightly. Put a cake on a plate. Spread a layer of frosting on top. Set the second cake on top.

12 Swirl the rest of the frosting all over the cake. Sprinkle with the toasted coconut and leave to set.

Energy 732kcal/3079kJ; Protein 7.3g; Carbohydrate 111g, of which sugars 59g; Fat 32g, of which saturates 20.5g; Cholesterol 155mg; Calcium 105.7mg; Fibre 2.1g; Sodium 221mg.

Cinnamon apple gâteau

Make this unusual cake for an autumn tea party. A light sponge is split and filled with a honey and cream cheese layer as well as softly cooked cinnamon apples and sultanas, then topped with glazed apples. Keep the sponge, unfilled, for 2 days in an airtight container. Fill and eat fresh.

SERVES 8–10

3 eggs
115g/4oz/generous ½ cup caster (superfine) sugar
75g/2½oz/⅔ cup plain (all-purpose) flour
5ml/1 tsp ground cinnamon

For the filling & topping
4 large eating apples
60ml/4 tbsp clear honey

75g/2½oz/generous ½ cup sultanas (golden raisins)
2.5ml/½ tsp ground cinnamon
350g/12oz/1½ cups soft cheese
60ml/4 tbsp fromage frais or crème fraîche
10ml/2 tsp lemon juice
45ml/3 tbsp sieved apricot jam
fresh mint sprigs, to decorate

1 Preheat the oven to 190°C/375°F/Gas 5. Generously grease and line a 23cm/9in round cake tin (pan) and line with baking parchment.

2 Put the eggs and sugar in a large bowl and beat with an electric whisk until thick and mousse-like and the beaters leave a trail on the surface of the mixture. This will take 5–10 minutes.

3 Sift the flour and cinnamon over the egg mixture and carefully fold in with a large metal spoon, until the flour is completely incorporated but without knocking out too much air.

4 Pour the mixture gently into the prepared tin and bake for 25–30 minutes, or until the cake springs back when lightly pressed in the centre.

5 Slide a knife between the cake and the tin to loosen the edge, then carefully turn the cake on to a wire rack to cool.

6 To make the filling, peel, core and slice three apples and put them in a pan. Add 30ml/2 tbsp of the honey along with 15ml/1 tbsp water. Cover and cook over a low heat for 10 minutes, or until the apples have softened.

7 Add the sultanas and cinnamon, stir, replace the lid and leave to cool.

8 Put the soft cheese in a bowl with the remaining honey, the fromage frais or crème fraîche and half the lemon juice. Beat until smooth.

9 Cut the cake into two equal rounds. Put half on a serving plate and drizzle over any liquid from cooking the apples.

10 Spread the surface with two-thirds of the cheese mixture, then top with the apple filling. Fit the top of the cake in place.

11 Swirl the remaining cheese mixture over the top of the sponge.

12 Core and slice the remaining apple, sprinkle with lemon juice and place around the edge of the cake. Brush the apple with jam and decorate with mint sprigs.

Energy 305kcal/1281kJ; Protein 4.6g; Carbohydrate 39.6g, of which sugars 31.6g; Fat 15.4g, of which saturates 9.6g; Cholesterol 37mg; Calcium 132mg; Fibre 0.4g; Sodium 120mg.

Raspberry & hazelnut meringue cake

Toasted and ground hazelnuts add a nutty flavour to this simple cake of meringue rounds sandwiched together with fresh cream and raspberries. Chill before serving, then eat fresh. You can store baked meringue bases, unfilled, for 1 week.

SERVES 8

150g/5oz/1¼ cups hazelnuts
4 egg whites
200g/7oz/1 cup caster (superfine) sugar
2.5ml/½ tsp vanilla extract

300ml/½ pint/1¼ cups whipping cream, whipped to soft peaks
450g/1lb/4 cups raspberries
icing (confectioners') sugar, for dusting

1 Preheat the oven to 180°C/350°F/Gas 4. Grease and line the bases of two 20cm/8in round cake tins (pans) with baking parchment.

2 Spread the hazelnuts on a baking sheet and bake for 8 minutes, or until lightly toasted.

3 Leave to cool slightly. Rub the hazelnuts vigorously in a clean dish towel to remove the skins. Reduce the oven temperature to 150°C/300°F/Gas 2.

4 Grind the nuts in a food processor, until they are the consistency of coarse sand.

5 Put the egg whites into a clean, grease-free bowl and whip until they form stiff peaks. Beat in 30ml/2 tbsp of the sugar, then fold in the remaining sugar, a few spoonfuls at a time. Fold in the vanilla and hazelnuts.

6 Divide the mixture between the tins and smooth the top. Bake for 1¼ hours until firm.

7 Leave to cool for 5 minutes, then run a knife around tins to loosen. Turn out to cool on a wire rack.

8 Spread half the cream on one cake and top with half the raspberries. Top with the other cake, the remaining cream and raspberries. Dust with icing sugar just before serving.

Energy 298kcal/1252kJ; Protein 3.2g; Carbohydrate 39.5g, of which sugars 39.5g; Fat 15.3g, of which saturates 9.5g; Cholesterol 39mg; Calcium 55mg; Fibre 1.4g; Sodium 44mg.

Summer celebration shortcake

A departure from the usual summer shortcake, this teatime treat contains crunchy almonds, which go particularly well with the juicy strawberries and cream filling. The top layer is divided into portions, giving it an attractive appearance as well as making it easier to serve.

SERVES 8

175g/6oz/¾ cup butter
150g/5oz/1¼ cups plain (all-purpose) flour
115g/4oz/1 cup ground almonds
50g/2oz/¼ cup caster (superfine) sugar
25g/1oz/¼ cup flaked (sliced) almonds

For the filling & decoration

450g/1lb/4 cups strawberries
300ml/½ pint/1¼ cups double (heavy) cream
15ml/1 tbsp amaretto (optional)
icing (confectioners') sugar, for dusting

1 Preheat the oven to 180°C/350°F/Gas 4. Grease two baking sheets.

2 Rub the butter into the flour until it forms fine crumbs, then stir in the ground almonds and sugar. Mix to a soft dough and knead until smooth.

3 Roll half of the dough into a 20cm/8in round and cut out neatly. Put on a baking sheet and sprinkle over half the almonds.

4 Knead the trimmings and the rest of the dough to make a second shortcake round. Sprinkle over the almonds. Prick each with a fork.

5 Bake for 20 minutes, or until pale golden. While still warm, mark the flattest shortbread into eight even triangles and leave to cool. Cut the triangles when cold.

6 For the filling, reserve nine strawberries. Hull and chop the rest. Whip the cream to soft peaks. Place a quarter in a piping or pastry bag with a star nozzle.

7 Fold the berries into the remaining cream with the liqueur, if using.

8 Put the whole shortbread on a serving plate. Pile the fruit filling on top and arrange the eight triangles on top with points facing inwards.

9 Pipe a cream rosette on each one and top with a strawberry, then put the last strawberry in the centre. Dust lightly with icing sugar. Serve immediately.

Energy 240kcal/1000kJ; Protein 5.6g; Carbohydrate 22.2g, of which sugars 13.4g; Fat 14.9g, of which saturates 8.6g; Cholesterol 81mg; Calcium 74mg; Fibre 1g; Sodium 155mg.

No-bake berry crispy cake

Everyone loves a crispy cake – and this is a grown-up version fit for a teatime table. It looks utterly kitsch but offers the irresistible combination of rich cream with a crunchy marshmallow base and ripe fresh strawberries, blueberries and raspberries.

SERVES 8
For the base
225g/8oz marshmallows
50g/2oz/4 tbsp butter
100g/3½oz/3½ cups rice crispies
90g/3oz white chocolate, broken into pieces

For the topping
250ml/8½fl oz/1¼ cups clotted or whipped cream
400g/14oz/3 cups fresh berries
icing (confectioners') sugar, for dusting

1 Grease and line a 23cm/9in round springform tin (pan) with baking parchment.

2 Place the marshmallows and butter in a pan over a gentle heat until they have melted and are combined, stirring all the time.

3 Add the rice crispies to the pan and stir well so that all the crispies are coated in the marshmallow mixture.

4 Spoon the crispy mixture into the prepared tin and press down to an even layer with the back of a spoon.

5 Break the white chocolate into pieces and place in a heatproof bowl over a pan of simmering water. Leave to melt, making sure that the base of the bowl does not touch the water.

6 Spread the melted chocolate over the top of the crispy cake layer and leave to set.

7 When you are ready to serve and the white chocolate has set, take the cake out of the tin and remove the lining paper.

8 Place the cake on a serving plate and cover the white chocolate layer with the thick cream. Top with the mixed fresh berries and finish off with a light dusting of icing sugar.

9 As the cake contains fresh cream serve it straight away or store in the refrigerator. This cake should be eaten on the day it is made and will not keep.

Cook's tip
White chocolate can be a bit tricky to melt, since if it gets too hot, or if you stir it too much, it very easily seizes, which means it goes lumpy. In fact the cheaper brands of white chocolate tend to be more stable, and don't taste remarkably different from more expensive types, so are often a good choice.

Energy 440kcal/1837kJ; Protein 3.8g; Carbohydrate 46g, of which sugars 30.4g; Fat 28.1g, of which saturates 17.4g; Cholesterol 64mg; Calcium 111mg; Fibre 0.9g; Sodium 157mg.

White chocolate & blueberry cheesecake

This cake has such a pretty delicate purple and white colour that it looks simply spectacular as the centrepiece of a teatime table. You can make your own flapjacks for the base (see page 126, omitting the cherries) but for a quick and easy cake it is fine to use ready-made.

SERVES 10–12

For the blueberry compote & syrup

50g/2oz/¼ cup caster (superfine) sugar
250g/9oz/1 cup blueberries
juice of 2 lemons

For the base & topping

300g/10oz soft flapjacks
115g/4oz white chocolate
150ml/5fl oz/⅔ cup crème fraîche
250g/9oz/1 cup mascarpone cheese

1 Grease and line a 23cm/9in round loose-bottomed cake tin (pan).

2 Place the sugar, blueberries and lemon juice in a pan and simmer over a gentle heat for about 5 minutes until the fruit is very soft and the liquid is syrupy.

3 Place a fine-mesh sieve or strainer over a bowl and pour in the cooked blueberries to separate the fruit and the syrup. Do not press the fruit down as you want the fruit to remain juicy. Leave to cool.

4 Press the flapjacks into the base of the tin, pressing them down with your hands so that they form a complete layer.

5 Using a swivel peeler, make chocolate curls with around 20g/¾oz of the white chocolate by pulling the peeler along the long edge of the chocolate bar. It is important that the chocolate is at room temperature.

6 Place the remaining white chocolate in a heatproof bowl resting over a pan of simmering water and heat until the chocolate has melted.

7 Spoon the melted white chocolate over the flapjack base and spread out evenly, then spread over the blueberry fruit.

8 In a separate bowl, whisk together most of the blueberry syrup, crème fraîche and mascarpone cheese until the mixture is thick.

9 Spoon the creamy mixture into the tin on top of the fruit and spread out into an even layer.

10 Drizzle over the remaining blueberry syrup and swirl in, using a fork to make a decorative pattern. Top the dessert with the white chocolate curls and chill in the refrigerator for 3 hours. This will store for up to 3 days in the refrigerator.

Energy 305kcal/1281kJ; Protein 4.6g; Carbohydrate 39.6g, of which sugars 31.6g; Fat 15.4g, of which saturates 9.6g; Cholesterol 37mg; Calcium 132mg; Fibre 0.4g; Sodium 120mg.

Praline chocolate cheesecake

Chocolate, bananas and walnut praline – are there many better combinations? Use ripe bananas for full flavour. This cheesecake is also delicious with pecans or Brazil nuts in place of the walnuts, or use a mixture of all three.

SERVES 10–12

For the walnut praline & decoration
90g/3oz/½ cup caster (superfine) sugar
90g/3oz/scant 1 cup walnut halves
200ml/7fl oz/⅔ cup double (heavy) cream

For the biscuit case
300g/10oz Oreo or similar chocolate cookies
115g/4oz/½ cup butter

For the cheesecake
400ml/14fl oz/1⅔ cups double (heavy) cream
5ml/1 tsp ground cinnamon

5 sheets leaf gelatine (platinum grade)
2 ripe bananas
juice of 1 lemon
500g/1lb2oz/2 cups full-fat cream cheese

For the chocolate sauce
250ml/8½fl oz/1¼ cups double (heavy) cream
90g/3oz/7 tbsp butter
150g/5oz plain (semisweet) chocolate
30ml/2 tbsp golden (light corn) syrup

1 Grease and line a 23cm/9in loose-bottomed round springform cake tin (pan).

2 Begin by preparing the walnut praline. Heat the sugar in a pan until melted and lightly golden brown. Take care towards the end of cooking as the caramel can burn quickly. Do not stir the pan as the sugar is cooking but swirl it to ensure that the sugar does not burn.

3 Spread the walnuts out on a silicone mat or greased baking sheet, mostly in a flat layer – place around 10–12 individually as these will be used to decorate the top of the cheesecake. Using a spoon or fork drizzle swirls of the caramel over the individual walnuts in pretty patterns, then carefully pour the remaining caramel over the rest of the walnuts.

4 Once cool put the individual walnut decorations into an airtight container and blitz the larger walnut praline in a food processor or blender to very fine crumbs.

5 For the biscuit case, crush the cookies to fine crumbs in a food processor or use a rolling pin to crush them in a clean plastic bag.

6 Melt the butter in a pan and stir in the biscuit crumbs. Press the biscuit crumb mixture into the base and sides of the prepared tin using the back of a spoon. You want the crumbs to come about 2.5cm/1in up the sides of the cake tin.

7 For the cheesecake filling, heat the cream and cinnamon in a pan until warm. Soak the gelatine leaves in water until they are soft, then squeeze out the water.

8 Add the gelatine to the warm cream and stir the mixture until the gelatine has dissolved. Pass the mixture through a fine mesh sieve or strainer.

9 Wrap the tin in clear film (plastic wrap) to ensure there are no leaks. Peel the bananas and discard the skins.

10 In a bowl, whisk the bananas, lemon juice and walnut praline powder together until you have a smooth purée. Add the cream cheese and whisk again, then whisk in the cinnamon cream mixture.

11 Pour the cheesecake filling into the biscuit case. Chill the cheesecake in the refrigerator for at least 3 hours or overnight.

12 To make the chocolate sauce simmer the cream, butter, chocolate and syrup in a pan over a gentle heat until the butter and chocolate have melted. Allow to cool slightly.

13 For the decoration, whisk the cream to stiff peaks in a clean bowl and then spoon into the piping bag. Pipe stars of cream around the edge of the cheesecake and top with the whole caramelized walnut decorations.

14 Serve the cheesecake with the warm chocolate sauce drizzled over. This cheesecake will store for up to 3 days in the refrigerator.

Energy 1180kcal/4882kJ; Protein 7.6g; Carbohydrate 48.4g, of which sugars 36.4g; Fat 107.5g, of which saturates 62.7g; Cholesterol 232mg; Calcium 140mg; Fibre 1.2g; Sodium 451mg.

St Clement's cheesecake

This zesty tangy cheesecake makes a perfect teatime treat – citrus flavours are so refreshing. You can use limes, lemons or oranges in any combination you want. Ginger work well with citrus but you can substitute digestive biscuits or graham crackers instead.

SERVES 10–12

For the base
300g/10oz ginger biscuits or cookies
150g/5oz/⅔ cup butter

For the cheesecake
300g/10oz good-quality lemon curd

500g/1lb2oz/2½ cups mascarpone
500g/1lb2oz/2½ cups crème fraîche
30ml/2 tbsp icing (confectioners') sugar, plus extra for dusting
zest and juice of 1 small orange
zest and juice of 1 lemon

1 Grease and line a 23cm/9in round loose-bottomed cake tin (pan).

2 Crush the ginger biscuits to fine crumbs in a food processor or blender, or use a rolling pin to crush the biscuits in a clean plastic bag.

3 Gently melt the butter in a large pan over a low heat, then pour in the biscuit crumbs and stir to combine well. Press into the base of the prepared tin using the back of a spoon.

4 Spread two-thirds of the lemon curd evenly over the biscuit base.

5 In a mixing bowl, whisk together the mascarpone and crème fraîche until smooth.

6 Sift in the icing sugar, add the lemon and orange zest and juice and remaining lemon curd then whisk again. Taste the mixture and add a little more icing sugar if you wish it to be sweeter.

7 Spoon the cheesecake mixture over the biscuit base and level with a knife or spatula. Chill in the refrigerator for at least 3 hours or until set.

8 To decorate, dust with a little icing sugar and sprinkle over a little grated zest if you wish. Alternatively you could reserve a few spoonfuls of the buttery biscuit crumb mixture and sprinkle that over the top.

Variation
For a lemon and lime version replace the orange juice with the juice of 2 limes.

Energy 523kcal/2176kJ; Protein 6.6g; Carbohydrate 40.6g, of which sugars 22.6g; Fat 38.2g, of which saturates 24.1g; Cholesterol 99mg; Calcium 103mg; Fibre 0g; Sodium 328mg.

Small cakes, muffins & fancies

The highlight of a teatime table is a selection of small but perfectly formed sweet treats, arranged pleasingly on a plate or tiered cake stand. Whether simple, everyday cakes or elaborate fondant fancies, cake pops, and extravagently iced cupcakes, they are sure to elicit 'oohs' and 'aahs' as they are brought out. Some of these creations are very quick and easy to make, while others are more involved and are intended for special occasions. All are delicious.

Left Miniature cake pops offer everything – sponge, jam and cream – in one delectable mouthful. Make up a selection of light and delicate little cakes for a special tea party.

Brandy snaps with cream

There are historical accounts of brandy snaps being sold at fairs in the north of England in the 19th century, and they were a special treat for high days and holidays. They make a lovely surprise for afternoon tea.

MAKES 12

50g/2oz/4 tbsp butter
50g/2oz/¼ cup caster (superfine) sugar
30ml/2 tbsp golden (light corn) syrup
50g/2oz/½ cup plain (all-purpose) flour

2.5ml/½ tsp ground ginger
5ml/1 tsp brandy
150ml/5fl oz/⅔ cup double (heavy) or whipping cream

1 Preheat the oven to 180°C/350°F/Gas 4. Line two or three baking sheets with baking parchment.

2 Gently heat the butter, sugar and golden syrup in a small pan until melted and the sugar dissolved.

3 Remove the pan from the heat. Sift the flour and ginger and stir into the mixture with the brandy

4 Put small spoonfuls of the mixture on the baking sheets, spacing them 10cm/4in apart for spreading. Bake for 7–8 minutes or until bubbling and golden. Meanwhile, grease the handles of several wooden spoons.

5 Allow the wafers to cool on the sheet for about 1 minute then loosen with a metal spatula and quickly roll around the spoon handles. Leave to set for 1 minute, then slide them off the handles and cool completely on a wire rack.

6 Just before serving, whip the cream to soft peaks and pipe some into both ends of each brandy snap.

Energy 121kcal/505kJ; Protein 0.6g; Carbohydrate 11.7g, of which sugars 10g; Fat 7.9g, of which saturates 5g; Cholesterol 21mg; Calcium 16mg; Fibre 0.1g; Sodium 24mg.

Coconut macaroons

These delicate, aromatic cakes are simple for children to make with a little supervision, as just a few ingredients are needed. They are best served warm, straight from the oven, but will keep reasonably well in an airtight container.

MAKES 14

225g/8oz/2½ cups desiccated (dry unsweetened shredded) coconut

300g/10oz/scant 1½ cups caster (superfine) sugar

3 egg whites

Cook's tip
These easy three-ingredient cakes won't freeze but they are very quick to rustle up when needed.

1 Preheat the oven to 180°C/350°F/Gas 4. Line a cake or muffin tin (pan) with paper cases.

2 Put the coconut, sugar and egg whites in a large heavy pan and stir over a low heat with a wooden spoon for about 5 minutes, or until just warmed through.

3 Spoon a heaped tablespoonful of the mixture into each paper case, and bake for about 15 minutes until pale golden. Allow to cool on a wire rack.

Energy 190cal/793kJ; Protein 1.5g; Carbohydrate 16g, of which sugars 16g; Fat 13.9g, of which saturates 10.6g; Cholesterol 25mg; Calcium 17mg; Fibre 2g; Sodium 12mg.

Chocolate mini macaroons

These bite-sized macaroons are just right for a tea party. They combine moist coconut with dark chocolate, making a chewy macaroon with a slightly toasted outer edge. Eat quickly before the chocolate sets firm, for the ultimate taste sensation.

MAKES 18

2 egg whites
125g/4¼oz/⅔ cup caster (superfine) sugar
pinch of salt
10ml/2 tsp clear honey

100g/3½oz/generous 1 cup (dry unsweetened shredded) coconut
2.5ml/½ tsp vanilla extract
100g/3½oz dark (bittersweet) chocolate, broken into pieces

1 Preheat the oven to 160°C/325°F/Gas 3. Line a baking sheet with baking parchment.

2 Combine all of the ingredients, except the chocolate, in a heavy pan and cook over a medium heat for about 7 minutes until the mixture is opaque and sticky. The coconut should just begin to scorch on the bottom of the pan. Transfer the mixture to a clean bowl and allow it to cool.

3 Drop tablespoonfuls of the mixture on to the baking sheet. Using the end of a wooden spoon, make small depressions in the centre of each macaroon. Place in the oven and bake for about 12 minutes, until the macaroons are just golden around the edges.

4 Place the chocolate in a heatproof bowl and position over a pan of barely simmering water, making sure the water does not touch the bottom of the bowl. Leave, stirring occasionally, until the chocolate has melted.

5 Transfer the melted chocolate to a piping or pastry bag with a fine nozzle and fill the centre of each macaroon. Leave till almost set then serve immediately. These are best eaten on the day they are made while the chocolate is still slightly soft, but they can be stored in an airtight container for up to 2 days.

Energy 93kcal/390kJ; Protein 0.9g; Carbohydrate 11.6g, of which sugars 11.3g; Fat 5.1g, of which saturates 3.9g; Cholesterol 1mg; Calcium 7mg; Fibre 0.8g; Sodium 9mg.

Madeleines

These small shell-shaped sponge cakes are light as a feather and traditionally served with a cup of tea. In France on Christmas Eve, however, you'll find them coloured a delicate pink and accompanied by a glass of champagne. Eat these fresh on the day they are made. Do not freeze.

MAKES 15

2 eggs
50g/2oz/¼ cup vanilla caster (superfine) sugar
50g/2oz/½ cup plain (all-purpose) flour, plus extra for dusting
50g/2oz/4 tbsp unsalted butter, melted, plus extra for greasing
a few drops of orange flower water
icing (confectioners') sugar, for dusting
caramel or chocolate sauce, to serve (optional)

1 Preheat the oven to 200°C/400°F/Gas 6. Lightly grease a scalloped madeleine mould with a little melted butter, making sure all the indentations are greased well, so the cakes are released easily. Dust with a little flour, shake the tin, then tap out any excess.

2 Put the eggs and sugar in a heatproof bowl set over a pan of hot water. Whisk until very thick and mousse-like, and the mixture leaves a thick ribbon trail when the beaters are lifted away. Remove from the heat and continue whisking for 2 minutes.

3 Sift half the flour over the surface and fold in gently with a large metal spoon, then repeat with the remaining flour. Gently fold in the cooled melted butter and the orange flower water.

4 Spoon the mixture into the moulds to just level with the top. Smooth level and bake for 10 minutes, or until firm and pale golden.

5 Cool in the tin for a few minutes, then turn out to cool on a wire rack. Re-grease and flour the madeleine moulds, then use up the remaining batter and bake in the same way.

6 Serve the madeleines with the shell sides upward, dusted with icing sugar, accompanied by caramel or chocolate sauce for dipping, if you like.

Variation
If you like you could colour the batter with a few drops of pink food colouring.

Energy 130kcal/547kJ; Protein 2.4g; Carbohydrate 17.3g, of which sugars 6.8g; Fat 6.2g, of which saturates 3.5g; Cholesterol 45mg; Calcium 28mg; Fibre 0.4g; Sodium 50mg.

Honey & spice cakes

These little golden cakes are fragrant with honey and cinnamon and are ideal for an autumnal afternoon tea. Though their appearance is more traditional when they are cooked directly in a bun tin, they tend to rise higher and are therefore lighter when baked in paper cases.

MAKES 18

250g/9oz/2¼ cups plain (all-purpose) flour
5ml/1 tsp ground cinnamon
5ml/1 tsp bicarbonate of soda (baking soda)
130g/4½oz/generous ½ cup butter, softened
125g/4¼oz/⅔ cup soft dark brown sugar
1 egg, separated
125g/4¼oz/10 tbsp clear honey
60ml/4 tbsp milk

1 Preheat the oven to 200°C/400°F/ Gas 6. Grease the cups of two bun tins (pans) or line them with paper cases.

2 Sift the flour into a large mixing bowl, together with the ground cinnamon and the bicarbonate of soda.

3 Beat the butter with the sugar in another large mixing bowl until the mixture is very light and fluffy.

4 Beat in the egg yolk, then gradually add the honey.

5 Lightly fold the flour, spice and bicarbonate of soda into the mixture until just combined.

6 Add sufficient milk from the measured amount to make a soft mixture that will just drop off the spoon. Do not make the mixture too wet or the cakes will be heavy.

7 In a separate bowl, whisk the egg white until stiff peaks form. Using a large metal spoon, fold the egg white gently into the cake mixture.

8 Divide the mixture among the tins or cases. Bake for about 25 minutes, until lightly coloured.

9 Leave to stand for 5 minutes before transferring to a wire rack to cool.

Energy 152kcal/639kJ; Protein 1.9g; Carbohydrate 23.6g, of which sugars 13g; Fat 6.3g, of which saturates 3.8g; Cholesterol 26mg; Calcium 30mg; Fibre 0.4g; Sodium 49mg.

Gooey butterscotch cakes

If you like, you can make up the two mixtures for these cakes the night before a tea party and stir them together first thing next day for an irresistible mid-afternoon treat. Instead of butterscotch, you could try adding chocolate chips, marshmallows or blueberries.

MAKES 9–12

150g/5oz butterscotch sweets
225g/8oz/2 cups plain
(all purpose) flour, plus extra for
dusting
90g/3oz/½ cup golden caster
(superfine) sugar
10ml/2 tsp baking powder

pinch of salt
1 egg, beaten
150ml/5fl oz/⅔ cup milk
50ml/2fl oz/4 tbsp sunflower oil
or melted butter
75g/2½oz/¾ cup chopped
hazelnuts

1 Preheat the oven to 200°C/400°F/ Gas 6. Arrange 9–12 paper cases in a muffin tin (pan).

2 With floured fingers, break the butterscotch sweets into small chunks. Toss them in a little flour, if necessary, to prevent them from sticking together.

3 Sift together the flour, sugar, baking powder and salt into a large mixing bowl.

4 Whisk together the egg, milk and oil or melted butter, then stir the mixture into the dry ingredients with the sweets and nuts. Stir together only lightly – the mixture should be lumpy.

5 Spoon the batter evenly into the paper cases, filling about half full.

6 Bake for 20 minutes, until risen and golden. They should spring back when pressed lightly in the centre.

7 Leave the muffins in the tin for 5 minutes, then remove and transfer to a wire rack to cool.

Energy 224kcal/941kJ; Protein 3.9g; Carbohydrate 31.7g, of which sugars 14.6g; Fat 10g, of which saturates 2.1g; Cholesterol 19mg; Calcium 66mg; Fibre 1g; Sodium 55mg.

Chocolate chip cupcakes

Nothing could be easier – or nicer – than these classic cakes. The cake mixture is plain, but has a surprise layer of chocolate chips inside. Sprinkle a few chocolate chips on top of the cakes to make them look irresistible. They are delicious eaten warm with your favourite tea.

MAKES 10

115g/4oz/½ cup butter, softened
75g/2½oz/scant ½ cup caster
(superfine) sugar
30ml/2 tbsp soft dark
brown sugar
2 eggs
175g/6oz/1½ cups plain
(all-purpose) flour
5ml/1 tsp baking powder
120ml/4fl oz/½ cup milk
175g/6oz/1 cup plain (semisweet)
chocolate chips

Variation
You can add all sorts of other flavours to these simple, popular little cakes. These include vanilla extract and grated orange rind as well as ground spices such as ginger or cinnamon, or even finely ground cardamom seeds or a tiny pinch of chilli powder.

1 Preheat the oven to 190°C/375°F/ Gas 5. Arrange 10 paper cases in a muffin tin (pan).

2 n a large bowl, beat the butter until it is pale and light. Add the caster and dark brown sugars and beat until the mixture is light and fluffy.

3 Beat in the eggs, one at a time, beating thoroughly after each addition.

4 Sift the flour and baking powder together twice. Fold into the butter mixture, alternating with the milk.

5 Divide half the mixture among the paper cases. Sprinkle with half the chocolate chips, then cover with the remaining mixture and the rest of the chocolate chips.

6 Bake for about 25 minutes, until golden. Leave to stand for 5 minutes then transfer to a wire rack to cool.

Energy 296kcal/1241kJ; Protein 4.2g; Carbohydrate 36.5g, of which sugars 22.3g; Fat 15.9g, of which saturates 9.5g; Cholesterol 67mg; Calcium 59mg; Fibre 0.5g; Sodium 110mg.

Chunky chocolate & banana cupcakes

Luxurious and moist but not overly sweet, these cakes are simple and quick to make for afternoon tea. They taste best if served while still warm, when the chocolate is soft and gooey. The cakes will keep for a couple of days.

MAKES 12

90ml/3fl oz/6 tbsp semi-skimmed (low-fat) milk
2 eggs
150g/5oz/⅔ cup butter, melted
225g/8oz/2 cups plain (all-purpose) flour
5ml/1 tsp baking powder
150g/5oz/¾ cup golden caster (superfine) sugar
150g/5oz plain (semisweet) chocolate, cut into chunks
2 small bananas, mashed

Cook's tip
Choose bananas that are fully ripe and can be mashed easily.

1 Preheat the oven to 200°C/400°F/ Gas 6. Arrange 12 paper cases in a muffin tin (pan).

2 In a small bowl, whisk the milk, eggs and melted butter together until combined.

3 Sift together the flour and baking powder into a separate bowl. Add the sugar, chocolate and bananas to the flour mixture.

4 Stir gently to combine, gradually stirring in the milk and egg mixture, but do not beat it. Spoon the mixture into the paper cases.

5 Bake for about 20 minutes until the cakes are risen and golden.

6 Allow to stand for 5 minutes, then turn out and leave to cool on a wire rack.

Energy 303kcal/1268kJ; Protein 4g; Carbohydrate 40g, of which sugars 24.6g; Fat 15.2g, of which saturates 9.3g; Cholesterol 62mg; Calcium 54mg; Fibre 0.8g; Sodium 112mg.

Lemon cream cakes

Add a zing to teatime with the freshly baked citrus aromas of these lemony cakes. They are topped with a fresh lemon crème fraîche frosting, decorated with candied lemon rind, and dusted with icing sugar.

MAKES 8–9

225g/8oz/2 cups plain (all-purpose) flour
10ml/2 tsp baking powder
150g/5oz/¾ cup caster (superfine) sugar, or 75ml/5 tbsp clear honey
1 egg, beaten
350ml/12fl oz/1½ cups natural (plain) yogurt
15ml/1 tbsp grated lemon rind
75g/2½oz/6 tbsp butter, melted

For the frosting

150g/5oz/⅔ cup butter, softened
350g/12oz/3 cups icing (confectioners') sugar, plus extra for dusting
150g/5oz/⅔ cup crème fraîche
juice and rind of 1 lemon
candied lemon rind, to decorate

1 To make the frosting, put the softened butter in a bowl, and whisk at low speed, gradually adding the icing sugar and crème fraîche in alternate amounts. Continue to beat the mixture with a wooden spoon, adding the lemon juice and rind, for about 3 minutes until thick and creamy. Cover and chill for an hour or more to firm up while you make the cakes.

2 Preheat the oven to 180°C/350°F/Gas 4. Line the cups of a bun tin (pan) with paper cases.

3 Sift the flour and baking powder into a large bowl and stir in the sugar (but not the honey, if using).

4 In another bowl, mix together the egg, yogurt, lemon rind, honey (if using) and melted butter. Add to the dry ingredients and fold lightly together until just mixed.

5 Spoon the mixture into the paper cases, to about two-thirds full. Bake for 25 minutes until springy to the touch. Leave to cool on a wire rack.

6 Spread the frosting over the cakes, dust liberally with icing sugar and garnish with candied lemon rind.

Energy 211kcal/887kJ; Protein 2.1g; Carbohydrate 32.7g, of which sugars 25.4g; Fat 8.9g, of which saturates 5.5g; Cholesterol 54mg; Calcium 32mg; Fibre 0.3g; Sodium 85mg.

Vanilla cream cupcakes

These cakes have at their base a simple vanilla sponge, transformed by a snowy topping, which is a velvety-smooth, luxurious meringue-style frosting. Serve fresh for the best flavour, or store for up to 3 days.

MAKES 8–9

175g/6oz/¾ cup butter, softened
150g/5oz/¾ cup caster (superfine) sugar
5ml/1 tsp vanilla extract
4 eggs, lightly beaten
175g/6oz/1½ cups self-raising (self-rising) flour, sifted

For the topping

175g/6oz/scant 1 cup caster (superfine) sugar
3 egg whites
175g/6oz/¾ cup butter, softened
1 vanilla pod (bean), split for the seeds, and the pods cut into strips to decorate
icing (confectioners') sugar, for dusting

1 Preheat the oven to 180°C/350°F/Gas 4. Line the cups of a bun tin (pan) with paper cases.

2 Beat the softened butter with the sugar using an electric mixer until light and creamy. Add the vanilla extract. Gradually add the eggs, beating well after each addition. Add the sifted flour and fold in lightly until just combined.

3 Spoon the mixture into the paper cases and bake for 20 minutes until golden brown and firm to the touch. Allow the cakes to cool a little in the tin, then turn them out on to a wire rack to cool completely.

4 To make the topping, put 45ml/3 tbsp water in a pan with the sugar and heat gently to dissolve. Bring to the boil until it reaches 121°C/250°F. Remove from the heat.

5 Beat the egg whites to form peaks. Gradually pour the syrup in a thin steady stream over the egg whites, whisking constantly at a low speed, until the meringue is thick and cold (about 10–15 minutes). Set aside.

6 In a separate bowl, beat the butter until creamy. Gradually add the meringue with the vanilla seeds, whisking well after each addition.

7 Put the meringue in a piping bag and pipe small balls over the cupcakes; add strips of vanilla if you like to decorate, and a dusting of icing sugar.

Energy 618kcal/2587kJ; Protein 5g; Carbohydrate 76.8g, of which sugars 62.4g; Fat 34.5g, of which saturates 21.7g; Cholesterol 174mg; Calcium 118mg; Fibre 0.6g; Sodium 396mg.

Butterfly cakes

These pretty little cakes are filled with a simple vanilla buttercream. The butterfly 'wings' are so easy to make, but when dusted with icing sugar make a really elegant decoration.

MAKES 8–10

175g/6oz/¾ cup unsalted butter, softened

175g/6oz/¾ cup caster (superfine) sugar

5ml/1 tsp vanilla extract

4 eggs, lightly beaten

175g/6oz/1½ cups self-raising (self-rising) flour, sifted

For the buttercream

75g/2½oz/6 tbsp unsalted butter, softened

175g/6oz/1½ cups icing (confectioners') sugar, plus extra for dusting

½ vanilla pod (bean), or a few drops of vanilla extract

1 Preheat the oven to 180°C/350°F/Gas 4. Line a bun tin (pan) with paper cases.

2 Beat the butter and sugar together until light and creamy. Add the vanilla.

3 Gradually add the eggs, beating well after each addition. Add the sifted flour and fold into the mixture until just combined.

4 Divide the mixture among the paper cases and bake for 20 minutes until the cakes are golden brown and the centres feel firm to the touch.

5 Remove from the oven. Leave to cool in the tin for 5 minutes, then turn out on to a wire rack to cool completely.

6 To make the buttercream filling, beat the butter and icing sugar together until smooth. For the best vanilla flavour, split the vanilla pod in half and scrape out the seeds. Discard the pod and mix the seeds into the buttercream. Alternatively, add a few drops of vanilla extract to the mixture.

7 When the cakes have cooled, carefully cut round the lightly domed tops with a small sharp knife and remove the top of each cake. Slice the tops in half to form two semicircles, to make the butterfly wings. Set aside.

8 Use a piping or icing bag with a star nozzle to pipe a whirl of buttercream into each cake.

9 Press the wings into the cream and dust with icing sugar.

Energy 455kcal/1905kJ; Protein 4.8g; Carbohydrate 55.3g, of which sugars 40.9g; Fat 25.4g, of which saturates 15.7g; Cholesterol 148mg; Calcium 106mg; Fibre 0.6g; Sodium 312mg.

Carrot & apple passionettes

These treats are popular with children and adults, and are perfect for an autumn tea table with their apple and carrot sponge, warming mixed spice flavouring, and walnut topping.

MAKES 24

150g/5oz/⅔ cup butter, melted
200g/7oz/1 cup soft light brown sugar
115g/4oz carrots, peeled and finely grated
50g/2oz dessert apples, peeled and finely grated
pinch of salt
5–10ml/1–2 tsp mixed (apple pie) spice
2 eggs
200g/7oz/1¾ cups self-raising (self-rising) flour

10ml/2 tsp baking powder
115g/4oz/1 cup walnuts, finely chopped

For the topping

175g/6oz/¾ cup cream cheese
75ml/5 tbsp single (light) cream
50g/2oz/½ cup icing (confectioners') sugar
24 walnut halves
10ml/2 tsp unsweetened cocoa powder

1 Preheat the oven to 180°C/350°F/ Gas 4. Arrange 24 small paper cases in muffin or cupcake trays.

2 Beat the butter, sugar, carrot, apple, salt, mixed spice and eggs together until well combined. Sift in the flour and baking powder, add the walnuts and fold in evenly.

3 Half-fill the cases and bake for 20–25 minutes until golden or they spring back when pressed lightly. Leave the cakes in the tins for a few minutes then transfer them to a wire rack to cool.

4 To make the topping, beat the cream cheese, cream and icing sugar in a mixing bowl together until smooth.

5 Put a spoonful of the topping in the centre of each cake, then decorate with the walnut halves. Dust with sifted cocoa powder and allow the icing to set before serving.

Energy 194kcal/808kJ; Protein 3.1g; Carbohydrate 18.3g, of which sugars 11.8g; Fat 12.6g, of which saturates 5.5g; Cholesterol 37mg; Calcium 38mg; Fibre 0.7g; Sodium 75mg.

Raspberry crunch friands

In this recipe egg whites are combined with ground nuts, melted butter and very little flour. The raw mixture has quite a loose consistency, but don't worry – as the cakes bake they will become just as firm and well risen as other cakes with a higher proportion of flour.

MAKES 12

175g/6oz/¾ cup butter, plus extra for greasing
115g/4oz/1 cup ground almonds
225g/8oz/2 cups icing (confectioners') sugar, sifted
65g/2½oz/generous ½ cup plain (all-purpose) flour, sifted, plus extra for dusting
6 egg whites
115g/4oz/1 cup fresh raspberries

For the sugar frosting

juice of 1 small lemon
150g/5oz/¾ cup caster (superfine) sugar
very finely cut strips of candied lemon rind
icing (confectioners') sugar, for dusting

1 Preheat the oven to 200°C/400°F/ Gas 6. Grease the cups of a friand or bun tin (pan) with a little melted butter and dust lightly with flour. Turn the tin upside down and tap it sharply on the work surface to get rid of any excess flour.

2 Melt the butter, remove from the heat and set aside to cool slightly.

3 Put the ground almonds, icing sugar and flour in a mixing bowl and stir together.

4 In a separate bowl, beat the egg whites lightly for about 15 seconds, or just enough to break them up. Add the egg whites to the dry ingredients and mix them together gently.

5 Add the melted butter and mix until just combined.

6 Pour the mixture into the cups of the baking tin and press one raspberry into the centre of each.

7 Bake for 20–25 minutes until the friands are pale golden and springy to the touch. Leave to cool slightly then turn them out on to a wire rack.

8 To make the sugar frosting, mix the lemon juice with the sugar and set aside for 10 minutes for the sugar to partly dissolve.

9 Drizzle over the tops of the cooled cakes and leave to set for several hours. Top with a few curls of candied lemon rind and dust with icing sugar if you like.

Energy 317kcal/1330kJ; Protein 4.4g; Carbohydrate 38.3g, of which sugars 33.6g; Fat 17.4g, of which saturates 8.4g; Cholesterol 34mg; Calcium 53mg; Fibre 1.1g; Sodium 143mg.

Little Madeira cakes with cream & jam

These cakes look as good as they taste. The Madeira cake mixture, enriched with ground almonds and Calvados, rises beautifully into a perfect dome. When the cakes have cooled the domes are sliced away to make room for a mouthwatering filling of buttercream and jam.

MAKES 14

225g/8oz/1 cup butter, softened
225g/8oz/generous 1 cup caster
(superfine) sugar
4 eggs
225g/8oz/2 cups self-raising
(self-rising) flour
115g/4oz/1 cup plain
(all-purpose) flour
60ml/4 tbsp ground almonds
5ml/1 tsp finely grated lemon rind
30ml/2 tbsp Calvados, brandy or
milk

For the filling

175g/6oz/¾ cup butter, softened
350g/12oz/3 cups icing
(confectioners') sugar, plus extra
for dusting
20ml/4 tsp lemon juice
20ml/4 tsp warm water
60ml/4 tbsp raspberry jam

1 Preheat the oven to 180°C/350°F/ Gas 4. Line cups of two muffin tins (pans) with paper cases.

2 Cream the butter and caster sugar together until light and fluffy. Add two of the eggs, a little at a time, mixing well after each addition.

3 Sprinkle 15ml/1 tbsp of the flour into the mixture and beat it in. Add the other eggs gradually, beating well, then beat in another spoon of flour until just combined.

4 Sift the remaining flours into the mixture and fold in lightly with the ground almonds, lemon rind and Calvados, brandy or milk.

5 Fill the prepared cups almost to the top. Bake for 20–22 minutes until the tops spring back when touched and the cakes are light golden. Transfer to a wire rack.

6 Beat the butter with the icing sugar until smooth and fluffy. Stir in the juice and water and beat until smooth.

7 When the cakes have cooled completely, slice a round from the top of each. Using a large piping or pastry bag fitted with a plain nozzle, pipe a circle of buttercream.

8 Add a spoonful of jam to fill each cake before replacing the dome on top. Dust lightly with icing sugar and serve.

Energy 574kcal/2406kJ; Protein 5.2g; Carbohydrate 75.5g, of which sugars 54g; Fat 29.5g, of which saturates 18.6g; Cholesterol 140mg; Calcium 81mg; Fibre 0.9g; Sodium 278mg.

Fresh raspberry & fig cakes

Beautiful purple figs, with their luscious red flesh, nestle with fresh raspberries in this delicious cake batter, which puffs up around them in a golden dome as it bakes. Cakes made with fresh summer fruit are a seasonal treat and best eaten while still warm from the oven.

MAKES 8–9

150g/5oz/1¼ cups fresh raspberries
150g/5oz/¾ cup and 15ml/1 tbsp golden caster (superfine) sugar
3 fresh figs
225g/8oz/2 cups plain (all-purpose) flour
10ml/2 tsp baking powder
90g/3oz/7 tbsp butter, melted, plus extra for greasing
1 egg, beaten
300ml/½ pint/scant 1¼ cups buttermilk
grated rind of ½ small orange

1 Preheat the oven to 180°C/350°F/Gas 4. Grease the cups of a large muffin tin (pan) or line with paper muffin cases.

2 Arrange the fresh raspberries in a single layer on a large plate and sprinkle them evenly with the 15ml/ 1 tbsp sugar. Slice the figs vertically into eighths and set them aside with the raspberries.

3 Sift the flour and baking powder into a large mixing bowl and mix in the 150g/5oz sugar. Make a well in the centre of the dry ingredients.

4 In another bowl, mix the cooled melted butter with the egg, buttermilk and grated orange rind. Pour this mixture into the dry ingredients and fold in gently until just blended. Do not overwork the mixture.

5 Set aside a small quantity of the raspberries and figs. Sprinkle the remaining fruit over the surface of the batter and fold in lightly.

6 Spoon the mixture into the tin or the paper cases, filling each not more than two-thirds full. Lightly press the reserved fruit into the top of the batter.

7 Bake for 22–25 minutes until the muffins are risen and golden.

8 Leave in the tin for 5 minutes, then turn out on to a wire rack to cool a little before serving.

Energy 260kcal/1098kJ; Protein 4.7g; Carbohydrate 43.2g, of which sugars 24.2g; Fat 8.9g, of which saturates 5.4g; Cholesterol 44mg; Calcium 107mg; Fibre 1.7g; Sodium 102mg.

Frosted fruit mini loaves

These tasty cakes are simple to make using a basic cupcake recipe. Dust your choice of seasonal fruits with a sugar frosting, then mound them up on top of the cakes just before serving, for an elegant teatime treat. Serve with fresh cream, if you like.

MAKES 8

175g/6oz/¾ cup butter, softened
175g/6oz/scant 1 cup golden
(superfine) caster sugar
5ml/1 tsp vanilla extract, or
5ml/1 tsp finely grated lemon rind
4 eggs, lightly beaten
175g/6oz/1½ cups self-raising
(self-rising) flour, sifted

For the frosted fruits

seasonal soft fruits, rinsed
a few leaves, for decoration
1 egg white, lightly beaten
caster (superfine) sugar,
for dusting
icing (confectioners') sugar,
for dusting

1 Preheat the oven to 180°C/350°F/Gas 4. Set 8 oblong silicone cake cases on a baking sheet.

2 In a bowl, beat together the butter and sugar until creamy. Add the vanilla or lemon rind, then the eggs, beating well after each addition.

3 Fold in the flour. Divide the batter among the cake cases. Bake for 20 minutes until the cakes are golden and firm to the touch.

4 Leave to go cold on a wire rack. Remove the cases.

5 To frost the fruit, first rinse the berries and leaves, then pat them dry with kitchen paper. Brush each fruit, stem and leaf with beaten egg white. Dredge each item with caster sugar while the egg white is wet, then leave to dry on baking parchment in a warm place.

6 Arrange the sugar-frosted pieces on top of each cake. Dust with a light sprinkling of icing sugar.

Cook's tip

If you don't have oblong cake cases, you can achieve a similar effect by baking the batter in a square tin and then slicing the cake into 8 rectangles. These slices won't have quite the same loaf shape, but will still look smart.

Energy 317kcal/1326kJ; Protein 35g; Carbohydrate 20.6g, of which sugars 18.6g; Fat 11.2g, of which saturates 7.5g; Cholesterol 129mg; Calcium 94mg; Fibre 0.6g; Sodium 248mg.

Double apricot and amaretto cakes

Amaretto has a special affinity with apricots (both fresh and dried ones are used here), and although it is an expensive addition, the scent alone makes it worthwhile. A glass of milk or an espresso is the ideal accompaniment to these Italian-style muffins. Best served fresh.

MAKES 8–9

225g/8oz/2 cups plain (all-purpose) flour
12.5ml/2½ tsp baking powder
2.5ml/½ tsp ground cinnamon
115g/4oz/generous ½ cup caster (superfine) sugar
75g/2½oz/6 tbsp butter, melted
1 egg, beaten
150ml/5fl oz/⅔ cup buttermilk
a handful ready-to-eat dried apricots, cut into strips
2–3 amaretti, crumbled

For the glazed fruit

300g/10oz fresh apricots
15ml/1 tbsp apricot jam
15ml/1 tbsp clear honey
30ml/2 tbsp amaretto liqueur

1 Preheat the oven to 200°C/400°F/Gas 6. Lightly grease the cups of a muffin tin (pan) or line with paper cases.

2 To cook the fruit, pit the apricots, cut into quarters and put on a baking tray. Add the jam and honey.

3 Bake for 5 minutes, basting once. Drizzle with the amaretto. Leave to cool.

4 Reduce the oven temperature to 180°C/350°F/Gas 4. Sift the dry ingredients into a large bowl.

5 Mix the melted butter with the beaten egg and buttermilk. Pour into the dry ingredients and mix together gently. Add the cooked apricots, reserving the syrup.

6 Spoon the batter into the paper cases, then bake for 28 minutes, until well risen and firm to the touch.

7 Decorate the tops with the dried apricot strips and crumbled amaretti. Return to the oven for 4–5 minutes until the tops look golden. Leave to cool slightly.

8 Heat the reserved syrup in a small pan for 30 seconds, then brush the hot glaze on top of the muffins.

9 When the cakes are cool enough to handle, transfer them to a wire rack to go cold.

Energy 216kcal/909kJ; Protein 3.8g; Carbohydrate 34.5g, of which sugars 15g; Fat 7.9g, of which saturates 4.8g; Cholesterol 41mg; Calcium 68mg; Fibre 0.8g; Sodium 84mg.

Coffee cakes with fudge frosting

With a dense texture and complex flavours these coffee muffins are truly a cake to savour. The rich and sweet smooth fudgy frosting is a contrast to the grainy-textured cake. The candy-coated coffee beans add a bittersweet taste. Store for up to 3 days in an airtight container.

MAKES 10

100ml/3½fl oz/scant ½ cup single (light) cream

10ml/2 tsp instant coffee granules

15ml/1 tbsp fine-ground roasted coffee

175g/6oz/¾ cup butter, softened

175g/6oz/scant 1 cup soft light brown sugar

2 eggs

100g/3½oz/¾ cup spelt flour

100g/3½oz/¾ cup self-raising (self-rising) flour

For the frosting

75g/2½oz/6 tbsp butter

75g/2½oz/scant ½ cup light muscovado (brown) sugar

15ml/1 tbsp golden (light corn) syrup

5ml/1 tsp instant coffee granules

130g/4½oz/generous 1 cup icing (confectioners') sugar, sifted

5ml/1 tsp lemon juice

candy-coated coffee beans, to decorate

1 Place the cream and coffees in a small pan and bring to the boil. Remove from the heat. Set aside to cool.

2 Preheat the oven to 180°C/350°F/Gas 4. Line the cups of a muffin tin (pan) with paper cases.

3 Beat the butter and sugar until light and creamy, then gradually beat in the eggs. Beat in the coffee mixture.

4 Sift the two flours into the creamed mixture and fold in until just combined. Do not overmix.

5 Three-quarters fill the paper cases with the batter. Bake for 20–25 minutes. Leave to stand for 5 minutes before turning out on to a wire rack to go cold.

6 To make the frosting, melt 50g/2oz/4 tbsp of the butter with the sugar and golden syrup in a pan over a low heat, stirring occasionally.

7 Dissolve the coffee in 50ml/2fl oz/¼ cup boiling water and add to the ingredients in the pan. Bring slowly to the boil, stirring frequently, then simmer for 3 minutes, stirring once or twice. Pour into a large bowl.

8 Whisk in the icing sugar, then the lemon juice and remaining butter. Beat until smooth. Stand the bowl in iced water and stir until the mixture thickens. Spread on to the tops of the muffins. Decorate with coffee beans.

Energy 441kcal/1846kJ; Protein 3.6g; Carbohydrate 56.7g, of which sugars 41.5g; Fat 23.8g, of which saturates 15.1g; Cholesterol 101mg; Calcium 56mg; Fibre 1.5g; Sodium 213mg.

Dark chocolate cakes

Ground almonds replace most of the flour in these chocolatey sponge cakes, giving a very rich, deliciously moist result that needs very little adornment: instead of frosting, the cakes have been simply finished with a generous dusting of icing sugar.

MAKES 12

175g/6oz/¾ cup unsalted butter

50g/2oz plain (semisweet) chocolate, broken up

7.5ml/1½ tsp finely grated orange rind

115g/4oz/1 cup ground almonds

115g/4oz/1 cup icing (confectioners') sugar, sifted

65g/2½oz/generous ½ cup plain (all-purpose) flour, sifted

15ml/1 tbsp unsweetened cocoa powder

6 egg whites

1 Preheat the oven to 190°C/375°F/Gas 5. Grease the cups of a bun tin (pan). Melt the butter with the chocolate and add the orange rind. Set aside to cool slightly.

2 Put the almonds in a large bowl and sift in the icing sugar, flour and cocoa powder.

3 In a separate bowl, beat the egg whites for 15 seconds, just to break them up. Add the egg white to the dry ingredients and mix. Add the melted mixture to the bowl and mix until just combined.

4 Pour the mixture into the bun tin and bake for about 18 minutes, until the cakes are springy to the touch. Leave to cool slightly then turn out on to a wire rack.

5 Dust the cakes with icing sugar to serve, laying a card heart template over each one before dusting. Remove the template carefully.

Variation

Decorate the cakes with chocolate hearts. Spread melted chocolate on to a cool surface. Leave until just set, then cut out the shapes. Dust with cocoa and chill. Attach a single heart to the top of each cake with a little sieved jam or icing.

Energy 255kcal/1063kJ; Protein 4.6g; Carbohydrate 18.1g, of which sugars 13g; Fat 18.8g, of which saturates 9.2g; Cholesterol 34mg; Calcium 42mg; Fibre 1g; Sodium 154mg.

Espresso & mascarpone cakes

Mascarpone adds a delicious nuance to these Marsala- and mocha-flavoured little cakes, and also to the Italian-style cream cheese topping, which itself has a double coffee hit. A sophisticated addition to the afternoon tea table.

MAKES 8–10

150g/5oz/⅔ cup butter, softened

200g/7oz/1 cup golden caster (superfine) sugar

3 eggs

175g/6oz/¾ cup mascarpone

5ml/1 tsp grated lemon rind

30ml/2 tbsp buttermilk

15ml/1 tbsp unsweetened cocoa powder

25ml/1½ tbsp espresso coffee

15ml/1 tbsp Marsala

250g/9oz/2¼ cups self-raising (self-rising) flour

For the topping

175g/6oz/¾ cup butter, softened

2.5ml/½ tsp finely grated lemon rind

350g/12oz/3 cups icing (confectioners') sugar, sifted

225g/8oz/scant 1 cup mascarpone

10ml/2 tsp strong espresso coffee

25g/1oz plain (semisweet) chocolate, melted, to drizzle (optional)

10ml/2 tsp instant coffee granules, to decorate (optional)

1 Preheat the oven to 180°C/350°F/Gas 4. Line a muffin tin (pan) with paper cases.

2 Beat the butter and sugar together until light and creamy. Gradually beat in the eggs, one at a time. Stir in the mascarpone, lemon rind, buttermilk, cocoa, coffee and Marsala, then fold in the flour.

3 Fill the prepared paper cases. Bake for 25 minutes, or until firm to the touch. Turn out on to a wire rack to cool.

4 Meanwhile make the topping. Beat the butter in a bowl until soft. Add the lemon rind and gradually mix in the sugar and mascarpone alternately, in small amounts, until the mixture is smooth and creamy. Stir in the coffee.

5 Spoon the topping on to the top of the cakes. To decorate, if you like, pipe on lines of melted chocolate and sprinkle on a few coffee granules.

Energy 167kcal/703kJ; Protein 2.7g; Carbohydrate 27.6g, of which sugars 11.8g; Fat 5.9g, of which saturates 3.6g; Cholesterol 30mg; Calcium 41mg; Fibre 0.7g; Sodium 79mg.

Montebianco cupcakes

This recipe is based on a pudding called Marrons Mont Blanc in France and Montebianco in Italy: a sweetened chestnut purée is covered in thick vanilla cream. Anyone with a sweet tooth and a passion for chestnuts will find these little cakes especially delicious.

MAKES 10

75g/2½oz/6 tbsp butter, softened
175g/6oz/scant 1 cup golden caster (superfine) sugar
115g/4oz/1 cup icing (confectioners') sugar
5ml/1 tsp vanilla extract
15ml/1 tbsp rum
4 eggs, separated
200g/7oz cooked and peeled whole chestnuts, ground
150g/5oz/1¼ cups plain (all-purpose) flour
10ml/2 tsp baking powder

For the topping

300ml/½ pint/1¼ cups double (heavy) cream
5ml/1 tsp vanilla extract
10ml/2 tsp caster (superfine) sugar
sifted cocoa powder, to dust

1 Preheat the oven to 180°C/350°F/Gas 4. Line the cups of a bun tin (pan) with paper cases.

2 Place the butter, caster sugar and icing sugar in a large bowl and beat until light and smooth using an electric mixer. Mix in the vanilla extract and rum.

3 Beat the egg yolks lightly and add them in a thin stream, beating well until the mixture is very smooth.

4 Add the ground chestnuts and beat them in, then fold in the flour sifted together with the baking powder.

5 In a separate bowl beat the egg whites into fairly firm peaks and fold them lightly into the chestnut mixture until evenly combined.

6 Fill the cups three-quarters full with the cake mixture, and bake for 20–25 minutes, until the cakes are golden and the centres feel springy. Remove from the oven.

7 Leave the cakes in the tins for 5 minutes to cool, then turn them out on to a wire rack to cool.

8 To make the topping, beat the cream with the vanilla extract and caster sugar into soft peaks that hold their shape.

9 Transfer to a large piping or pastry bag fitted with a plain 5mm/¼in nozzle and pipe into tall piles on top of the cakes.

10 To finish, dust the cream with sifted cocoa powder.

Energy 429kcal/1796kJ; Protein 5g; Carbohydrate 51.1g, of which sugars 33.8g; Fat 25.2g, of which saturates 13.8g; Cholesterol 132mg; Calcium 74mg; Fibre 1.3g; Sodium 100mg.

Cupcakes with raspberry buttercream

This mouthwatering raspberry pink cream is great for party cakes, when it is piped into little rosettes. Top these cakes with a few fresh raspberries for an elegant finish.

MAKES 8–9

175g/6oz/¾ cup butter, softened
175g/6oz/scant 1 cup caster (superfine) sugar
5ml/1 tsp vanilla extract, or finely grated lemon rind
4 eggs, lightly beaten
175g/6oz/1½ cups self-raising (self-rising) flour, sifted

For the topping

175g/6oz/¾ cup butter, softened
350g/12oz/3 cups icing (confectioners') sugar, sifted
25ml/1½ tbsp lemon juice
25ml/1½ tbsp raspberry jam
few drops red food colouring
fresh raspberries, to decorate

1 Preheat the oven to 180°C/350°F/Gas 4. Line cups of a bun tin (pan) with paper cases.

2 Beat the butter and sugar together until light and creamy. Add the vanilla or lemon rind.

3 Gradually add the eggs, beating well after each addition. Add the sifted flour and fold into the mixture until just combined.

4 Divide the mixture among the paper cases and bake for 20 minutes until the cakes are golden brown and the centres feel firm to the touch. Remove from the oven.

5 Leave to cool in the tin for 5 minutes, then turn out on to a wire rack to cool completely.

6 For the topping, beat the butter with the icing sugar until smooth and fluffy. Stir in the lemon juice and raspberry jam and continue to beat until smooth.

7 Add the food colouring and beat until the buttercream is evenly coloured a pale pink.

8 Fill a piping or pastry bag fitted with a star nozzle with the buttercream, and pipe small rosette shapes on to the cooled cakes. Decorate with fresh raspberries.

Energy 618kcal/2587kJ; Protein 5g; Carbohydrate 76.8g, of which sugars 62.4g; Fat 34.5g, of which saturates 21.7g; Cholesterol 174mg; Calcium 118mg; Fibre 0.6g; Sodium 396mg.

Fancy floral cupcakes

Add a touch of indulgence to a summer tea party with these gloriously pretty cupcakes. The recipe is simple, as the focus is the fruit-juice flavoured icings and the decorative flowers.

MAKES 12

225g/8oz/1 cup butter, softened
225g/8oz/generous 1 cup caster (superfine) sugar
4 eggs, lightly beaten
50g/2oz/½ cup plain (all-purpose) flour
150g/5oz/1¼ cups ground almonds
5ml/1 tsp vanilla extract
15ml/1 tbsp single (light) cream

For the topping

350g/12oz white sugarpaste
food colouring
royal icing
artificial flower stamens
candy sugar, for sprinkling
350g/12oz/3 cups icing (confectioners') sugar, sifted
15ml/1 tbsp fresh raspberry juice
15ml/1 tbsp fresh orange juice
15ml/1 tbsp fresh lime juice

1 Preheat the oven to 180°C/350°F/Gas 4. Line the cups of a bun tin (pan) with paper cases. Beat the butter and sugar until light and creamy.

2 Add the eggs in small amounts, beating after each addition. Sift in the flour and beat well. Add the ground almonds, vanilla extract and cream and combine.

3 Part fill the paper cases and bake for 20 minutes until golden brown and firm. Cool in the tin for 5 minutes, then turn on to a wire rack to cool completely.

4 To make the flowers, tint pieces of paste as desired. Roll out and stamp out individual petals. Stick together in a flower shape. Mount some stamens in royal icing. Leave to dry. Cut out small flowers using plunger cutters. Leave to dry.

5 For the icing, divide the sugar among three bowls and mix each batch with one of the fruit juices and about 5ml/1 tsp hot water to make a smooth fluid icing.

6 Spread each icing on top of the cakes. Arrange the decorations on the cakes before the icing sets. Once it is dry, sprinkle over a little candy sugar.

Energy 240kcal/1000kJ; Protein 5.6g; Carbohydrate 22.2g, of which sugars 13.4g; Fat 14.9g, of which saturates 8.6g; Cholesterol 81mg; Calcium 74mg; Fibre 1g; Sodium 155mg.

Crystallized flower cupcakes

This traditional method of preserving summer flowers is simple to do and makes charming and very effective decorations for delicately iced cupcakes.

MAKES 10

2 eggs

115g/4oz/generous ½ cup caster (superfine) sugar

50ml/2fl oz/¼ cup double (heavy) cream

finely grated rind of 1 lemon

115g/4oz/1 cup self-raising (self-rising) flour

2.5ml/½ tsp baking powder

50g/2oz/4 tbsp butter, melted

For the icing

225g/8oz/2 cups icing (confectioners') sugar

15–30ml/1–2 tbsp hot water

For the decoration

selection of petals and/or flowers

1 egg white

50g/2oz/¼ cup caster (superfine) sugar

1 Preheat the oven to 180°C/350°F/Gas 4 and line 10 holes of a bun tin (pan) with paper cases. Beat the eggs with the sugar. Beat in the cream for 1 minute, then add the lemon rind. Sift the flour with the baking powder, then fold it into the mixture, followed by the butter.

2 Three-quarters fill the paper cases with the cake mixture. Bake in the centre of the oven for 12–15 minutes until risen and golden brown. Remove from the oven and leave to cool in the bun tin for 5 minutes, then turn the cakes out on to a wire rack to cool completely.

3 To make the crystallized flowers, gather flowers when they are dry, and select clean, perfect specimens. Trim and prepare individual petals or whole flowers. Beat the egg white lightly and put it and the caster sugar in separate saucers.

4 Pick up each petal or flower and paint the entire surface, front and back, carefully with the egg white, using an artist's brush. Dredge on both sides with caster sugar so that it sticks to the egg white and coats the flower or petal.

5 Lay the flowers and petals on baking parchment and leave them in a warm, dry place until dry and crisp.

6 To make the icing, sift the icing sugar into a bowl, then gradually mix in the water, a few drops at a time, beating until the mixture is the consistency of thick pouring cream.

7 Use the icing immediately to cover the cakes, while it is smooth and fluid. Before the icing dries, carefully arrange the flowers on top of the cakes.

Energy 284kcal/1199kJ; Protein 2.7g; Carbohydrate 49.8g, of which sugars 40.8g; Fat 9.5g, of which saturates 5.5g; Cholesterol 68mg; Calcium 29mg; Fibre 0.5g; Sodium 51mg.

Salted caramel cornflake cakes

Easy-to-make, no-bake cornflake cakes aren't just popular with children; these deliciously salted caramel-flavoured crispy bites make a surprisingly sophisticated addition to a tea table. Do choose sugar-free cereal as you are adding your own sweetness.

MAKES 15

100g/3½oz/½ cup caster (superfine) sugar
200g/7oz/scant 1 cup unsalted butter
pinch of sea salt flakes
300g/10oz marshmallows
200g/7oz/6 cups cornflakes

Variation
You can add salt to your own taste – start with a pinch and add a little more if you want a real salty kick.

1 In a pan, heat the sugar and butter until the sugar has melted, then continue to heat, stirring all the time until the mixture starts to caramelize and goes golden brown. You want the caramel to be a deep golden brown colour but take care that the mixture does not overcook and burn or it will taste bitter.

2 Add the salt to the pan with the marshmallows and stir the mixture over a gentle heat until all the marshmallows have melted.

3 Stir in the cornflakes and toss well in the salted caramel mixture so that each flake is coated.

4 Place 15 cake cases in muffin tins and place a large spoonful of mixture in each, piling each one high above the tops.

5 Leave to cool for about 30 minutes then store in an airtight container for up to 3 days.

Energy 241kcal/1013kJ; Protein 1.9g; Carbohydrate 35.6g, of which sugars 21.1g; Fat 11.1g, of which saturates 7g; Cholesterol 28mg; Calcium 5mg; Fibre 0.4g; Sodium 220mg.

Peanut butter cashew cakes

Another variant of rice crispie squares, these are rich with peanut butter and white chocolate, and are a quick and tasty teatime treat. If you can't find honey-roasted cashews then you can happily substitute with honey-roasted peanuts instead.

MAKES 24

150g/5oz/1¼ cups honey-roasted
cashew nuts
300g/10oz marshmallows
130g/4½oz/generous ½ cup butter
150g/5oz/⅔ cup peanut butter
200g/7oz/7 cups rice crispies
200g/7oz white chocolate

Variation
For an almond version of these cakes, replace the peanut butter with almond butter and the honey-roasted cashew nuts with honey-roasted or plain roasted blanched almonds instead.

1 Grease and line a 30 x 20cm/12 x 8in tin (pan). Roughly chop the cashew nuts on a chopping board. Set aside until needed.

2 In a large heavy pan, melt the marshmallows and butter over a gentle heat, stirring all the time so that the marshmallows do not burn. The mixture will become very gooey. Stir in the peanut butter and mix in well.

3 Working quickly so that the marshmallow mixture does not cool, stir in the rice crispies and half of the chopped cashews (reserving the remainder for the topping) and stir well so that everything is coated.

4 Spoon the mixture into the prepared tin and press down with the back of a spoon.

5 Break the white chocolate into pieces and place in a heatproof bowl rested over a pan of simmering water. Heat until the chocolate has melted and then drizzle over the top of the crispy cake using a spoon. Sprinkle over the reserved chopped cashews and leave to set. You can chill in the refrigerator, if you wish.

6 Once the chocolate has set, cut the cake into 24 squares and place in cake cases to serve. These cakes will store for up to 3 days in an airtight container.

Energy 191kcal/802kJ; Protein 2.8g; Carbohydrate 24.2g, of which sugars 14.1g; Fat 10g, of which saturates 4.9g; Cholesterol 11mg; Calcium 64mg; Fibre 0.4g; Sodium 99mg.

Fondant fancies

These fancies are extra special, and nostalgic; you might serve them at a children's celebration tea party or a baby shower. They will keep for 2 days in an airtight container so can easily be made ahead. You could also freeze the undecorated base for up to 3 months.

MAKES 28

50g/2oz/4 tbsp unsalted butter
oil, for greasing
3 large eggs
100g/3½oz/generous ½ cup caster (superfine) sugar
100g/3½oz/scant 1 cup plain (all-purpose) flour
15ml/1 tbsp cornflour (cornstarch)
pinch of salt

For the icing & decoration

500g/1lb2oz/5 cups fondant icing sugar, sifted
food colourings

1 Melt the butter in a small pan over a gentle heat and allow to cool.

2 Preheat the oven to 180°C/350°F/Gas 4. Oil and line a 28 × 18cm/11 × 7in baking tin with baking parchment.

3 In a bowl, whisk the eggs and sugar together, using an electric mixer, until it is pale, thick and creamy, and the mixture leaves a trail on the surface when the beaters are lifted away.

4 Sift the flour, cornflour and salt over the surface and pour the melted butter around the sides of the bowl. Gently fold together, taking care not to knock out the air, then pour into the lined tin.

5 Bake for 20 minutes, or until light golden and just firm to the touch. Cool in the tin for 5 minutes, then turn out, peel away the paper and cool on a wire rack.

6 Cut out squares using a 3.5cm/1½in cutter, and put on a wire rack standing over a tray.

7 Put the sifted fondant icing sugar into a bowl and add enough cold water to give a coating consistency. Divide the icing among several bowls and colour each delicately with a few drops of food colouring. Keep each bowl covered with a damp cloth until needed.

8 Working quickly, spoon the icing over each cake and smooth down to cover the tops and sides. Put in paper cases to serve.

Energy 121kcal/513kJ; Protein 1.2g; Carbohydrate 25.7g, of which sugars 22.3g; Fat 2.2g, of which saturates 1.1g; Cholesterol 29mg; Calcium 10mg; Fibre 0.2g; Sodium 12mg.

Mini lemon whoopie pies

Whoopie pies are a contemporary addition to a tea table. These lemon-flavoured pies are a delight with their citrus burst and zesty undertone. The hint of limoncello in the ganache filling gives them a truly scrumptious grown-up flavour.

MAKES 24

125g/4¼oz/½ cup unsalted butter, softened
175g/6oz/scant 1 cup soft light brown sugar
seeds of 1 vanilla pod (bean)
5ml/1 tsp lemon extract
1 egg
350g/12oz/3 cups plain (all-purpose) flour
7.5ml/1½ tsp bicarbonate of soda (baking soda)
5ml/1 tsp salt
250ml/8½fl oz/1 cup buttermilk

For the ganache filling

150g/5oz white chocolate
65g/2¼oz/5 tbsp unsalted butter, softened
100ml/3½fl oz/scant ½ cup double (heavy) cream
30ml/2 tbsp limoncello

For the lemon glaze

100g/3½oz/¾ cup icing (confectioners') sugar
finely grated rind and juice of 1 large lemon

1 Preheat the oven to 180°C/350°F/Gas 4. Line two baking trays with baking parchment or silicone mats.

2 Whisk the butter, sugar, vanilla and lemon in a bowl until light and fluffy. Whisk in the egg. In a separate bowl, sift the flour with the bicarbonate of soda and salt. Fold half into the butter mixture. Mix in the buttermilk, then the remaining dry ingredients.

3 Using a piping or pastry bag fitted with a large plain nozzle, pipe 24 3cm/1¼in rounds 4cm/1½in apart on each baking tray. Bake for 10–12 minutes, until the cakes bounce back when pressed. Cool on a wire rack.

4 For the ganache, break the chocolate and put with the butter in a bowl. Heat the cream until nearly boiling, pour over the chocolate, and stir until smooth. Stir in the limoncello. Chill, covered, to thicken.

5 To make the glaze, mix everything to a paste. Spread ganache on the flat side of one cake, then sandwich with another cake. Spoon glaze over each cake.

Energy 215kcal/904kJ; Protein 3g; Carbohydrate 27g, of which sugars 16g; Fat 11g, of which saturates 7g; Cholesterol 34mg; Calcium 59mg; Fibre 0.5g; Sodium 172mg.

Mini mint & chocolate whoopies

The classic combination of mint and chocolate works beautifully in these decadent whoopie pies, which make a dainty and interesting addition to a special tea table. For a stronger minty flavour, finely chop some dark mint chocolates and add to the buttercream filling.

MAKES 24
For the cakes
125g/4¼oz/½ cup unsalted butter, softened
175g/6oz/scant 1 cup soft light brown sugar
seeds of 1 vanilla pod (bean)
1 egg
300g/10oz/2½ cups plain (all-purpose) flour
40g/1½oz unsweetened cocoa powder
7.5ml/1½ tsp bicarbonate of soda (baking soda)
5ml/1 tsp salt
250ml/8½fl oz/1 cup buttermilk

For the filling
2 egg whites
125g/4¼oz/⅔ cup caster (superfine) sugar
225g/8oz/1 cup unsalted butter, softened
40g/1½oz unsweetened cocoa powder
4–5 drops peppermint extract

For the topping
100g/3½oz dark (bittersweet) chocolate, melted
24 fresh mint leaves

1 Preheat the oven to 180°C/350°F/Gas 4. Line two baking trays with baking parchment, or use silicone mats if you have them.

2 To make the cakes, whisk the butter, sugar and vanilla seeds together until light and creamy. Whisk in the egg.

3 In a separate bowl, sift the flour with the cocoa powder, bicarbonate of soda and salt. Fold half into the butter mixture, mix in the buttermilk, then add the remaining dry ingredients and stir to combine.

4 Using a piping or pastry bag fitted with a large plain nozzle, pipe 24 3cm/1¼in rounds of cake mixture 4cm/1½in apart on each baking tray.

5 Bake for 10–12 minutes, or until the cakes bounce back when gently pressed. Transfer the cakes to a wire rack to cool.

6 To make the filling, put the egg whites and sugar in a heatproof bowl and place the bowl over a pan of gently simmering water. Using an electric whisk, whisk the ingredients together until the sugar has dissolved and the mixture is white and hot.

7 Remove the bowl from the heat and continue to whisk the mixture on high speed until the bottom of the bowl starts to cool down. Turn the speed down to low and whisk in the butter, about 15g/½oz/1 tbsp at a time, making sure that each addition is fully incorporated before adding the next. Fold in the sifted cocoa powder and peppermint extract and mix gently until fully incorporated.

8 To assemble the pies, place a tablespoon of filling on to the flat side of one cake and top with the flat side of another. Repeat with the remaining cakes and filling to make 24 pies. When you are ready to serve them, spread a little melted chocolate over the tops, and place a mint leaf on each one.

Energy 238kcal/1001kJ; Protein 3g; Carbohydrate 26g, of which sugars 16g; Fat 14g, of which saturates 9g; Cholesterol 44mg; Calcium 44mg; Fibre 0.5g; Sodium 196mg.

Mini Victoria sponge pops

The Victoria sponge is one of England's most popular teatime treats – light vanilla cakes sandwiched together with buttercream and jam, and elegantly dusted with icing sugar. These mini versions are perfect for serving with a pot of freshly brewed tea for an afternoon tea party.

MAKES 10
For the cakes
50g/2oz/4 tbsp butter, softened
50g/2oz/¼ cup caster
(superfine) sugar
1 egg
5ml/1 tsp vanilla extract
50g/2oz/½ cup self-raising
(self-rising) flour, sifted
5ml/1 tsp baking powder

For the filling
100g/3½oz/¾ cup icing
(confectioners') sugar, plus extra
for dusting
30g/1¼oz/2 tbsp butter, softened
30g/1¼oz/2 tbsp cream cheese
5ml/1 tsp vanilla extract
a little milk, for mixing (optional)
60–75ml/4–5 tbsp strawberry jam

1 Preheat the oven to 180°C/350°F/Gas 4. Grease a 10-cup straight-sided mini muffin tin (pan) or silicone mould.

2 To make the cakes, cream the butter and sugar together until fluffy. Beat in the egg and vanilla extract.

3 Sift the flour and baking powder into the butter mixture, then fold in. Divide the cake mixture (batter) between the cups of the prepared tin or mould. Bake for 12–15 minutes, until the cakes spring back when gently pressed. Transfer to a wire rack to cool.

4 For the buttercream, sift the icing sugar into a bowl, add the butter, cream cheese and vanilla extract, and whisk together for 3 minutes, or until light and creamy, adding a little milk if necessary.

5 Cut each of the cakes in half horizontally. Using a piping or pastry bag fitted with a small star-shaped nozzle, pipe the buttercream on to the bottom half of each cake. Using a teaspoon, add a little strawberry jam to each. Top with the other cake halves and dust with sifted icing sugar. Insert a wooden skewer into the top of each cake and tie a ribbon around it.

Energy 177kcal/742kJ; Protein 2g; Carbohydrate 24g, of which sugars 20g; Fat 9g, of which saturates 5g; Cholesterol 45mg; Calcium 33mg; Fibre 0.3g; Sodium 136mg.

Key lime pops

The inspiration for these little pops is the American favourite, key lime pie, which comprises a sharp lime mousse in a buttery crumb case and topped with whipped cream. Here, cake is instead used as the base so they are not too heavy to stay on the little sticks.

MAKES 36

For the cakes
50g/2oz/4 tbsp butter, softened
50g/2oz/¼ cup caster (superfine) sugar
1 egg
50g/2oz/½ cup self-raising (self-rising) flour
15ml/1 tbsp crème fraîche
finely grated rind of 1 lime

For the filling
120ml/4fl oz/½ cup crème fraîche
125g/4¼oz/½ cup mascarpone

juice of 1 lime
15ml/1 tbsp icing (confectioners') sugar
15ml/1 tbsp sweetened condensed milk
green food colouring gel (optional)

For the crumb topping
45g/1¾oz/3½ tbsp butter
6 digestive biscuits (graham crackers), crushed into crumbs

1 Preheat the oven to 180°C/350°F/Gas 4. Grease and line a 20cm/8in square loose-bottomed cake tin (pan).

2 To make the sponge cake, cream the butter and sugar together until light and creamy. Beat in the egg.

3 Sift in the flour, then fold in with the crème fraîche and lime rind.

4 Spoon into the cake tin and level the surface. Bake for 15–20 minutes, or until it springs back when pressed and the tip of a knife comes out clean when inserted into the centre. Leave the cake to cool in the tin.

5 For the filling, whisk the crème fraîche, mascarpone, lime juice, icing sugar and condensed milk until smooth. Add a few drops of green food colouring gel (optional), and mix in until uniform. Spoon the mousse on top of the cake in the tin and smooth it level.

6 To prepare the crumb topping, melt the butter in a pan, then stir in the biscuit crumbs. Sprinkle the crumbs over the mousse, then chill for 2 hours, or until set.

7 To serve, remove from the tin and cut into 36 squares, wiping the knife clean between each cut. Thread the cake squares on little wooden skewers to serve.

Energy 74kcal/139 kJ; Protein 585g; Carbohydrate 19g, of which sugars 17g; Fat 7g, of which saturates 3g; Cholesterol 30mg; Calcium 28mg; Fibre 0.g; Sodium 48mg.

Biscuits, macarons & meringues

A plate of elegant biscuits, macarons or meringues forms a traditional part of a formal teatime table, but these treats also provide a tasty lift served with a pot of tea or cup of coffee at any time of the day. Choose from simple yet flavoursome classics such as sugar-crusted shortbreads, Viennese whirls or oat biscuits, or perhaps opt for the decadent dipped chocolate cookies or light-as-air meringues.

Left Dainty, flavoursome biscuits, such as melting moments, make the ideal accompaniment to a pot of tea.

Tea fingers

The unusual ingredient in these cookies is Lady Grey tea – similar to Earl Grey but with the addition of Seville orange and lemon peel, which imparts a subtle citrus flavour. As you might expect, they make the ideal accompaniment to a pot of tea.

MAKES ABOUT 36

150g/5oz/⅔ cup unsalted butter, diced and softened
115g/4oz/generous ½ cup light muscovado (brown) sugar
15–30ml/1–2 tbsp Lady Grey tea leaves

1 egg, beaten
200g/7oz/1¾ cups plain (all-purpose) flour, plus extra for dusting
demerara (raw) sugar, for sprinkling

1 Preheat the oven to 190°C/375°F/Gas 5. Line two or three baking sheets with baking parchment.

2 In a large bowl, beat the butter and sugar until light and creamy. Stir in the tea until combined. Add the egg, then carefully fold in the flour using a metal spoon.

3 Using your hands, roll the dough on a lightly floured surface into a log, about 23cm/9in long.

4 Gently press down on the top of the log with the palm of your hand to flatten slightly. Wrap the dough in clear film (plastic wrap) and chill for about 1 hour until the dough is firm enough to slice.

5 Using a sharp knife, cut the dough log widthways into 5mm/¼in slices and place, slightly apart, on the prepared baking sheets.

6 Sprinkle the cookies with a little demerara sugar, then bake for 10–15 minutes until lightly browned. Transfer the cookies to a wire rack and leave to cool.

Energy 65kcal/270kJ; Protein 0.7g; Carbohydrate 7.7g, of which sugars 3.4g; Fat 3.7g, of which saturates 2.2g; Cholesterol 14mg; Calcium 11mg; Fibre 0.2g; Sodium 28mg.

Sugar-crusted shortbreads

Shortbread is one of the most popular biscuits, commonly enjoyed with a cup of tea or coffee at any time of the day, and this melt-in-the-mouth version, with its crunchy sugar rim, is elegant enough to grace any teatime table.

MAKES ABOUT 24

450g/1lb/2 cups butter

225g/8oz/generous 1 cup caster (superfine) sugar

450g/1lb/4 cups plain (all-purpose) flour

5ml/1 tsp salt

225g/8oz/scant 1½ cups ground rice or rice flour

demerara (raw) sugar, to decorate

golden caster (superfine) sugar, for dusting

1 Place the butter and sugar in a large bowl and cream together until light, pale and fluffy. Alternatively, process them in a food processor, then scrape the mixture into a bowl.

2 Sift together the flour, salt and ground rice or rice flour and stir into the butter and sugar with a wooden spoon, until the mixture resembles fine breadcrumbs.

3 Working quickly, gather the dough together with your hand, then put it on a clean work surface. Knead lightly together until it forms a ball, but take care not to over-knead or the shortbread will be tough and greasy.

4 Lightly roll into a sausage shape, about 7.5cm/3in thick. Wrap the roll of dough in clear film (plastic wrap) and chill until firm.

5 Preheat the oven to 190°C/375°F/Gas 5. Line two baking sheets with baking parchment.

6 Pour the demerara sugar on to a sheet of baking parchment. Unwrap the dough and roll it in the sugar until evenly coated.

7 Using a large, sharp knife, slice the roll into discs about 1cm/½in thick.

8 Place the discs on to the baking sheets, spacing them well apart. Bake for 20–25 minutes until very pale gold in colour.

9 Remove from the oven and sprinkle with golden caster sugar. Leave to cool on the baking sheet for 10 minutes before transferring to a wire rack to cool completely.

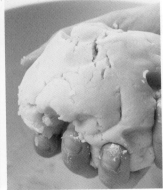

Energy 275kcal/1147kJ; Protein 2.5g; Carbohydrate 32g, of which sugars 10.2g; Fat 15.7g, of which saturates 9.8g; Cholesterol 40mg; Calcium 37mg; Fibre 0.8g; Sodium 197mg.

Melting moments

As the name suggests, these crisp biscuits really do melt in the mouth. They have a texture like shortbread but are covered in rolled oats to give a crunchy surface and extra flavour, and are traditionally topped with a piece of cherry. They look especially attractive on the tea table.

MAKES 16–20

40g/1½oz/3 tbsp butter, at room temperature
65g/2¼oz/5 tbsp lard
75g/2½oz/scant ½ cup caster (superfine) sugar
1 egg yolk, beaten
few drops of vanilla or almond extract
150g/5oz/1¼ cups self-raising (self-rising) flour

rolled oats, for coating
4–5 glacé (candied) cherries

Variation

You could ring the changes and flavour these biscuits with a little cinnamon or grated orange or lemon rind, if you like.

1 Preheat the oven to 180°C/350°F/Gas 4. Grease two or three baking sheets.

2 Beat together the butter, lard and sugar, then beat in the egg yolk and vanilla or almond extract. Sift the flour over the mixture and stir to make a soft dough.

3 Gather up the dough, divide into 16–20 pieces and roll into small balls.

4 Spread rolled oats on a sheet of baking parchment and toss the balls in them until evenly coated.

5 Space the dough balls slightly apart, on two baking sheets. Flatten each ball a little with your thumb.

6 Cut the cherries into quarters and place a piece on top of each flat ball. Bake for 15–20 minutes, until they are lightly browned.

7 Allow to cool for a few minutes on the baking sheets before transferring them to a wire rack to cool completely.

Energy 88kcal/370kJ; Protein 0.7g; Carbohydrate 10.9g, of which sugars 5.4g; Fat 5g, of which saturates 2.4g; Cholesterol 7mg; Calcium 30mg; Fibre 0.3g; Sodium 40mg.

Viennese whirls

The mixture for these cookies is piped into rosette shapes on to a baking sheet, then each piece is sandwiched together with sweet, coffee-flavoured buttercream icing. Fabulously soft and elegant to look at, these are delicious for a special tea.

MAKES 20

175g/6oz/¾ cup butter
50g/2oz/½ cup icing
(confectioners') sugar
2.5ml/½ tsp vanilla extract
115g/4oz/1 cup plain
(all-purpose) flour
50g/2oz/½ cup cornflour
(cornstarch)
icing (confectioners') sugar and
cocoa powder, to dust

For the filling

15ml/1 tbsp ground coffee
60ml/4 tbsp single (light) cream
75g/2½oz/6 tbsp butter, softened
115g/4oz/1 cup icing
(confectioners') sugar, sifted

1 Preheat the oven to 180°C/350°F/Gas 4. Grease two or three baking sheets.

2 Cream together the butter, icing sugar and vanilla extract until light and fluffy. Sift in the flour and cornflour, and mix together until just smooth, but do not overmix.

3 Spoon the mixture into a piping bag fitted with a 1cm/½in fluted nozzle. Do not overfill the bag. Pipe even-sized rosettes on the greased baking sheets.

4 Bake for 12–15 minutes until golden. Transfer to a wire rack to cool.

5 Put the coffee in a bowl. Heat the cream to near-boiling and pour it over. Infuse (steep) for 4 minutes, then strain.

6 Beat together the butter, icing sugar and coffee cream. Use to sandwich the whirls in pairs. Dust with icing sugar and cocoa powder.

Energy 210Kcal/877kJ; Protein 2.2g; Carbohydrate 21.3g, of which sugars 11.2g; Fat 13.5g, of which saturates 7.6g; Cholesterol 22mg; Calcium 28mg; Fibre 0.8g; Sodium 64mg.

Honey crunch creams

Greek honey works well in this recipe, as it has a strong flavour of liquorice and aniseed. If you prefer a more subtle taste, use heather or lavender honey. These cookies will bring an aroma of the countryside to the tea table.

MAKES 20

250g/9oz/2¼ cups self-raising (self-rising) flour

10ml/2 tsp bicarbonate of soda (baking soda)

50g/2oz/¼ cup caster (superfine) sugar

115g/4oz/½ cup unsalted butter, diced

finely grated rind of 1 large orange

115g/4oz/½ cup honey

25g/1oz/¼ cup pine nuts or chopped walnuts

For the filling

50g/2oz/4 tbsp unsalted butter, at room temperature, diced

115g/4oz/1 cup icing (confectioners') sugar, sifted

15ml/1 tbsp honey

Variation

Try chopped peanuts instead of pine nuts or walnuts, and sandwich the cookies with peanut butter mixed with honey instead of buttercream.

1 Preheat the oven to 200°C/400°F/Gas 6. Line three baking sheets with baking parchment.

2 Place the flour, bicarbonate of soda and caster sugar in a large mixing bowl. Add the butter and rub in with your fingers until the mixture resembles breadcrumbs. Stir in the orange rind.

3 Put the honey in a small pan and heat until over a low heat until it is just runny but not hot. Pour it over the flour and sugar mixture and mix to a firm dough, taking care not to overmix.

4 Divide the dough in half and shape one half into 20 small balls about the size of a hazelnut. Place the balls on the baking sheets, spaced well apart, and gently flatten.

5 Bake for 6–8 minutes, until golden brown. Leave to cool and firm up on the baking sheets. Use a metal spatula to transfer the cookies to a wire rack to allow them to cool completely.

6 Shape the remaining dough into 20 even-sized balls and dip one side of each one into the pine nuts or chopped walnuts.

7 Place the cookies, nut sides up, on the baking sheets, gently flatten and bake for 6–8 minutes, until golden brown. Keep a close eye on them.

8 Leave to cool and firm up slightly on the baking sheets before carefully transferring the cookies to a wire rack, still nut sides up, to cool completely.

9 To make the filling, put the butter, icing sugar and honey in a small mixing bowl and beat together until light and fluffy.

10 When the cookies are completely cool, use the filling to sandwich the cookies together in pairs using a plain cookie for the bottom and a nut-coated one for the top.

Energy 164Kcal/688kJ; Protein 1.5g; Carbohydrate 23.4g, of which sugars 13.9g; Fat 7.8g, of which saturates 4.4g; Cholesterol 18mg; Calcium 24mg; Fibre 0.4g; Sodium 52mg.

Oat biscuits

These crisp and crunchy biscuits are wonderfully quick and easy to make, as well as being utterly delicious. They are homely and comforting at any time of day, and are filling enough to keep hunger pangs at bay – just right with a cup of tea.

MAKES 18

115g/4oz/½ cup butter
115g/4oz/generous ½ cup soft light brown sugar
115g/4oz/⅓ cup golden (light corn) syrup
150g/5oz/1¼ cups self-raising (self-rising) flour
150g/5oz rolled oats

Variation
Add 25g/1oz finely chopped toasted almonds or walnuts, or a small handful of dried fruit (raisins or currants) to the mixture in step 3.

1 Preheat the oven to 180°C/350°F/Gas 4. Lightly grease or line two or three baking sheets with sheets of baking parchment.

2 Gently heat the butter, sugar and golden syrup in a heavy pan until the butter has melted and the sugar has dissolved, taking care not to let it get too hot as the mixture will easily burn.

3 Remove from the heat and leave to cool slightly.

4 Sift the flour and stir into the mixture in the pan, together with the oats, to make a soft dough.

5 Roll the dough into small balls and arrange them on the prepared baking sheets, leaving plenty of room for them to spread out.

6 Flatten each ball with a spatula. Bake for 12–15 minutes until golden brown, longer if more than one tray is in the oven.

7 Leave to cool on the baking sheet briefly, then transfer to a wire rack to crisp up and cool completely.

Energy 151kcal/637kJ; Protein 1.8g; Carbohydrate 23.9g, of which sugars 11.9g; Fat 6g, of which saturates 3.3g; Cholesterol 14mg; Calcium 22mg; Fibre 0.8g; Sodium 59mg.

Double ginger cookies

These are a supreme treat for ginger lovers – richly spiced cookies packed with chunks of succulent preserved stem ginger as well as ground ginger. They are perfect for an afternoon tea party.

MAKES 20

350g/12oz/3 cups self-raising (self-rising) flour
pinch of salt
200g/7oz/1 cup golden caster (superfine) sugar
15ml/1 tbsp ground ginger
5ml/1 tsp bicarbonate of soda (baking soda)

115g/4oz/½ cup unsalted butter
90g/3oz/generous ¼ cup golden (light corn) syrup
1 large egg, beaten
150g/5oz preserved stem ginger in syrup, drained and coarsely chopped

1 Preheat the oven to 160°C/325°F/Gas 3. Line three baking sheets with baking parchment.

2 Sift the flour into a bowl, add the salt, sugar, ground ginger and bicarbonate of soda and stir to combine.

3 Dice the butter and put it in a pan with the syrup. Heat gently, stirring, until the butter has melted. Remove from the heat and set aside to cool until just warm.

4 Pour the butter mixture over the dry ingredients, then add the egg and two-thirds of the ginger. Mix, then use your hands to bring the dough together.

5 Shape the dough into 20 large balls, depending on the size you require. Place them, spaced well apart, on the baking sheets.

6 Gently flatten the balls, then press a few pieces of the remaining preserved stem ginger into the top of each.

7 Bake for about 12–15 minutes, depending on the size of your cookies, until light golden in colour. Leave to cool for 1 minute on the baking sheets to firm up.

Energy 114kcal/479kJ; Protein 1.4g; Carbohydrate 20.4g, of which sugars 11.5g; Fat 3.5g, of which saturates 2.1g; Cholesterol 15mg; Calcium 23mg; Fibre 0.4g; Sodium 42mg.

Rich peanut crunch cookies

These delicious sweet and nutty cookies are so easy to make. They puff up into lovely domed rounds during baking, giving them a very appealing look. If you prefer cookies with a slightly less 'nutty' texture, use smooth peanut butter rather than the crunchy variety.

MAKES 25

150g/5oz/1¼ cups self-raising (self-rising) flour
2.5ml/½ tsp baking powder
115g/4oz/½ cup butter, diced
115g/4oz/½ cup light muscovado (brown) sugar

1 egg
150g/5oz/generous ½ cup crunchy peanut butter
icing (confectioners') sugar, for dusting

1 Preheat the oven to 190°C/375°F/Gas 5. Lightly grease two baking sheets.

2 Sift the flour and baking powder together into a bowl. Put the butter and sugar in a mixing bowl and beat until pale and creamy.

3 Beat in the egg, then add the flour mixture and the peanut butter. Beat until thoroughly mixed.

4 Place heaped teaspoonfuls of the mixture on to the baking sheets; space well apart to allow the cookies to spread while baking. (Work in batches, if necessary.)

5 Bake the cookies for about 20 minutes until risen; they will still be quite soft to the touch.

6 Leave on the baking sheets to set for about 5 minutes, then transfer to a wire rack and leave to cool completely.

7 To serve, lightly dust with icing sugar. Store in an airtight container for 2–3 days.

Energy 112kcal/466kJ; Protein 2.1g; Carbohydrate 10.3g, of which sugars 5.3g; Fat 7.2g, of which saturates 3.2g; Cholesterol 18mg; Calcium 15mg; Fibre 0.5g; Sodium 50mg.

Dark chocolate fingers

With their understated elegance and distinctly grown-up flavour, these moreishly decadent chocolate fingers are perfect for a stylish afternoon tea. If you want to make them more child-friendly, you could use milk chocolate for dipping.

MAKES ABOUT 26

115g/4oz/1 cup plain (all-purpose) flour

pinch of baking powder

30ml/2 tbsp unsweetened cocoa powder

50g/2oz/¼ cup caster (superfine) sugar

50g/2oz/4 tbsp butter, softened

20ml/4 tsp golden (light corn) syrup

150g/5oz dark (bittersweet) chocolate

chocolate mini flakes, for sprinkling

1 Preheat the oven to 160°C/325°F/Gas 3. Line two baking sheets with baking parchment.

2 Sift the dry ingredients into a bowl.

3 Add the butter and golden syrup and work the ingredients together with your hands to form a dough.

4 Roll the dough out between sheets of baking parchment to an 18 x 24cm/7 x 9in rectangle. Remove the top sheet. Cut in half lengthways, then cut each half into 13 slices. Place on the baking sheets.

5 Bake the cookies for about 15 minutes. Transfer to a wire rack to cool.

6 Melt the chocolate in a heatproof bowl set over a pan of simmering water. Half-dip the cookies, place on baking parchment, sprinkle with chocolate flakes, then leave to set.

Energy 72kcal/303kJ; Protein 0.9g; Carbohydrate 9.9g, of which sugars 6.3g; Fat 3.5g, of which saturates 2.1g; Cholesterol 4mg; Calcium 11mg; Fibre 0.4g; Sodium 25mg.

Cappuccino swirls

These melt-in-the-mouth, mocha-flavoured cookies are prettily drizzled with melted white and dark chocolate, and have a wonderful texture and delicious warm fragrance. Just the thing for a special teatime, they go really well with a cup of coffee too.

MAKES 18

10ml/2 tsp instant coffee powder
10ml/2 tsp boiling water
150g/5oz/1¼ cups plain (all-purpose) flour
115g/4oz/1 cup cornflour (cornstarch)
15ml/1 tbsp (unsweetened) cocoa powder
225g/8oz/1 cup unsalted (sweet) butter, at room temperature, diced
50g/2oz/¼ cup golden caster (superfine) sugar

For the decoration

50g/2oz white chocolate
25g/1oz dark (bittersweet) chocolate

Cook's tip
As for most biscuits, it is important not to overbake these cookies, as this not only makes them dry, but can also make them taste a little bitter.

1 Preheat the oven to 190°C/375°F/Gas 5. Line two baking sheets with baking parchment. Put the coffee powder in a cup, add the boiling water and stir until dissolved. Set aside to cool. Sift together the flour, cornflour and cocoa powder.

2 Put the butter and sugar in a bowl and beat until creamy. Add the coffee and flour and mix well. Spoon into a piping or pastry bag fitted with a plain nozzle. Pipe 18 spirals, slightly apart, on to the prepared baking sheets.

3 Bake for 10–15 minutes, until firm but not browned. Remove from the oven and leave on the baking sheets for 1 minute, then transfer to a wire rack to cool.

4 Melt the white and dark chocolate separately in heatproof bowls set over a pan of hot water.

5 Place the cooled cookies close together on a few pieces of kitchen paper. Using a teaspoon, take some white chocolate and flick over the cookies, moving your hand speedily from left to right to create small lines of chocolate drizzle over them.

6 When all the white chocolate has been used, repeat the process with the dark chocolate, flicking it over the cookies at an angle to the white chocolate streaks. Leave until the chocolate has set and then remove the cookies from the paper.

Energy 179kcal/746kJ; Protein 1.3g; Carbohydrate 18.1g, of which sugars 5.7g; Fat 11.8g, of which saturates 7.3g; Cholesterol 27mg; Calcium 19mg; Fibre 0.5g; Sodium 88mg.

Black & white ginger florentines

Florentines are special-occasion cookies packed with luxurious ingredients and topped with a thick coating of melted chocolate. Traditionally they are made for Christmas and would make a perfect centrepiece for a festive afternoon tea.

MAKES 30

120ml/4fl oz/½ cup double (heavy) cream
50g/2oz/4 tbsp unsalted butter
50g/2oz/¼ cup granulated (white) sugar
30ml/2 tbsp honey
150g/5oz/1¼ cups flaked (slivered) almonds
40g/1½oz/⅓ cup plain (all-purpose) flour
2.5ml/½ tsp ground ginger

50g/2oz/⅓ cup diced candied orange peel
75g/2½oz/generous ½ cup diced stem ginger
50g/2oz milk chocolate, chopped into small pieces
150g/5oz plain (semisweet) chocolate, chopped into small pieces
150g/5oz white chocolate, chopped into small pieces

1 Preheat the oven to 180°C/350°F/Gas 4. Lightly grease two large baking sheets.

2 In a small pan over medium heat, stir the cream, butter, sugar and honey until the sugar dissolves. Bring the mixture to the boil, stirring.

3 Remove the pan from the heat and stir in the almonds, flour and ground ginger. Stir in the candied peel, ginger and milk chocolate.

4 Drop teaspoons of the mixture on to the baking sheets at least 7.5cm/3in apart. Spread each round thinly with the back of a spoon.

5 Bake for 8–10 minutes or until the edges are golden brown and the cookies are bubbling.

6 Allow to cool on the baking sheets for 10 minutes, then transfer to a wire rack to go cold.

7 Melt the plain chocolate in a heatproof bowl over a pan of gently simmering water. Melt the white chocolate in a separate bowl in the same way.

8 Using a spatula, spread half the florentines with plain chocolate and the other half with white chocolate. Use a fork to mark on wiggly lines. Place on a wire rack, chocolate side up. Chill for 10–15 minutes to set.

Energy 71kcal/298kJ; Protein 0.9g; Carbohydrate 8.6g, of which sugars 7.8g; Fat 3.9g, of which saturates 1.3g; Cholesterol 2mg; Calcium 16mg; Fibre 0.3g; Sodium 11mg.

Macadamia & Champagne macarons

These macarons exude elegance. The flavours are light, sophisticated and indulgent, making them a good option to serve for a special-occasion tea, such as at a christening or for an engagement party. You could sprinkle these with edible glitter for extra wow factor, if you like.

MAKES 12
For the shells
65g/2¼oz egg whites
65g/2¼oz/generous ¼ cup caster (superfine) sugar
7.5ml/1½ tsp egg white powder
120g/4¼oz/generous 1 cup icing (confectioners') sugar
30g/1¼oz/generous ¼ cup ground almonds

20g/¾oz/3½ tbsp ground macadamias, plus extra for sprinkling

For the filling
80g/2¾oz/scant ¾ cup icing (confectioners') sugar
40g/1½oz/3 tbsp butter, softened
20ml/4 tsp Champagne

1 Line a baking tray with non-stick baking parchment. Fit a piping or pastry bag with a plain round tip.

2 Place the egg whites in a clean bowl, and sift the caster sugar and egg white powder over the egg whites. Whisk with an electric mixer until stiff peaks form.

3 In a separate bowl, sift together the icing sugar, ground almonds and macadamias. Add the egg white mixture to the almond mixture. Using a spatula, gently fold the mixture until the batter falls in ribbons when lifted with the spatula.

4 Fill the piping bag with the mixture and pipe 24 4cm/1½in rounds on to the lined baking tray. Sprinkle half the piped shells with ground macadamias (these will be the tops).

5 Preheat the oven to 130°C/250°F/Gas ½. Leave the baking tray containing the macarons out in a warm, dry room for at least 15 minutes.

6 Place the tray in the middle of the oven and bake the macarons for 10 minutes. Remove from the oven and allow to cool.

7 To make the filling, place the icing sugar and softened butter in a large bowl, and whisk until crumbly. Add the Champagne and whisk until smooth and of a spreadable consistency.

8 To fill the macarons, place a teaspoonful of buttercream on to the flat side of an undecorated macaron shell and top with the flat side of a decorated shell. Repeat to make 12 macarons.

Energy 141kcal/593kJ; Protein 1.8g; Carbohydrate 23.1g, of which sugars 22.8g; Fat 5.1g, of which saturates 1.9g; Cholesterol 7mg; Calcium 13mg; Fibre 0g; Sodium 42mg.

Raspberry & white chocolate macarons

These tangy raspberry macaron shells pack a lot of flavour into a delicate mouthful. They contain freeze-dried raspberries, which have an intense flavour, and this works perfectly with the creamy white chocolate filling to create an irresistible combination.

MAKES 12

For the shells
65g/2¼oz egg whites
65g/2¼oz/generous ¼ cup caster (superfine) sugar
7.5ml/1½ tsp egg white powder
120g/4¼oz/generous 1 cup icing (confectioners') sugar
50g/2oz/½ cup ground almonds
5g/⅛oz ground freeze-dried raspberries, plus extra for sprinkling

For the filling
50g/2oz white chocolate
75ml/5 tbsp double (heavy) cream

1 Line a baking tray with non-stick greaseproof baking paper. Fit a piping (pastry) bag with a plain round tip.

2 Place the egg whites in a clean bowl, and sift the caster sugar and egg white powder over the egg whites. Whisk with an electric mixer until stiff peaks form.

3 In a separate bowl, sift together the icing sugar, ground almonds and freeze-dried raspberries. Add the egg white mixture to the almond mixture. Using a spatula, gently fold the mixture until the batter falls in ribbons when lifted with the spatula.

4 Fill the piping bag with the mixture, and pipe 24 4cm/1½in rounds on to the lined baking tray. Sprinkle half of the shells with the extra ground raspberries (these will be the tops).

5 Preheat the oven to 130°C/250°F/Gas ½. Leave the baking tray containing the macarons out in a warm, dry room for at least 15 minutes.

6 Place the tray in the middle of the oven and bake for 10 minutes. Remove from the oven and allow to cool.

7 To make the ganache filling, melt the white chocolate with the double cream in a non-stick pan over a low heat. Remove the pan from the heat and stir occasionally, until thickened.

8 To fill, place a teaspoonful of ganache on to the flat side of an undecorated shell and top with the flat side of a decorated one. Repeat to make 12 macarons.

Energy 141kcal/594kJ; Protein 2.3g; Carbohydrate 18.6g, of which sugars 18.4g; Fat 7g, of which saturates 3g; Cholesterol 9mg; Calcium 27mg; Fibre 0g; Sodium 27mg.

Apple macarons

These macarons invoke the perfect flavour combination of apple and cinnamon. The apple buttercream gives a light and fragrant balance to the macaron shells. As an alternative, try filling with peeled eating apples, cut into tiny chunks and folded into some whipped cream.

MAKES 12
For the shells
65g/2¼oz egg whites
65g/2¼oz/generous ¼ cup caster (superfine) sugar
7.5ml/1½ tsp egg white powder
120g/4¼oz/generous 1 cup icing (confectioners') sugar
65g/2¼oz/generous ½ cup ground almonds
2.5ml/½ tsp ground cinnamon
pink food colouring gel

For the filling
80g/2¾oz/scant ¾ cup icing (confectioners') sugar
40g/1½oz/3 tbsp unsalted butter, softened
20ml/4 tsp apple preserve

Variation
You could colour these macarons a pale green, if you prefer.

1 Line a baking tray with non-stick baking parchment. Fit a piping or pastry bag with a plain round tip.

2 Place the egg whites in a clean bowl, and sift the caster sugar and egg white powder over the egg whites. Whisk with an electric mixer until stiff peaks form.

3 In a separate bowl, sift together the icing sugar, almonds and cinnamon. Add the egg white mixture to this. Dip a cocktail stick or toothpick into the colouring gel and scrape on to the tip of a spatula. Use the spatula to fold the mixture gently, until the colour is even and the batter falls in ribbons when lifted with the spatula.

4 Fill the piping bag with the mixture and pipe 24 4cm/1½in rounds on to the lined baking tray. Preheat the oven to 130°C/250°F/Gas ½. Leave the baking tray out in a warm, dry room for at least 15 minutes.

5 Place the tray in the middle of the oven and bake for 10 minutes. Remove from the oven and allow to cool.

6 To make the buttercream filling, place the icing sugar and butter in a bowl, and whisk until crumbly. Add the apple preserve and whisk until smooth.

7 To fill the macarons, place a teaspoonful of buttercream on to the flat side of one macaron shell and top with the flat side of another shell. Repeat to make 12 macarons.

Energy 146kcal/614kJ; Protein 2g; Carbohydrate 23.5g, of which sugars 23.1g; Fat 5.5g, of which saturates 2g; Cholesterol 7mg; Calcium 17mg; Fibre 0g; Sodium 43mg.

Cinnamon meringues

These meringues are flavoured with a hint of cinnamon and almond and have a slightly chewy texture – both attributes that mean they go well with luscious summer fruits and amaretto-flavoured cream. They make a light and attractive addition to a teatime table.

MAKES 10

4 egg whites
1.25ml/¼ tsp cream of tartar
225g/8oz/generous 1 cup caster (superfine) sugar
2.5ml/½ tsp ground cinnamon
few drops of almond extract
40g/1½oz/generous ⅓ cup ground almonds

For the filling

300ml/½ pint/1¼ cups double (heavy) cream
15ml/1 tbsp amaretto liqueur
350g/12oz/2½ cups raspberries
tiny sprigs of fresh mint
icing (confectioners') sugar, for dusting

1 Preheat the oven to 110°C/225°F/Gas ¼. Line two baking sheets with baking parchment.

2 Rinse out a clean mixing bowl with boiling water, then dry with kitchen paper to make sure it is totally grease-free.

3 Put the egg whites into the bowl and whisk until they form stiff peaks. Add the cream of tartar.

4 Gradually whisk in the sugar with the cinnamon and almond extract in small batches until the mixture is thick and stiff. Fold in the almonds.

5 Spoon 20 rough dessertspoonfuls on to the baking sheets, then bake for 2 hours, or until crisp and dry, swapping over the position of the baking sheets halfway through the cooking time.

6 Leave to cool completely, then peel off from the baking parchment.

7 Whip the cream until soft peaks form. Fold in the liqueur, then fill a piping or pastry bag.

8 Pipe the whipped cream on to 10 meringue bases. Arrange the fruits, mint and meringue lid on each base and serve immediately, dusted with icing sugar.

Cook's tip

If you don't want to make the meringues immediately, store them, undecorated, in an airtight container for up to 2 weeks.

Energy 177kcal/742kJ; Protein 2g; Carbohydrate 24g, of which sugars 20g; Fat 9g, of which saturates 5g; Cholesterol 45mg; Calcium 33mg; Fibre 0.3g; Sodium 136mg.

Mini meringue pops

These dainty pink meringues are the lightest of treats and are perfect for an afternoon tea party. They are filled with chocolate ganache, but you could replace this with rose petal jam and buttercream, if you prefer. Make sure the meringues are small enough to be just one mouthful.

MAKES 20

For the meringues
3 egg whites
175g/6oz/scant 1 cup caster
(superfine) sugar
5ml/1 tsp vanilla extract
few drops of pink food
colouring gel

For the chocolate ganache
100g/3½oz plain (semisweet)
chocolate, roughly
chopped
15g/½oz/1 tbsp butter
50ml/2fl oz/¼ cup double
(heavy) cream

1 Preheat the oven to 140°C/275°F/Gas 1. Grease and line two baking sheets.

2 For the meringues, place the egg whites and sugar in a heatproof bowl set over a pan of simmering water. It is important that the bottom of the bowl does not touch the water. Using an electric whisk, whisk over the heat for 5 minutes, or until the mixture is foamy.

3 Remove the bowl from the heat and whisk the mixture for 5 minutes more, or until the meringue is stiff. Fold in the vanilla extract and food colouring.

4 Using a piping (pastry) bag fitted with a large plain nozzle, pipe 40 rounds of meringue on to the prepared baking sheets. Bake for 1–1¼ hours, or until the meringues are dried and crisp.

5 Leave the meringues to cool completely on the baking sheets, then peel of the baking parchment.

6 To make the ganache, put the chocolate, butter and cream in a heatproof bowl over a pan of simmering water.

7 Stir until the chocolate has melted and the mixture is smooth and glossy, then remove from the heat and leave to cool for about 1 hour, or until thickened.

8 Using a piping bag fitted with a plain nozzle, pipe a round of ganache on to the flat side of half of the meringues. Top with the flat sides of the remaining meringue halves. Allow to set. Press a cocktail stick into the filling to serve.

Energy 74kcal/139 kJ; Protein 585g; Carbohydrate 19g, of which sugars 17g; Fat 7g, of which saturates 3g; Cholesterol 30mg; Calcium 28mg; Fibre 0.g; Sodium 48mg.

Sweet pastries

This winning collection of sweet and delicate pastries includes a wide range of individual treats as well as tarts to slice and share. All the classics are included here, from favourite jam tarts that are the perfect treat for children, to a luxurious summer berry tart, packed with seasonal fruits. The pastry selection includes fabulous suggestions from around the world, too. Try irresistible custard tarts, flaky and flavoursome apple strudel, or for the ultimate indulgence nothing beats a chocolate éclair.

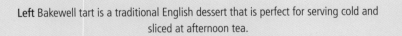

Left Bakewell tart is a traditional English dessert that is perfect for serving cold and sliced at afternoon tea.

Peach & blueberry tart

With its attractive lattice pastry top, this colourful tart is bursting with plump blueberries and juicy peaches. As tasty to eat as it is pretty to look at, it makes a great centrepiece.

SERVES 8
For the pastry
225g/8oz/2 cups plain (all-purpose) flour
2.5ml/½ tsp salt
5ml/1 tsp granulated (white) sugar
150g/5oz/⅔ cup cold butter or margarine, diced
1 egg yolk
30–45ml/2–3 tbsp iced water
30ml/2 tbsp milk, for glazing

For the filling
6 peaches, peeled, pitted and sliced
225g/8oz/2 cups fresh blueberries
150g/5oz/¾ cup granulated sugar
30ml/2 tbsp fresh lemon juice
40g/1½oz/⅓ cup plain (all-purpose) flour
pinch of grated nutmeg
25g/1oz/2 tbsp margarine or butter, diced

1 For the pastry, sift the flour, salt and sugar into a bowl. Rub the butter or margarine into the dry ingredients as quickly as possible until the mixture is crumbly and resembles breadcrumbs.

2 Mix the egg yolk with 30ml/2 tbsp of iced water and sprinkle over the flour mixture. Combine with a fork until the pastry holds together. If it is too crumbly, add a little more water, 5ml/1 tsp at a time. Gather the pastry into a ball and flatten into a disk. Wrap in clear film (plastic wrap) and chill for at least 20 minutes.

3 Roll out two-thirds of the pastry between sheets of baking parchment to a thickness of about 3mm/⅛in. Use to line a 23cm/9in fluted tin (pan). Trim all around, leaving a 1cm/½in overhang, then trim the edges.

4 Gather the trimmings and remaining pastry into a ball, and roll out to a thickness of about 6mm/¼in. Using a pastry wheel or sharp knife, cut strips 1cm/½in wide. Chill the pastry case and the strips for 20 minutes. Preheat the oven to 200°C/400°F/ Gas 6.

5 Line the pastry case with baking parchment and fill with dried beans. Bake blind until the pastry case is just set, 12–15 minutes. Remove from the oven and carefully lift out the paper with the beans. Prick the bottom of the pastry case all over with a fork, then return to the oven and bake for 5 minutes more.

6 Let the pastry case cool slightly before filling. Leave the oven on.

7 In a mixing bowl, combine the peach slices with the blueberries, sugar, lemon juice, flour and nutmeg. Spoon the fruit mixture evenly into the pastry case. Dot with the pieces of butter or margarine.

8 Weave a lattice top with the chilled pastry strips, pressing the ends to the baked pastry-case edge. Brush the strips with the milk.

9 Bake the pie for 15 minutes. Reduce the heat to 180°C/350°F/Gas 4, and bake until the filling is tender and bubbling and the lattice is golden, about 30 minutes more. If the pastry gets too brown, cover loosely with a piece of foil. Serve warm or at room temperature.

Energy 391kcal/1640kJ; Protein 4.7g; Carbohydrate 53g, of which sugars 27.7g; Fat 19.3g, of which saturates 11.7g; Cholesterol 72mg; Calcium 86mg; Fibre 2.9g; Sodium 139mg.

Treacle tart

Traditional shortcrust pastry is perfect for this old-fashioned teatime favourite, with its sticky lemon and syrup filling and twisted lattice topping. It's delicious warm or cold with cream and is equally at home on the tea table as for dessert.

SERVES 4–6

For the pastry

150g/5oz/1¼ cups plain (all-purpose) flour
pinch of salt
130g/4½oz/generous ½ cup butter, chilled and diced
45–60ml/3–4 tbsp chilled water

For the filling

275g/9½oz/generous ¾ cup golden (light corn) syrup
75g/2½oz/1½ cups fresh white breadcrumbs
grated rind of 1 lemon
30ml/2 tbsp lemon juice

1 To make the pastry, combine the flour and salt in a bowl. Rub in the butter until the mixture resembles coarse crumbs. With a fork, stir in enough water to bind the dough.

2 Gather into a ball, knead lightly for a few seconds until smooth, then wrap in clear film (plastic wrap) and chill for 20 minutes.

3 On a lightly floured surface, roll out the pastry to a thickness of 3mm/⅛in. Use to line a 20cm/8in fluted flan tin (pan) and trim off the overhang.

4 Chill the pastry case (pie shell) for 20 minutes. Reserve the pastry trimmings. Put a baking sheet in the oven and preheat to 200°C/ 400°F/Gas 6.

5 To make the filling, warm the syrup in a pan until it melts. Remove the syrup from the heat and stir in the breadcrumbs and lemon rind. Leave to stand for 10 minutes, then add more breadcrumbs if it is too runny. Stir in the lemon juice, then spread evenly in the pastry case.

6 Roll out the pastry trimmings and cut into 10–12 thin strips. Twist the strips and arrange half on the filling and the rest at right angles to form a lattice. Press the ends on to the rim.

7 Place the tart on the hot baking sheet and bake for 10 minutes. Lower the oven temperature to 190°C/ 375°F/Gas 5. Bake for 15 minutes more, until golden. Cool on a wire rack before serving.

Energy 420kcal/1764kJ; Protein 4.1g; Carbohydrate 63.5g, of which sugars 35.1g; Fat 18.4g, of which saturates 11.3g; Cholesterol 46mg; Calcium 62mg; Fibre 1.1g; Sodium 344mg.

Bakewell tart

A light version of an old-fashioned English tart, the frangipane topping of ground almonds, sugar and butter on a puff pastry base is not too sweet and contrasts perfectly with the jam. Served in wedges, warm or cold, it tastes wonderful at teatime.

SERVES 6–8

225g/8oz puff pastry, thawed if frozen
30ml/2 tbsp raspberry or apricot jam
2 eggs, plus 2 egg yolks
115g/4oz/generous ½ cup caster (superfine) sugar

115g/4oz/½ cup butter, melted
50g/2oz/½ cup ground almonds
a few drops almond extract
icing (confectioners') sugar, for dusting

1 Preheat the oven to 200°C/400°F/Gas 6.

2 Roll out the pastry on a lightly floured surface and use to line an 18cm/7in tart tin (pan). Trim the edges with a sharp knife.

3 Prick the pastry case (pie shell) all over, then spread jam over the base.

4 Whisk the eggs, egg yolks and sugar together in a large bowl until thick and pale. Stir the melted butter, ground almonds and almond extract into the whisked egg mixture.

5 Pour the mixture into the pastry case and bake for about 30 minutes, or until the filling is just set and lightly browned.

6 Dust with icing sugar before serving hot, warm or cold, with cream, if you like.

Cook's tip
This recipe uses puff pastry, but you could substitute a more traditional sweet, rich shortcrust pastry instead, if you prefer.

Energy 350kcal/1460kJ; Protein 5.4g; Carbohydrate 28.6g, of which sugars 18.5g; Fat 25g, of which saturates 8.7g; Cholesterol 129mg; Calcium 55mg; Fibre 0.5g; Sodium 197mg.

Lemon meringue pie

This classic tart, with its zesty lemon curd filling and sweet, crunchy top, is always extremely popular and is as welcome on a teatime table as it is for dessert. The pie is best served at room temperature, with or without cream, and should be eaten on the day of making.

SERVES 8

For the pastry
115g/4oz/1 cup plain (all-purpose) flour
pinch of salt
25g/1oz/2 tbsp cold lard, diced
25g/1oz/2 tbsp cold unsalted butter, diced

For the filling
50g/2oz/¼ cup cornflour (cornstarch)

175g/6oz/scant 1 cup caster (superfine) sugar
finely grated rind and juice of 2 lemons
2 egg yolks
15g/½oz/1 tbsp butter, diced

For the meringue
2 egg whites
75g/2½oz/scant ½ cup sugar

1 To make the pastry, sift the flour and salt into a bowl and add the lard and butter. With the fingertips, lightly rub the fats into the flour until the mixture resembles fine crumbs.

2 Stir in about 20ml/1½ tbsp cold water until the mixture can be gathered together into a smooth ball of dough. (Alternatively make the pastry using a food processor.) Wrap the pastry and chill for at least 30 minutes. Preheat the oven to 200°C/400°F/Gas 6.

3 Roll out the pastry on a lightly floured surface and use to line a 20cm/8in flan tin (pan). Prick the base with a fork, line with baking parchment or foil and add a layer of baking beans to prevent the pastry rising.

4 Put the pastry case (pie shell) into the hot oven and bake blind for 15 minutes. Remove the beans and parchment or foil, return the pastry to the oven and cook for a further 5 minutes until crisp and golden brown. Reduce the oven temperature to 150°C/300°F/Gas 2.

5 To make the lemon filling, put the cornflour into a pan and add the sugar, lemon rind and 300ml/½ pint/1¼ cups water. Heat the mixture, stirring continuously, until it comes to the boil and thickens. Reduce the heat and simmer very gently for 1 minute. Remove the pan from the heat and stir in the lemon juice.

6 Add the egg yolks to the lemon mixture, one at a time and beating after each addition, and then stir in the butter. Tip the mixture into the baked pastry case and level the surface.

7 To make the meringue topping, whisk the egg whites until stiff peaks form then whisk in half the sugar. Fold in the rest of the sugar using a metal spoon.

8 Spread the meringue over the lemon filling, covering it completely. Cook for about 20 minutes until lightly browned. Leave to stand until it is room temperature, then serve in slices.

Energy 391kcal/1640kJ; Protein 4.7g; Carbohydrate 53g, of which sugars 27.7g; Fat 19.3g, of which saturates 11.7g; Cholesterol 72mg; Calcium 86mg; Fibre 2.9g; Sodium 139mg.

Summer berry tart

A simple crisp pastry case is all that is needed to set off this classic filling of vanilla-flavoured custard, topped with luscious berry fruits and drizzled with syrup. Use whatever fruits are available locally for a colourful tart that is ideal to serve at a summer tea table.

SERVES 6–8

For the pastry
190g/6½oz/1⅔ cups plain (all-purpose) flour
pinch of salt
115g/4oz/½ cup butter, diced
1 egg yolk
30ml/2 tbsp chilled water

For the filling
3 egg yolks
50g/2oz/¼ cup caster (superfine) sugar
30ml/2 tbsp cornflour (cornstarch)
30ml/2 tbsp plain (all-purpose) flour
5ml/1 tsp vanilla extract
300ml/½ pint/scant 1¼ cups milk
150ml/5fl oz/⅔ cup double (heavy) cream
800g/1lb12oz/7 cups mixed summer berries
60ml/4 tbsp redcurrant jelly
30ml/2 tbsp raspberry liqueur
icing (confectioners') sugar, for dusting

1 To make the pastry, sift the flour and salt into a large mixing bowl. Rub in the butter until the mixture resembles fine breadcrumbs.

2 Mix the egg yolk with the chilled water and sprinkle over the dry ingredients. Mix to a firm dough using a round-bladed knife.

3 Knead the dough on a lightly floured surface for a few seconds, until smooth. Wrap in clear film (plastic wrap) and chill for 30 minutes.

4 Roll out the pastry and use to line a 23cm/9in round flan tin (pan). Wrap in clear film and chill. Preheat the oven to 200°C/400°F/Gas 6.

5 Prick the base of the pastry, line it with baking parchment, fill with baking beans and bake on a tray for 15 minutes. Remove the baking parchment and beans and bake for 10 minutes more. Leave to cool.

6 To make the filling, beat the egg yolks, caster sugar, cornflour, flour and vanilla together in a large mixing bowl until smooth.

7 Pour the milk into a pan, and heat gently until almost boiling. Slowly pour the milk on to the egg mixture, whisking all the time.

8 Pour the custard back from the bowl into the pan and stir constantly over low heat, until it has thickened. Work quickly or lumps will form.

9 Return to a clean mixing bowl, cover the surface with a piece of clear film and set aside to cool.

10 Whip the cream until thick, then fold into the cooled custard. Spoon the custard into the pastry case (pie shell) and spread out evenly.

11 Wash and dry the fruit, then arrange it attractively on top of the custard.

12 In a small pan, gently heat the redcurrant jelly and liqueur together until melted. Allow to cool, then brush liberally over the surface of the fruit.

13 Serve the tart within 3 hours of assembling. Dust with a little icing sugar for a finishing touch before serving.

Energy 432Kcal/1807kJ; Protein 6.7g; Carbohydrate 47.6g, of which sugars 21.8g; Fat 25.7g, of which saturates 14.6g; Cholesterol 160mg; Calcium 130mg; Fibre 2g; Sodium 150mg.

Raspberry & lemon tartlets

Fresh raspberries and lemon curd team up in these colourful pastries. Use the best lemon curd you can find, as it makes such a difference to the flavour. This makes 4 substantial tartlets but you could make smaller tarts if you prefer.

MAKES 4

For the pastry

115g/4oz/1 cup plain (all-purpose) flour, plus extra for dusting

15ml/1 tbsp caster (superfine) sugar

50g/2oz/4 tbsp butter, diced

about ½ egg, lightly beaten

For the filling

120ml/8 tbsp good-quality lemon curd, preferably homemade (see page 264)

115g/4oz/1 cup fresh raspberries

1 Sift the flour and sugar into a bowl. Rub in the butter until the mixture resembles fine crumbs. Stir in as much egg as required to form a smooth dough ball. Wrap in clear film (plastic wrap) and chill for 30 minutes.

2 Preheat the oven to 190°C/375°F/Gas 5. Roll out the pastry thinly on a floured surface and use to line four 9cm/3½in tartlet tins or muffin pans.

3 Line each tin with a circle of baking parchment and fill with baking beans or uncooked rice.

4 Bake blind in the preheated oven for 15–20 minutes, or until golden and cooked through.

5 Remove the baking beans or rice and paper and take the pastry cases out of the tins. Leave the cases to cool completely on a wire rack.

6 Set aside 12 raspberries for decoration and fold the remaining ones into the lemon curd. Spoon the mixture into the pastry cases and top with the reserved raspberries.

Energy 289Kcal/1214kJ; Protein 3.1g; Carbohydrate 40.6g, of which sugars 13.8g; Fat 13.9g, of which saturates 4.3g; Cholesterol 13mg; Calcium 47mg; Fibre 1.6g; Sodium 195mg.

Jam tarts

These nostalgic jam tarts are the perfect treat for afternoon tea, especially when children are present. Fill with your favourite jams, homemade if possible. Keep an eye on the tarts towards the end of the cooking time, and try not to overfill, or they look less neat.

MAKES 12

For the pastry

175g/6oz/1½ cups plain (all-purpose) flour
pinch of salt
30ml/2 tbsp caster (superfine) sugar
75g/2½oz/6 tbsp butter, diced
1 egg, lightly beaten

For the filling

60–75ml/4–5 tbsp fruit jam (see pages 262–3)

1 Sift the flour, salt and sugar into a bowl. Rub in the butter until the mixture resembles fine crumbs. Stir in the egg and gather into a smooth dough ball. Wrap in clear film (plastic wrap) and chill for 30 minutes.

2 Preheat the oven to 220°C/425°F/Gas 7. Lightly grease a 12-hole (or two 6-hole) tartlet tins or muffin pans.

3 Roll out the pastry on a floured surface to about 3mm/⅛in thick and, using a 7.5cm/3in cutter, stamp out 12 circles. Gather the trimmings, re-roll and cut out more.

4 Press the pastry circles into the prepared tartlet tin. Place a heaped teaspoonful of jam into the centre of each.

5 Bake for 15–20 minutes until the pastry is cooked through and light golden brown in colour.

6 Carefully lift the tarts out of the tin on to a wire rack and leave to cool before serving.

Energy 114kcal/479kJ; Protein 1.1g; Carbohydrate 18.8g, of which sugars 12.5g; Fat 4.3g, of which saturates 2.6g; Cholesterol 18mg; Calcium 16mg; Fibre 0.3g; Sodium 39mg.

Custard tarts

These luxurious little tarts are an indulgent treat. The silky texture of the custard combined with the rich vanilla-flavoured pastry is truly unsurpassable. The nutmeg-dusted delights are perfect served still warm with tea, but can be cooled and kept in the refrigerator for up to 2 days.

MAKES ABOUT 8

For the pastry
175g/6oz/1½ cups plain (all-purpose) flour
pinch of salt
75g/2½oz/6 tbsp unsalted butter
75g/2½oz/scant ½ cup sugar
3 egg yolks, at room temperature
few drops of vanilla extract

For the filling
600ml/1 pint/2½ cups full-fat (whole) milk
6 egg yolks
75g/2½oz/scant ½ cup caster (superfine) sugar
freshly grated nutmeg

1 To make the pastry, sift the flour and salt into a bowl. Put the butter, sugar, egg yolks and vanilla extract in a food processor and process until the mixture resembles scrambled eggs. Add the flour and blend briefly.

2 Transfer the dough to a floured surface and knead gently until smooth. Form into a ball, flatten and wrap in clear film (plastic wrap). Chill for at least 30 minutes. Bring back to room temperature before rolling out.

3 Roll out the pastry and use to line 8 individual 10cm/4in loose-bottomed tartlet tins (pans). Place on a baking sheet and chill for 30 minutes.

4 Preheat the oven to 200°C/400°F/Gas 6. To make the custard filling, gently heat the milk in a pan until just warmed but not yet boiling.

5 In a bowl, vigorously beat the egg yolks and sugar together until they become pale and creamy in texture. Pour the milk on to the yolks and stir well to mix. Do not whisk as this will produce too many bubbles.

6 Strain the milk mixture into a jug, then pour liquid into the tart cases. Liberally grate over fresh nutmeg.

7 Bake for about 10 minutes, then lower the heat to 180°C/350°F/Gas 4 and bake for 10 minutes, or until the filling has set and is just turning golden. The custard should be a bit wobbly when they come out of the oven.

8 Remove from the oven and lift the tarts out of the tins. Serve warm or cold.

Energy 336kcal/1409kJ; Protein 7.9g; Carbohydrate 40g, of which sugars 23.4g; Fat 17.1g, of which saturates 8.6g; Cholesterol 257mg; Calcium 157mg; Fibre 0.7g; Sodium 101mg.

Mince pies

These small pies have become synonymous with Christmas; to eat one per day for the 12 days of Christmas was thought to bring happiness for the coming year. They make a wonderful addition to a festive teatime, being neither too sweet nor too savoury.

MAKES 12

For the pastry

225g/8oz/2 cups plain (all-purpose) flour

45ml/3 tbsp caster (superfine) sugar

115g/4oz/½ cup butter, diced, plus extra for greasing

1 egg, lightly beaten

For the filling

350g/12oz mincemeat (see page 265)

icing (confectioners') sugar for dusting

1 To make the pastry, sift the flour and stir in the sugar. Rub in the butter until the mixture resembles fine crumbs. Stir in the egg and gather into a smooth dough.

2 Chill the pastry for 30 minutes. Preheat the oven to 220°C/425°F/Gas 7 and grease a 12-hole bun tray.

3 Roll out the pastry on a lightly floured surface to about 3mm/⅛in thick and, using a 7.5cm/3in cutter, cut out 12 circles. Press into the prepared tray. Gather up the offcuts and roll out again, cutting slightly smaller circles to make 12 lids.

4 Spoon mincemeat into each case, dampen the edges and top with a pastry lid. Make a small slit in each pie.

5 Bake for 15–20 minutes until golden brown. Transfer to a wire rack to cool and serve dusted with sugar.

Energy 236kcal/993kJ; Protein 2.5g; Carbohydrate 36.7g, of which sugars 22.4g; Fat 9.8g, of which saturates 5.2g; Cholesterol 37mg; Calcium 43mg; Fibre 1g; Sodium 70mg.

Apple strudel

The apfelstrudel – wafer-thin pastry layers with a luscious chopped apple filling – was first baked by the Hungarians, and then adopted by the Viennese. The longer sheets of filo are best for this recipe, but if you cannot find these, use two small sheets and overlap them. Eat fresh.

SERVES 8–10

900g/2lb cooking apples
grated rind and juice of 1 lemon
50g/2oz/¼ cup caster
(superfine) sugar
75g/2½oz/generous ½ cup
sultanas (golden raisins)
115g/4oz/½ cup unsalted butter
75g/2½oz/1½ cups fresh white
breadcrumbs

50g/2oz/½ cup flaked
(sliced) almonds
2.5ml/½ tsp mixed (apple pie)
spice
400g/14oz filo pastry, thawed
if frozen
icing (confectioners') sugar,
for dusting

1 Peel, core and slice the apples. Put them in a pan with the lemon rind and juice and the sugar. Cook over a medium heat for 8–10 minutes, or until tender. Put in a bowl, add the sultanas and cool for 30 minutes.

2 Preheat the oven to 190°C/375°F/Gas 5. Grease a large baking sheet.

3 Melt 30ml/2 tbsp of the butter in a pan, add the breadcrumbs and cook, stirring, until golden brown. Stir in the almonds and spice. Cook for 1 minute, then set aside to cool.

4 Melt the remaining butter and brush over a large filo sheet. Reserve two sheets for decoration. Continue to butter the sheets and layer them on top of the first sheet. Brush the top layer with butter.

5 Sprinkle half the crumb mixture over, leaving a 5cm/2in border at the edges. Top with the cooked apples, then with the remaining crumbs.

6 Fold in the sides, then roll up like a Swiss roll (jelly roll) to enclose the filling. Put on the prepared baking sheet, join side down.

7 Make ruffles from the reserved filo and arrange on top. Brush all over with butter and bake for 25–30 minutes, or until light golden and crisp.

8 Cool slightly, dust with icing sugar and serve warm or cold with crème fraîche or plain (natural) yogurt.

Energy 397kcal/1676kJ; Protein 5.3g; Carbohydrate 66g, of which sugars 30.7g; Fat 14.4g, of which saturates 8.7g; Cholesterol 35mg; Calcium 82mg; Fibre 3.1g; Sodium 196mg.

Baklava

An eastern Mediterranean classic, baklava makes a wonderful addition to an afternoon tea spread, and pairs brilliantly with both tea and coffee. The delicate diamonds of flaky pastry contain a layer of chopped nuts and cinnamon, moistened with flavoursome syrup.

MAKES 12

175g/6oz/¾ cup clarified or unsalted butter

100ml/3½fl oz/scant ½ cup sunflower oil

450g/1lb filo pastry, thawed if frozen

450g/1lb/3½ cups walnuts, or a mixture of walnuts, pistachios and almonds, finely chopped

5ml/1 tsp ground cinnamon

For the syrup

450g/1lb/3 cups white sugar

juice of 1 lemon, or 30ml/2 tbsp rosewater

1 Preheat the oven to 160°C/325°F/ Gas 3. Melt the butter and oil in a pan, then brush a little over the bottom and sides of a 30cm/12in round or square cake tin (pan).

2 Place a sheet of filo in the bottom and brush it with melted butter and oil. Continue until you have used half the filo sheets. Ease the sheets into the corners and trim the edges if they flop over the rim of the tin.

3 Spread the nuts over the last buttered sheet and sprinkle with the cinnamon, then continue as before with the remaining filo sheets.

4 Brush the top one as well, then cut diagonal parallel lines through all the layers to the bottom to form small diamond shapes.

5 Bake the baklava for about 1 hour, until the top is golden – if it is still pale, increase the temperature for a few minutes at the end.

6 While the baklava is in the oven, make the syrup. Put the sugar into a heavy pan, pour in 250ml/8½fl oz/1 cup water and bring to the boil, stirring all the time.

7 When the sugar has dissolved, lower the heat and stir in the lemon juice, then simmer for about 15 minutes, until the syrup thickens. Leave to cool in the pan.

8 When the baklava is ready, remove it from the oven and slowly pour the cooled syrup over the hot pastry.

9 Return the tin to the oven for 2–3 minutes to soak up the syrup, then take it out and leave to cool.

10 Once cool, lift the baklava diamonds out of the tin and serve.

Cook's tip

To flavour the syrup, you can use lemon juice as here for a refreshing tang, or rosewater for its distinctive floral notes – both are traditional. Orange blossom water also works well.

Energy 275kcal/1147kJ; Protein 2.5g; Carbohydrate 32g, of which sugars 10.2g; Fat 15.7g, of which saturates 9.8g; Cholesterol 40mg; Calcium 37mg; Fibre 0.8g; Sodium 197mg.

Chocolate whirls

These pastry cookies are deceptively simple to rustle up from ready-made puff pastry, which is rolled out and filled with a quick chocolate and sultana paste. Drizzles of melted chocolate give the bakes a fancy-looking finish.

MAKES 20

75g/2½oz/scant ½ cup golden caster (superfine) sugar
40g/1½oz/6 tbsp unsweetened cocoa powder
2 eggs
500g/1lb2oz puff pastry, thawed if frozen
25g/1oz/2 tbsp butter, softened
75g/2½oz/scant ½ cup sultanas (golden raisins)
90g/3oz milk chocolate

Variation

You can use whatever type of chocolate you like to decorate these whirls, or a mixture – they look especially smart streaked with white and dark chocolate.

1 Preheat the oven to 220°C/425°F/Gas 7. Put the sugar, cocoa powder and eggs in a bowl and mix to a paste.

2 Roll out the pastry on a lightly floured surface to make a 30cm/12in square. Trim off any rough edges.

3 Dot the pastry all over with the butter, then spread with the cocoa paste. Sprinkle sultanas over the top.

4 Roll the pastry into a sausage shape, then cut the roll into 1cm/½in slices. Place the slices on the baking sheets, spacing them apart.

5 Bake for 10 minutes until risen and pale golden. Transfer to a wire rack and leave to cool.

6 Break the chocolate into pieces and put in a heatproof bowl set over a pan of simmering water. Heat, stirring until melted and smooth.

7 Spoon lines of melted chocolate over the cookies.

Cook's tips

• Use a sharp knife to cut the cookie slices from the pastry roll.
• Use a good-quality all-butter puff pastry if possible, for the best taste and texture.

Energy 165kcal/689kJ; Protein 2.9g; Carbohydrate 18.6g, of which sugars 9.4g; Fat 9.5g, of which saturates 1.9g; Cholesterol 23mg; Calcium 34mg; Fibre 0.4g; Sodium 117mg.

Chocolate & strawberry palmiers

Who could resist sweet and crisp puff pastry, with layers of chocolate, whipped cream and fresh strawberries, as a summer treat? These little pastries, formed into rounded swirls, may look complicated but are easy to make, and look delightful on the tea table.

MAKES 8

15g/½oz/2 tbsp unsweetened cocoa powder

375g/13oz puff pastry, thawed if frozen

25g/1oz/2 tbsp golden caster (superfine) sugar

175g/6oz/1½ cups strawberries, sliced

icing (confectioners') sugar, for dusting

For the filling

300ml/½ pint/1¼ cups whipping cream, whipped

45ml/3 tbsp chocolate spread

1 Preheat the oven to 220°C/425°F/Gas 7. Grease two large baking sheets.

2 Dust a clean, dry working surface lightly with 15ml/ 1 tbsp cocoa powder.

3 Keeping the long side of pastry towards you, roll it out on the cocoa powder to a rectangle 35 x 23cm/14 x 9in. Lightly brush the top of the pastry with cold water, then sprinkle over the caster sugar and remaining cocoa.

4 Measure and with a sharp knife mark the centre of the pastry. Roll up each of the short sides like a Swiss roll (jelly roll) so that they meet in the centre. Brush the join with a little water and press the rolls together to secure.

5 With a sharp knife, mark out and then cut the doubled pastry roll into 16 slices. Arrange on the baking sheets, using a metal spatula, spacing them well apart.

6 Bake for 8–10 minutes, or until risen, puffy and golden brown. Remove and cool on a wire rack.

7 To make the filling, put the cream in a piping or pastry bag fitted with a small plain nozzle. Spread half the pastries with the chocolate spread. Pipe the cream on to the remaining pastries and top with strawberries.

8 Sandwich the chocolate base with the cream and strawberry layer. Dust with icing sugar and serve.

Energy 368kcal/1533kJ; Protein 4.2g; Carbohydrate 27g, of which sugars 9.7g; Fat 28.3g, of which saturates 10.4g; Cholesterol 40mg; Calcium 60mg; Fibre 0.5g; Sodium 180mg.

Chocolate éclairs

These crisp choux pastry fingers are filled with fresh cream, and make an indulgent treat with afternoon tea. The finishing touch to the éclairs is a thick, glossy coat of dark chocolate. They are best served within 2 hours of making, but can be chilled for 24 hours if required.

MAKES 12

65g/2¼oz/generous ½ cup plain (all-purpose) flour
pinch of salt
50g/2oz/4 tbsp butter, diced
150ml/5fl oz/⅔ cup water
2 eggs, lightly beaten

10ml/2 tsp icing (confectioners') sugar, sifted
1.5ml/¼ tsp vanilla extract
115g/4oz plain (semisweet) chocolate
30ml/2 tbsp water
25g/1oz/2 tbsp butter

For the filling & topping
300ml/½ pint/1¼ cups double (heavy) cream

1 Preheat the oven to 200°C/400°F/Gas 6. Grease a large baking sheet and line it with baking parchment.

2 To make the pastry, sift the flour and salt on to a small sheet of baking parchment.

3 Heat the butter and water in a pan very gently until the butter melts, then increase the heat and bring to a rolling boil.

4 Remove the pan from the heat and add all the flour. Beat vigorously with a wooden spoon until the flour is incorporated. Return the pan to low heat, then beat until it leaves the sides of the pan and forms a ball.

5 Set the pan aside and allow the choux pastry mixture to cool for 2–3 minutes.

6 Add the beaten eggs a little at a time, beating well after each addition, until you have a smooth, shiny paste, which is thick enough to hold its shape.

7 Spoon the choux pastry into a piping or pastry bag fitted with a 2.5cm/1in plain nozzle. Pipe 10cm/4in lengths on to the prepared baking sheet. Use a wet knife to cut off the pastry at the nozzle.

8 Bake for 25–30 minutes, or until the pastry fingers are well risen and golden brown in colour. Remove from the oven. Make a neat slit along the side of each finger to release the steam.

9 Lower the oven temperature to 180°C/350°F/Gas 4 and bake for a further 5 minutes. Cool on a wire rack.

10 To make the filling, whip the cream with the icing sugar and vanilla extract until it just holds its shape. Spoon into a piping bag fitted with a 1cm/½in plain nozzle and use to fill the éclairs.

11 Place the chocolate and water in a heatproof bowl set over a pan of simmering water until melted. Remove from the heat and gradually stir in the butter.

12 Dip the top of each éclair in the melted chocolate, then place on a rack. Leave in a cool place until the chocolate is set.

Variation
To make profiteroles instead of chocolate éclairs, simply use the same choux pastry mixture to pipe rounds, instead of fingers, on to baking parchment. Dampen your finger and gently press down any peaks that may form when you lift off the piping bag, or these can burn. Bake the buns for a little less time than the fingers – about 20 minutes, keeping an eye on them towards the end of the cooking time to avoid letting them over-brown; they should be pale golden and risen. Instead of making a slit, poke a hole in the bottom of each bun with a skewer, then return to the oven briefly to dry out. Once cool, fill with cream and top with chocolate as you would éclairs.

 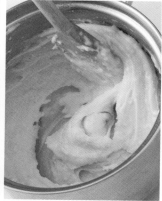

Energy 253kcal/1046kJ; Protein 2.7g; Carbohydrate 10.8g, of which sugars 6.5g; Fat 22.4g, of which saturates 13.5g; Cholesterol 86mg; Calcium 30mg; Fibre 0.4g; Sodium 58mg.

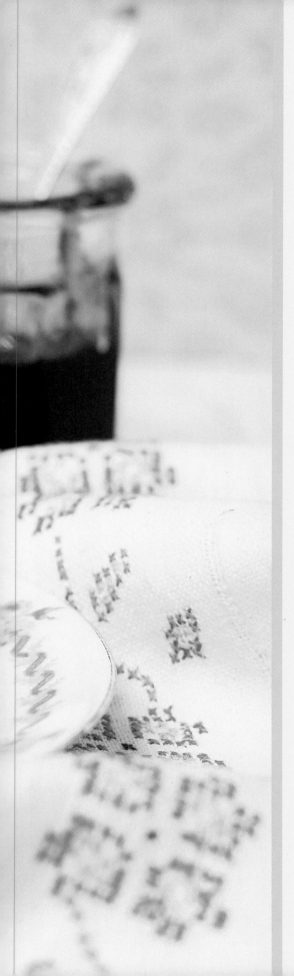

Useful basics

This section contains a range of recipes for some of the building blocks of afternoon tea: breads and rolls for slicing and making into delicate sandwiches; chutneys and other condiments to liven up the savouries; and jams for adding a special touch to scones and as fillings for teatime classics such as Victoria sponge cake or jam tarts. Although you can of course buy all of these preserves, making your own really makes a difference to the end result, and many can be made in bulk, divided into portions or jars, and brought out as required.

Left One of the most simple teatime pleasures has to be homemade jam on toasted homemade bread.

White sandwich loaf

Make this dough into any shape you like, such as braids, bloomers, or rolls. Bread must be made with strong bread flour as it has a high gluten content, which rises better. This mixture makes four loaves, so you can freeze some, or halve the quantities if you prefer.

MAKES 4 LOAVES

15g/1oz fresh yeast
10ml/2 tsp caster (superfine) sugar
900ml/1½ pints/3½ cups tepid water, or milk and water mixed
15ml/1 tbsp salt

1.3kg/3lb/12 cups strong white bread flour, preferably unbleached, plus extra for dusting
50g/2oz/4 tbsp white vegetable fat (shortening) or butter, or 50ml/2fl oz/3½ tbsp vegetable oil

1 Cream the yeast and caster sugar together in a measuring jug or cup, add about 150ml/5fl oz/⅔ cup of the measured liquid and leave in a warm place for about 10 minutes to froth up.

2 Meanwhile, mix the salt into the flour and rub in the fat (if using oil, add it to the remaining liquid).

3 Using an electric mixer with a dough hook attachment, or working by hand in a mixing bowl, add the yeast mixture and remaining liquid to the flour, and work it in to make a firm dough that leaves the bowl clean.

4 Knead well on a floured surface, or in the mixer, until the dough has become firm and elastic. Return to the bowl, cover lightly with a dish towel and leave in a warm place to rise for an hour, or until it has doubled in size. The dough will be springy and full of air. Meanwhile, oil four 450g/1lb loaf tins (pans).

5 Turn the dough out on to a floured work surface and knock back (punch down), flattening it out with your knuckles to knock the air out. Knead lightly into shape again, divide into four pieces and form into loaf shapes.

6 Place the dough in the loaf tins, pushing down well to fit into the corners, then leave to rise again for another 20–30 minutes. Meanwhile, preheat the oven to 230°C/450°F/Gas 8.

7 When the dough has risen just above the rims of the loaf tins, bake in the centre of the oven for 30 minutes, or until browned and shrinking a little from the sides of the tins; when turned out and rapped underneath they should sound hollow. Cool on wire racks.

Energy 1223kcal/5185kJ; Protein 30.7g; Carbohydrate 256.4g, of which sugars 7.5g; Fat 15.2g, of which saturates 6.3g; Cholesterol 0mg; Calcium 457mg; Fibre 10.1g; Sodium 1.48g.

Wholemeal loaf

This recipe is for a traditional wholemeal loaf with a lovely chewy texture from using a starter dough, and a nutty flavour from the wholemeal flour. For a lighter loaf, substitute some of the wholemeal flour with strong white bread flour.

MAKES 2 LOAVES

800g/1lb12oz/7 cups wholemeal (whole-wheat) flour, plus extra for dusting
45ml/3 tbsp sugar
40g/1½oz/3 tbsp butter, softened, plus extra for greasing
450ml/16fl oz/scant 2 cups lukewarm water
25ml/1½ tbsp salt

For the starter

200g/7oz/1¾ cups wholemeal (whole-wheat) flour
3 sachets easy-blend (rapid-rise) dried yeast
200–300ml/7–10fl oz/ scant 1–1¼ cups lukewarm water

1 For the starter, mix the flour and yeast in a large measuring jug or cup. Blend in enough of the water, a spoon at a time, until creamy. Cover and leave until it has foamed up to measure 1 litre/1¾ pints/4 cups.

2 Put the flour, sugar and butter in the bowl of an electric mixer with a dough hook. Add the starter and the 450ml/¾ pint lukewarm water and knead slowly.

3 Add the salt after a few minutes, then increase the speed and knead for about 10 minutes, until the dough comes away from the side of the bowl. Alternatively, knead by hand on a floured surface for 20 minutes.

4 Transfer the dough to a very large bowl. Cover with damp dish towels and leave until the dough has risen just above the bowl rim. Preheat the oven to 220°C/425°F/Gas 7. Grease two 30 x 10 x 10cm/12 x 4 x 4in loaf tins (pans) with butter.

5 Turn out the dough on to a lightly floured surface and with floured hands shape it into a rectangle 30cm/12in wide. Using scissors, cut the rectangle in half widthways. Dust both with flour and brush off any excess.

6 Roll up both dough rectangles and place in the tins, with the folds underneath. Slash the surface diagonally, cover with dampened dish towels and leave until the dough has risen well above the rims of the tins.

7 Bake for 20–25 minutes, until golden. Turn out the loaves on to wire racks and leave to cool.

Energy 1933kcal/8198kJ; Protein 47.2g; Carbohydrate 409.5g, of which sugars 28.5g; Fat 23g, of which saturates 11.4g; Cholesterol 43mg; Calcium 715mg; Fibre 15.5g; Sodium 1120mg.

Brown soda bread

Perhaps the easiest to make of all loaves, soda bread is yeast-free and so doesn't need time to rise. It is baked straight away and is best eaten on the day it is made. It tastes delicious spread with unsalted butter and topped with a fruity jam or a slice of farmhouse cheese.

MAKES 1 LOAF

450g/1lb/4 cups wholemeal (wholewheat) flour

175g/6oz/1½ cups plain (all-purpose) flour, plus extra for dusting

7.5ml/1½ tsp bicarbonate of soda (baking soda)

5ml/1 tsp salt

about 450ml/16fl oz/scant 2 cups buttermilk

1 Preheat the oven to 200°C/400°F/Gas 6, and grease a baking sheet.

2 Combine the dry ingredients in a mixing bowl and stir in enough buttermilk to make a fairly soft dough.

3 Turn on to a work surface dusted with wholemeal flour, and knead lightly until smooth.

4 Form the dough into a circle, about 4cm/1½in thick. Place it on the baking sheet and mark a deep cross in the top with the blunt side of a knife.

5 Bake for about 45 minutes, or until the bread is browned and sounds hollow when tapped on the base.

6 Leave the loaf to cool on a wire rack. If a soft crust is preferred, wrap the loaf in a clean dish towel while cooling.

Energy 2262kcal/9643kJ; Protein 88.5g; Carbohydrate 465.4g, of which sugars 31.4g; Fat 18.9g, of which saturates 6.5g; Cholesterol 27mg; Calcium 1.37g; Fibre 34.2g; Sodium 2.18g.

Soft white rolls

These rolls are delectable served warm, as soon as they are baked, preferably with a pat of fresh butter and homemade jams and jellies, or they can be left to cool, split and filled with a range of sandwich fillings for afternoon tea.

MAKES 10

450g/1lb/4 cups unbleached plain (all-purpose) white flour, plus extra for dusting
10ml/2 tsp salt
20g/³⁄₄oz fresh yeast

150ml/5fl oz/²⁄₃ cup lukewarm milk, plus extra for glazing
150ml/5fl oz/²⁄₃ cup lukewarm water

1 Grease two baking sheets. Sift the flour and salt together into a large bowl and make a well in the centre.

2 Mix the yeast with the milk, then mix in the water. Stir to dissolve. Add the yeast mixture to the centre of the flour and mix together to form a soft dough.

3 Knead the dough lightly then cover with lightly oiled clear film (plastic wrap) and leave to rise in a warm place for 1 hour, or until doubled in size.

4 Turn the dough out on to a floured surface and knock back (punch down).

5 Divide the dough into 10 equal pieces. Knead each roll lightly and, using a rolling pin, shape each piece to a flat 10 x 7.5cm/4 x 3in oval or a flat 9cm/3¹⁄₂in round.

6 Transfer the rolls to the prepared baking sheets and cover with oiled clear film. Leave to rise in a warm place for about 30 minutes.

7 Meanwhile, preheat the oven to 200°C/400°F/Gas 6.

8 Remove the clear film – the rolls should have risen slightly. Press each roll in the centre with your three middle fingers to equalize the air bubbles and to help prevent blistering.

9 Brush the tops with milk and dust with flour. Bake for 15–20 minutes, or until lightly browned.

10 As soon as you have taken the rolls out of the oven, dust with more flour and cool slightly on a wire rack. Serve warm with butter and jam, or leave to cool and fill with your choice of sandwich filling.

Energy 160kcal/682kJ; Protein 4.7g; Carbohydrate 35.7g, of which sugars 1.4g; Fat 0.8g, of which saturates 0.3g; Cholesterol 1mg; Calcium 81mg; Fibre 1.4g; Sodium 401mg.

Apricot jam

Sweet, tangy apricot and almond jam is delicous on scones, and in tarts and bakes.

MAKES 2KG/4½LB

675g/1lb8oz ready-to-eat dried apricots, soaked overnight in 900ml/1½ pints/3½ cups apple juice

juice and grated rind of 2 lemons
675g/1lb8oz/scant 3½ cups preserving sugar
50g/2oz/½ cup blanched almonds, coarsely chopped

1 Put the apricots and juice into a preserving pan and add the lemon juice and rind. Bring to the boil, then lower the heat and simmer for 15–20 minutes until soft.

2 Add the sugar to the pan and bring up to the boil, stirring until the sugar has completely dissolved. Boil for 15–20 minutes, or until setting point is reached.

3 Stir the chopped almonds into the jam and leave to stand for about 15 minutes, then pour the jam into warmed, sterilized jars (see page 265).

4 Seal, then leave to cool. Label and store in a cool, dark place for up to 1 year.

Strawberry jam

Perfectly ripe strawberries are the main ingredient of this most popular jam.

MAKES 1.3KG/3LB

1kg/2lb3oz/8 cups strawberries, hulled

900g/2lb/4½ cups preserving sugar
juice of 2 lemons

1 Layer the strawberries and sugar in a bowl. Cover and leave overnight. Put with the lemon juice into a large heavy pan. Bring to the boil, over low heat, stirring until the sugar has dissolved. Boil for 10–15 minutes, or until setting point is reached. Let stand for 10 minutes.

2 Pour into warm sterilized jars (see page 265), cover and seal. Store in a cool dark place for up to 1 year.

The setting point of jam

The point at which jam sets is 105°C/220°F. If you don't have a sugar thermometer, put 10ml/2 tsp of the jam on to a chilled saucer. Chill for 3 minutes, then push the jam gently with your finger; if wrinkles form it is ready. If not, continue boiling the jam, but keep checking regularly.

Apricot: Energy 4032kcal/17,163kJ; Protein 40.9g; Carbohydrate 955.2g, of which sugars 953.8g; Fat 31.9g, of which saturates 2.2g; Cholesterol 0mg; Calcium 970mg; Fibre 46.2g; Sodium 142mg.
Strawberry: Energy 3816kcal/16,259kJ; Protein 12.5g; Carbohydrate 1000.5g, of which sugars 1000.5g; Fat 1g, of which saturates 0g; Cholesterol 0mg; Calcium 637mg; Fibre 11g; Sodium 114mg.

Raspberry jam

For many, this is the best of all jams; it is delicious with scones and cream.

MAKES 3KG/7LB

1.8kg/4lb raspberries
juice of 1 large lemon

1.8kg/4lb/9 cups preserving sugar, warmed

1 Put 175g/6oz of the raspberries into a large, heavy pan and crush them. Add the rest and the lemon juice. Bring to the boil, and simmer until soft and pulpy.

2 Add the sugar and stir until dissolved. Bring back to the boil and boil rapidly until setting point is reached. Remove from the heat and leave to cool for 10 minutes.

3 Pour into warmed sterilized jars (see page 265), filling to the top. Cover and seal. Label when the jar is cold, then store in a cool, dark place for up to 1 year.

Damson jam

Dark, plump damsons produce a deeply coloured and richly flavoured jam.

MAKES 2KG/4½LB

1kg/2lb3oz damsons
400ml/14fl oz/1⅔ cups water

1kg/2lb3oz/5 cups preserving sugar, warmed

1 Put the damsons in a large, heavy pan and pour in the water. Bring to the boil, then reduce the heat and simmer until the damsons are soft. Stir in the sugar.

2 Bring the mixture to the boil. Skim off the stones (pits) as they rise to the surface. Boil to setting point. Remove from the heat and leave to cool for 10 minutes.

3 Pour into warmed sterilized jars (see page 265), cover and seal. Allow to cool, then label. Store in a cool, dark place for up to 1 year.

Raspberry: Energy 7542kcal/32,220kJ; Protein 34.2g; Carbohydrate 1963.8g, of which sugars 1963.8g; Fat 5.4g, of which saturates 1.8g; Cholesterol 0mg; Calcium 1.4mg; Fibre 45g; Sodium 162mg.
Damson: Energy 4320kcal/18,430kJ; Protein 10g; Carbohydrate 1141g, of which sugars 1141g; Fat 0g, of which saturates 0g; Cholesterol 0mg; Calcium 770mg; Fibre 18g; Sodium 80mg.

Lemon curd

This classic tangy, creamy curd is enduringly popular and delectable in cakes or on crumpets.

MAKES ABOUT 450G/1LB

3 unwaxed lemons

200g/7oz/1 cup caster (superfine) sugar

115g/4oz/½ cup unsalted butter, diced

2 large (US extra large) eggs and 2 large egg yolks

1 Wash the lemons, then grate the rind into a large heatproof bowl. Squeeze the juice into the bowl.

2 Set the bowl over a pan of gently simmering water and add the sugar and butter. Stir until the sugar has dissolved and the butter melted.

3 Beat the eggs and yolks in a bowl. Pour through a sieve (strainer) into the lemon mixture, and whisk well.

4 Stir the mixture constantly over the heat until the lemon curd thickens and lightly coats the back of a wooden spoon.

5 Remove the pan from the heat and pour the curd into small, warmed sterilized jars (see page 265). Cover and seal immediately. Allow to cool, then label.

6 Store in a cool, dark place, ideally in the refrigerator. Use within 3 months. Once opened, store the lemon curd in the refrigerator and use it up quickly.

Apple & sultana chutney

This versatile chutney pairs brilliantly with cheese or ham and really elevates sandwiches.

MAKES 900G/2LB

350g/12oz cooking apples, such as Bramley

115g/4oz/⅔ cup sultanas (golden raisins)

50g/2oz onions

25g/1oz/¼ cup blanched almonds

5ml/1 tsp white peppercorns

2.5ml/½ tsp coriander seeds

175g/6oz/scant 1 cup sugar

10ml/2 tsp salt

5ml/1 tsp ground ginger

450ml/16fl oz/scant 2 cups cider vinegar

1.5ml/¼ tsp cayenne pepper

red chillies (optional)

1 Peel, core and chop the apples. Chop the sultanas, onion and almonds. Tie the peppercorns and coriander seeds in muslin (cheesecloth), using a long piece of string, then tie to the handle of a preserving or stainless-steel pan.

2 Put the sugar, salt, ground ginger and vinegar into the pan, with the cayenne pepper to taste. Heat gently, stirring, until the sugar has completely dissolved.

3 Add the chopped fruit to the pan. Bring to the boil and simmer for 1½–2 hours, or until most of the liquid has evaporated.

4 Spoon into warmed, sterilized jars (see page 265) and place a chilli in each jar, if using. Once cold, cover, seal and label. Store in a cool dark place for up to 6 months.

Curd: Energy 1927kcal/8056kJ; Protein 20.7g; Carbohydrate 212.1g, of which sugars 212.1g; Fat 116.8g, of which saturates 66.2g; Cholesterol 1029mg; Calcium 294mg; Fibre 0g; Sodium 871mg.
Chutney: Energy 1299Kcal/5525kJ; Protein 10.9g; Carbohydrate 299.5g, of which sugars 297.7g; Fat 14.9g, of which saturates 1.1g; Cholesterol 0mg; Calcium 254mg; Fibre 10.4g; Sodium 3.97g

Mincemeat

In many mincemeat recipes, the raw ingredients are simply mixed together. Here, gentle cooking develops and intensifies the flavour, so that it may be used straight away without being left to mature. At the same time, heating helps prevent fermentation, allowing a much longer shelf-life.

MAKES 1.75KG/4LB

450g/1lb cooking apples
115g/4oz/²⁄₃ cup glacé (candied) citrus peel
115g/4oz/²⁄₃ cup glacé (candied) cherries
115g/4oz/²⁄₃ cup ready-to-eat dried apricots
115g/4oz/1 cup blanched almonds
150ml/5fl oz/²⁄₃ cup brandy
225g/8oz/1¹⁄₃ cups currants
225g/8oz/1¹⁄₃ cups sultanas (golden raisins)
450g/1lb/3 cups seedless raisins
225g/8oz/1 cup soft dark brown sugar
225g/8oz/1¹⁄₃ cups suet (chilled, grated shortening) or vegetarian suet
10ml/2 tsp ground ginger
5ml/1 tsp ground allspice
5ml/1 tsp ground cinnamon
2.5ml/½ tsp grated nutmeg
grated rind and juice of 1 lemon
grated rind and juice of 1 orange

1 Peel, core and chop the cooking apples, then roughly chop the citrus peel, glacé cherries, apricots and blanched almonds.

2 Reserve half the brandy and put the rest into a heavy pan with all the other ingredients. Stir well until thoroughly mixed.

3 Cover and place over a very low heat. Cook for about 1 hour, stirring halfway through cooking to prevent the mixture from overheating and sticking to the sides of the pan.

4 Remove the lid and leave the mixture to cool completely, stirring occasionally. Stir the reserved brandy into the mincemeat and spoon the mixture into sterilized jars.

5 Cover and store in a cool, dry place for up to 6 months. Once opened, store in the refrigerator and use within 2 weeks.

To sterilize jars

The easiest way to sterilize jars is to put them through the hot cycle in a dishwasher. Alternatively, place the open jars and lids on a baking sheet in a cold oven, bring up to 140°C/275°F/Gas 1 and bake for about 10 minutes.

Energy 7149Kcal/30087kJ; Protein 55.6g; Carbohydrate 1114g, of which sugars 1088.3g; Fat 267.7g, of which saturates 106.3g; Cholesterol 0mg; Calcium 1228mg; Fibre 47.3g; Sodium 774mg.

Mayonnaise

*Homemade mayonnaise is quick and easy
to make. The secret of success is having all
ingredients at room temperature.*

MAKES 225ML/8FL OZ

1 fresh egg yolk

5ml/1 tsp mustard powder or
made mustard

15ml/1 tbsp lemon juice or white
wine vinegar

salt and ground black pepper,
to taste

120–200ml/4–7fl oz/½–scant
1 cup vegetable oil or sunflower oil

1 Mix the egg yolk, mustard, lemon juice or vinegar,
salt and pepper in a bowl placed on a wet towel to
prevent it from moving while whisking. Pour the oil into
a jug or pitcher.

2 Whisk the mixture vigorously with one hand while
adding the oil slowly drop by drop with the other.
When it begins to thicken, the oil can be added more
quickly, in a thin and steady stream. It may not be
necessary to add all the oil. Stop when the mayonnaise
is thick and creamy. Check the seasoning is to your
taste, then serve.

Horseradish sauce

*Fiery, peppery horseradish sauce is the
essential accompaniment to roast beef, and
is also delicious with smoked salmon.*

MAKES 200ML/7FL OZ

45ml/3 tbsp freshly grated
horseradish root

15ml/1 tbsp white wine vinegar

5ml/1 tsp granulated white
sugar

pinch of salt

150ml/5fl oz/⅔ cup thick double
(heavy) cream

1 Place the grated horseradish in a bowl, then add the
white wine vinegar, granulated sugar and just a pinch of
salt. Stir the ingredients together, mixing them well until
they are thoroughly combined and smooth.

2 Pour the mixture into a sterilized jar (see page 265).
It will keep in the refrigerator for up to 6 months, but
use it up once the cream is added.

3 A few hours before you intend to serve the sauce, stir
the cream into the horseradish and leave to infuse. Stir
once again before serving.

Mayonnaise: Energy 958kcal/3940kJ; Protein 3.3g; Carbohydrate 0.5g, of which sugars 0.4g; Fat 104.8g, of which saturates 13.1g; Cholesterol 202mg; Calcium 27mg; Fibre 0g; Sodium 157mg.
Horseradish: Energy 774kcal/3190kJ; Protein 2.8g; Carbohydrate 9.9g, of which sugars 9.8g; Fat 80.7g, of which saturates 50.1g; Cholesterol 206mg; Calcium 98mg; Fibre 1.1g; Sodium 40mg.

Cranberry relish

Enriched with wine, this relish is perfect with slices of turkey or other cold meats, bringing a tart sweetness to sandwiches.

MAKES 900G/2LB

450g/1lb small red onions
30ml/2 tbsp olive oil
225g/8oz/1 cup soft light brown sugar
450g/1lb/4 cups cranberries
120ml/4fl oz/½ cup red wine vinegar
120ml/4fl oz/½ cup red wine
15ml/1 tbsp yellow mustard seeds
2.5ml/½ tsp ground ginger
30ml/2 tbsp orange liqueur or port
salt and ground black pepper, to taste

1 Halve the red onions and slice them very thinly. Heat the oil in a large pan, add the onions and cook over a very low heat for about 15 minutes, stirring occasionally, until softened.

2 Add 30ml/2 tbsp of the sugar and cook for a further 5 minutes, or until the onions are caramelized.

3 Meanwhile, put the cranberries in a pan with the remaining sugar, and add the vinegar, red wine, mustard seeds and ginger. Stir in thoroughly.

4 Heat gently, stirring continuously, until the sugar has dissolved, then cover and bring to the boil.

5 Simmer the relish for 12–15 minutes, until thickened and darker in colour, then add the caramelized onions. Stir them into the mixture.

6 Increase the heat slightly and cook uncovered for a further 10 minutes, stirring the mixture frequently, until well reduced and nicely thickened.

7 Remove the pan from the heat then season to taste with salt and ground black pepper.

8 Allow to cool completely, then transfer the relish to warmed sterilized jars (see page 265). Spoon a little of the orange liqueur or port over the surface of each, then cover, seal and label.

9 This relish can be stored for up to 6 months in a cool, dark place. Store in the refrigerator once opened and use within 1 month.

Honey mustard

This honey mustard is richly flavoured and is wonderful served with meats and cheeses in sandwiches or to flavour tarts.

MAKES 500G/1¼LB

225g/8oz/1 cup mustard seeds
15ml/1 tbsp ground cinnamon
2.5ml/½ tsp ground ginger
300ml/½ pint/scant 1¼ cups white wine vinegar
90ml/6 tbsp dark clear honey

1 Put the mustard seeds in a bowl with the cinnamon and ginger, and pour over the white wine vinegar. Stir, then cover and leave to soak overnight in a cool place.

2 Put the mustard in a mortar and pound with a pestle, adding the honey gradually. Continue pounding until the mustard resembles a stiff paste. If it becomes too stiff, add extra vinegar to achieve the desired consistency.

3 Spoon into sterilized jars (see page 265). Seal and label. Keep refrigerated after opening, and use within 4 weeks.

Cranberry: Energy 1532kcal/6486kJ; Protein 8g; Carbohydrate 314.6g, of which sugars 304.2g; Fat 23.3g, of which saturates 3.1g; Cholesterol 0mg; Calcium 259mg; Fibre 13.5g; Sodium 46mg.
Mustard: Energy 1276kcal/5345kJ; Protein 65.4g; Carbohydrate 115.3g, of which sugars 68.8g; Fat 101.5g, of which saturates 3.4g; Cholesterol 9mg; Calcium 747mg; Fibre 0g; Sodium 21mg.

Index

This edition is published by Lorenz Books
an imprint of Anness Publishing Ltd
info@anness.com; www.lorenzbooks.com
www.annesspublishing.com

© Anness Publishing Ltd 2022

A CIP catalogue record for this book is at the British Library.

Publisher: Joanna Lorenz
Editorial Director: Helen Sudell
Editor and Designer: Lucy Doncaster
Production Controller: Ben Worley
With thanks to all the recipe contributors and photographers.
Parts of this book have been previously published as
The Perfect Afternoon Tea Recipe Book.

COOK'S NOTES

• For all recipes, quantities are given in both metric
and imperial measures and, where appropriate, in
standard cups and spoons. Follow one set of
measures, but not a mixture, because they are not
interchangeable.
• Standard spoon and cup measures are level.
1 tsp = 5ml, 1 tbsp = 15ml, 1 cup = 250ml/8fl oz.
• Australian standard tablespoons are 20ml.
Australian readers should use 3 tsp in place of 1 tbsp
for measuring small quantities of gelatine, salt, etc.
• American pints are 16fl oz/2 cups. American
readers should use 20fl oz/2.5 cups in place of 1 pint
when measuring liquids.
• Electric oven temperatures in this book are for
conventional ovens. When using a fan oven, the
temperature will probably need to be reduced by
about 10–20°C/20–40°F. Since ovens vary, you
should check with your manufacturer's instruction
book for guidance.
• The nutritional analysis given for each recipe is
calculated per portion or item, unless otherwise
stated. If the recipe gives a range, such as Serves 4–6,
then the analysis will be for the smaller portion size,
ie 6 servings. The analysis does not include optional
ingredients.
• Medium (US large) eggs are used unless stated.